How We Sold Our Future

For Beatrice and Jasper
What world will you live in?

How We Sold Our Future

Future

The Failure to Fight Climate Change

JENS BECKERT

Translated by Ray Cunningham

polity

Originally published in German as *Verkaufte Zukunft: Warum der Kampf gegen den Klimawandel zu scheitern droht.* © Suhrkamp Verlag Berlin 2024. All rights reserved by and controlled through Suhrkamp Verlag Berlin.

The translation of this book was supported by a grant from the Goethe-Institut.

Polity Press
65 Bridge Street
Cambridge CB2 1UR, UK

Polity Press
111 River Street
Hoboken, NJ 07030, USA

ISBN-13: 978-1-5095-6509-2

A catalogue record for this book is available from the British Library.

Library of Congress Control Number: 2024939848

Typeset in 11 on 13 pt Sabon
by Cheshire Typesetting Ltd, Cuddington, Cheshire
Printed and bound in Great Britain by CPI Group (UK) Ltd, Croydon

For further information on Polity, visit our website:
politybooks.com

Contents

Nature always loses. When it comes to economic matters, that's the rule.

*– Renato Valencia**

* Valencia is Professor of Ecology and Evolution at the Pontificia Universidad Católica del Ecuador in Quito. Cited in Catrin Einhorn and Manuela Andreoni, 'Ecuador Tried to Curb Drilling and Protect the Amazon. The Opposite Happened', *The New York Times*, 14.01.2023 (https://www.nytimes.com/2023/01/14/climate/ecuador-drilling-oil-amazon.html).

1

Knowledge without change

Imagine Glacier Bay National Park in the south of Alaska, a spectacular landscape dominated by huge glaciers, with massive slabs of ice crashing into the Arctic Ocean. In 2022, Alaskan author Tom Kizzia watched this spectacle of glacial calving from a cruise ship.[1] He observed that this was once a sublime way to experience the power and beauty of untouched nature; today, however, it is impossible not to see in the breaking ice the accelerating and uncontrolled destruction of nature. Every roll of 'white thunder' feels like another loss.

We are surrounded by disturbing images of disrupted natural processes and the devastation of nature – the foundation of human life. These images often show tremendous suffering: we see families in Pakistan paddling boats through flooded villages; desperate people on the roofs of their flooded houses in Germany's Ahr Valley; or Californians standing aghast in front of the ruins of their burnt homes. None of these natural events can be causally attributed to climate change directly, but the significant rise in extreme weather events with disastrous consequences is indeed the result of human-induced global warming, caused by an increase in carbon dioxide and other greenhouse gases in the atmosphere. The broader public

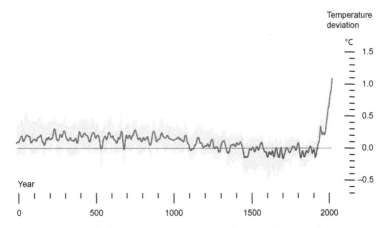

Figure 1.   Global air temperature over the past thousand years
Source: Based on IPCC (Intergovernmental Panel on Climate Change), *Climate Change 2021: The Physical Science Basis. Contribution of Working Group I to the Sixth Assessment Report of the Intergovernmental Panel on Climate Change*, New York, 2021, p. 6, Figure SPM.1.

has known that the destruction was coming for close to forty years; we have not stopped it.

Quite the opposite. Over this time period, annual global carbon dioxide emissions have not decreased, they have almost doubled. In the past thirty years alone, as much carbon dioxide was emitted into the atmosphere as in the previous two hundred years combined.[2] The result is a steep rise in the global average temperature, a development that climate researchers refer to as 'the great acceleration'. To date, the temperature has risen by almost 1.2 degrees Celsius compared to the early nineteenth century (see Figure 1). On our current path, with greenhouse gas emissions continuing to surge worldwide, the global average temperature is expected to increase by a further 1.3 degrees Celsius over the next eighty years – assuming that current climate action pledges are actually honoured.[3]

Human changes to the biosphere are damaging – or eliminating altogether – parts of the ecological niche in which our cultures can survive in relatively stable conditions. Global warming is now inevitable, and it is unclear if societies can adapt to the dramatically changed foundations of life that will result.[4] The increased incidence of floods, droughts, heat-waves, and wildfires, together with declining biodiversity and rising sea levels, has the potential to significantly destabilize our societies. We will be confronted with questions of social inequality as never before: inequality both between the global North and the particularly hard-hit global South and between affluent and poorer social groups. Climate refugees, water scarcity, famines, and – in rich countries, too – ever higher costs for protecting people against natural disasters will lead to new distributional conflicts and to the very real possibility of severe social disorder.

We by no means understand all the causal chains in the highly complex climate system, and must constantly refine and adapt our climate models to take account of new knowledge. Nonetheless, one thing is certain: we know where the journey is heading and how drastically living conditions on Earth will shift. In short, climate change is no longer just a research problem for the natural sciences. Nor is its solution simply a technical challenge. We have already developed many safe and effective technologies for reducing greenhouse gas emissions. We also know which policy choices, changes in economic activity, and behavioural shifts would make a difference. The greatest challenge, rather, is social and cultural. If we know what to do and how to do it, why don't societies act? That is the central question of this book.

The answer requires understanding the key social, political, and economic processes that drive our societies. I will sketch my answer by looking above all at the growth and profit rationale behind our capitalist economic system, together with its distribution of power, and the problems of political legitimacy in democratic political systems. Questions of cultural identity and status competition between consumers must also take centre stage. I will try to establish that the dominant role of power and culture in determining the social effects of climate change and how we fight it requires attending to the insights of social science. Natural scientists make the basic problem crystal clear and engineers propose technical solutions, but social scientists are uniquely equipped to investigate the economic, political, and cultural obstacles preventing us from taking urgent action against an ever-growing threat.

How do the workings of a capitalist market economy, of a parliamentary democracy, and of an individualistic culture shape the way we interact with the natural environment?[5] My thesis is simple: the power and incentive structures of capitalist modernity and its governance mechanisms are blocking a solution to climate change. They are responsible, of course, for much else too. Other fundamental social problems also come up against power structures that impede their solution: witness the persistent and scandalous forms of poverty and social inequality. But while we can always hope that poverty and social inequality will be lessened at some point in the future and that a fairer world will emerge, the temporal dimensions of climate change are different. The world is warming rapidly and the catastrophic consequences of postponing action are irreversible. As the Indian historian Dipesh Chakrabarty remarks, the problems of climate change 'confront us with finite calendars of urgent action. Yet powerful nations of the world have sought to deal with the problem with an apparatus that was meant for actions on indefinite calendars.'[6]

The 'finite calendar' has not spurred resolute action for the simple reason that the problem does not change the prevailing power and incentive structures, or not sufficiently. The fact is that the short-term gains of avoiding the costs of climate action exceed the current benefits of future climate security. This is because the positive effects of costly climate protection measures would only kick in when we are old, or dead, 'merely' benefiting later generations. Some people may also think that they can personally avoid the consequences of climate change, that they are protected by their wealth or by geography, that only 'others' will be affected. At best, an idealistic interest in the wellbeing of future generations – probably manifested most strongly when we picture the future lives of our own children and grandchildren – creates incentives to align our behaviour to more distant time horizons.

Since companies, politicians, and private citizens typically align their decision-making with short-term opportunities, we can expect them to overlook or downplay the future negative impacts caused by ignoring environmental damage.[7] The common good that is our natural environment remains an exploitable resource sold on the market for profit. Its sale leads to its destruction. This is what I mean when I say that we have 'sold' our future.[8]

Time and again, in political discussions on climate change, we hear statements such as, 'All *we* have to do is X', or, 'Why don't *we* finally agree on Y?' 'X' here might be the expansion of wind power, 'Y' setting limits on the use of natural resources or increasing the price of petrol and meat. However, the crucial question is: who is 'we'? Change requires actors who are willing to act and who command the resources necessary to implement changes in a contested field populated by a multitude of other actors with very different interests and goals. Every political action takes place within a dense thicket of rules, practices, and institutions, but also of values and habits. These bind actors to structures and opportunities that set specific incentives and define the scope for action, thereby shaping decisions. This brings us to the workings of capitalist modernity, which is the social system that has determined how we interact with the natural foundations of life for the past five hundred years. It also shapes our current responses to climate change, as I will show in the following chapters.

That our responses are far from adequate to deal with the problem is demonstrated by the uninterrupted rise in global warming (see Figure 1). But what would a commensurate

response look like? Implementing climate neutrality immediately? Three degrees of warming by the end of the century?
And 'commensurate' in whose eyes? An economic cost–benefit
calculation would not help here, because the assumptions
involved are far too arbitrary.[9] Rather, something like a norm
is needed, and in fact such a thing does exist: most countries
in the world have committed to climate targets, in particular under the 2015 Paris Climate Agreement, which has been
ratified by over 190 countries. This set the goal of limiting the
increase in the global average temperature compared to pre-
industrial levels to 1.5 degrees Celsius if possible, and in any
event to well below 2 degrees Celsius. Commensurate action
would therefore mean acting to achieve this goal.

How, then, are we doing? A well-known graph used by
the UN Intergovernmental Panel on Climate Change (IPCC)
illustrates the reductions in greenhouse gas emissions necessary to achieve the Paris climate targets (see Figure 2). This
graph serves to show how the measures taken so far are woe-
fully inadequate. Although the climate protection measures
taken to date are indeed flattening the curve of increasing
emissions, they are far from sufficient.[10] What is needed is
an emergency brake, and this is nowhere in sight. And so, in
all likelihood, not a single one of the signatory states to the
Paris Climate Agreement will succeed in meeting their agreed
climate targets.[11] Some actors clearly acknowledge this, while,
for political reasons, others maintain the illusion that we are
on the right track, fearing that without this illusion, even the
current inadequate commitments would weaken and resignation would set in.

This book seeks to understand why it has not been possible
to do what the future health of the world requires. My reflec-
tions have led me to a pessimistic conclusion: the necessary
measures are not being taken and will not be taken. I hasten to
add that we cannot see into the future and have all too often
been surprised by significant social developments. But climate

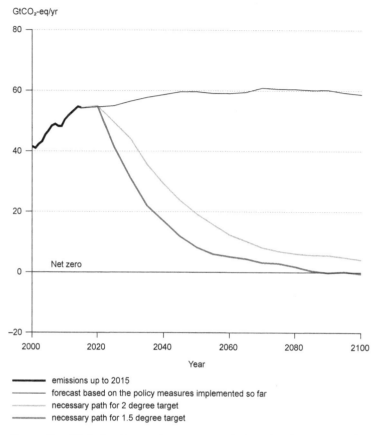

Figure 2. Global net greenhouse gas emissions in gigatonnes of CO_2 equivalents per year (mean values)
Source: IPCC, *Climate Change 2023: Synthesis Report: Summary for Policymakers*, ed. by The Core Writing Team, Hoesung Lee, and José Romero, Geneva, 2023, p. 22.

change is not a problem for the future. The destruction has already started. To repeat: we have known about the dangers of greenhouse gas emissions for decades. We know that over the past thirty years, despite regular high-level international climate conferences, annual global carbon dioxide emissions have increased by more than half and are hitting new peaks every year. And, truth be told, we also know that the measures currently planned are not sufficient to meet the agreed climate targets. For this to happen, according to the IPCC, annual global emissions would have to be halved by 2030; and by 2050, they would need to be as much as 85 per cent lower.[12] In Germany, for example, CO_2 emissions would have to fall by 6 per cent each year between now and 2030. Since 2010, however, the annual average fall has been just 2 per cent. Theoretically, of course, this could change, but this is not a plausible expectation; it is mere 'greenwishing'.[13]

This is because the changes needed would require radical reforms to our economic, political, and social structures. This kind of far-reaching transformation is nowhere in sight, and in any event would take a long time to implement. If a robust response to climate change comes at all, it will certainly come too late. The projections made by the International Energy Agency (IEA), which include the measures currently planned for the energy transition, show that global CO_2 emissions from fossil fuels will peak in 2025 at 37 billion tonnes, but then – and this is the kicker – they will fall only to 32 billion tonnes by 2050.[14] CO_2 savings are primarily being made in highly developed industrialized countries. Germany, for example, is planning to reduce its CO_2 emissions by two-thirds by 2030 compared to 1990.[15] As things stand, this is not likely to happen. But even if plans in Germany and perhaps some other countries do succeed, the impact will be limited. Globally, 60 per cent of energy demand will likely still be covered by fossil fuels in 2050.[16] Based on its own data, the IEA therefore expects global temperatures to rise by a total of 2.5 degrees Celsius by 2100.

I could have written this book as a parable, looking back on a past, idealistic society from a desolate future – this would probably have been interpreted as doom-mongering on my part. Instead, I propose something different: namely, considered realism based on empirical evidence. To paraphrase Walter Benjamin: I want to help 'organize' the pessimism that arises from sober observation of the situation[17] – to give it a conceptual structure that allows us to better understand the mechanisms behind the inadequate response to climate change. This 'considered realism' will include both a recognition that we will not be delivered from this clear and present danger and a collective mourning for what we will lose.[18] My hope is that a realistic perspective of this kind might help spark a change in political behaviour and strengthen our psychological capacity to adapt to the consequences of the altered living conditions on this planet.

So, to be blunt: the world is heading for further significant global warming. The consequences for nature and for humanity will be severe, but cannot be precisely specified in advance. Because the social consequences of climate change are so numerous and interdependent, we cannot know exactly how they will play out. At best, social scientists can develop a range of scenarios and anticipate how they might evolve – like strategists in a war room. My scenario does not postulate social collapse, but it does assume that climate change will exacerbate what is generally referred to as 'social stress' and will intensify social conflicts. Considerable economic, political, and social turmoil lies ahead. Although this will take different forms in different regions, societies overall will be thrown into unrest by increasingly virulent distributional conflicts. In a world that is 2 or 2.5 degrees warmer, and in which a significant proportion of our prosperity will have to be spent on repairing climatic damage and adapting to climate change, it will be much more difficult to organize a democratic social order, or even just peaceful coexistence. The damage caused by climate change (as opposed to financial crises or pandemics) is irreversible and the resultant peril is permanent. The world will be poorer than it is today. There will be greater suffering, and it will be extremely unevenly distributed.

And it will not be a world without capitalism. Even the climate crisis will not bring about 'the end of capitalism',[19] as some authors proclaim, because it is not a crisis of the economic system. Though this may sound cynical, climate change and the green transformation also represent a huge opportunity for companies. When temperatures go up, more air conditioning systems will be sold and new types of grain will have to be developed. Demand for solar panels will rise, dams will need to be built. It is quite possible that capitalist modernity is shedding its skin once again and adjusting to a new socio-economic regime, one geared towards increased decarbonization of the energy supply and adapted to fit the new climatic conditions, at least in the highly developed industrialized countries. This reorientation will take place precisely in the manner and to the degree permitted by the interests of profit and power, acting in concert with political and cultural structures. Neither the economic pursuit of profit maximization nor the growth imperative will be fundamentally called into question, and the same applies to overconsumption and global inequality. Rather, the pursuit of profit will merely shift its material reference points. Whether this will be compatible with social and political stability in a world that has warmed by 2.5 degrees is an open question. In such a world, the destruction caused to the natural foundations for human life by climate change will be dramatically visible everywhere.

However, predictions about the future are only marginal to the purpose of this book. The main focus, as mentioned, is on our inadequate response to climate change. I hope to contribute to the understanding of this phenomenon through the analysis of economic, political, and cultural processes. The fact that I concentrate on climate change and only touch on other environmental crises, such as pollution or biodiversity loss, does not mean that these are any less important. Rather, I believe that in many respects the way climate change has been handled exemplifies the approach to ecological crises in general. Climate change, like many other ecological crises, is what social scientists call a wicked problem.[20] The nature of wicked problems is such that there is no easily identifiable solution. This is what distinguishes them from tame problems, such as the hole in the ozone layer a few decades ago. In that instance, there was a clear cause which could be tackled using a comparatively straightforward measure: the phasing out and replacement (e.g. in refrigerators) of chlorofluorocarbons (CFCs).[21] Climate change is not tame, but, rather, is characterized by complex interdependencies on numerous levels that do not allow for a single universal solution. As with all wicked problems, climate change requires a step-by-step search for solutions and pragmatic ways of coping with it. This is why this book cannot offer simple messages along the lines of: 'the situation is serious, but here are ten ways to stop climate change.'

Instead, I seek to show how mechanisms in the economy, in politics, and in society block any adequate response to climate change. To do this, I demonstrate how the economy, politics, citizens, and consumers are in a conflictual relationship with each other, while at the same time depending on each other and mutually benefiting from the contribution they each provide. To a significant degree, they contribute to and manage their conflicts by tacitly tolerating the destruction of the natural foundations for successful human coexistence. Nature cannot 'defend' itself because it has no voice of its own. The climate crisis, as we will see, makes manifest the irreconcilable contradictions between the modus operandi of capitalist modernity and the preservation of the natural foundations for life. My analysis of these conflictual relationships is also intended to broaden our understanding of how it might still be possible, even if there is no ideal solution, to act wisely and responsibly in these muddled and bewildering circumstances.

This book is organized as follows. In Chapter 2, I lay the foundations of my argument. I describe the institutional and cultural mechanisms that spread throughout capitalist modernity and that determine the actions of companies, the state, citizens, and consumers in the climate crisis. Next, in Chapters 3, 4, 5, and 6, I show how these mechanisms translate into economic, state, and consumer behaviour and lead to the current inadequate response to climate change. In Chapters 7 and 8, I then address the widespread idea that the ecological crisis can be solved by a regime of 'green growth'. I do not deny that the decarbonization of energy consumption is tremendously important, but I show why, under the conditions created by an economic system designed for continuous and permanent growth, even this path does not lead to an adequate response.

Finally, in Chapter 9, I turn to possible options for action. My considered realism does not by any means lead of necessity to a state of resignation. Yes, the climate policy measures of the past thirty years have been inadequate, but if they are implemented consistently and rigorously, the global warming we can expect will probably be in the range of 2.2 to 2.9 degrees Celsius. This is not nothing, given that without them we would have ended up with warming between 3.6 and 4.2 degrees Celsius.[22] At the end of the book, I consider how climate protection can best be promoted under the conditions prevailing in capitalist modernity and how societies can adapt to life under altered climatic conditions. As already stated, lower greenhouse gas emissions certainly represent a worthwhile outcome.[23] The onset of some consequences of climate change could possibly be delayed, and the consequences themselves could be less severe. This would buy us time, time during which the social and technological conditions for action might change. In addition, precautions could be taken to better prepare us for what is to come.[24]

It falls to all concerned citizens, and not least to those of us in the social sciences, to identify potential political strategies without seeking to cover up the fact that we will not succeed in actually stopping climate change. How can societies shaped by capitalist modernity influence the collective social processes that determine how we interact with nature? Ultimately, it is a matter of encouraging business, politics, and citizens to treat the problem with much greater urgency and recalibrate the use and distribution of scarce economic resources. This will be a huge challenge in a world made more politically and socially volatile by climate change, as the resources required to make a difference will be that much greater. This will involve trade-offs: between financing measures to reduce greenhouse gas emissions and measures to adapt to climatically altered living conditions; and also between all spending on climate policy and spending on the countless other social challenges that will still be with us – from poverty and dilapidated infrastructure to underfunded public healthcare systems. However, we must bear in mind that the problem is not just financial: we will also need to mobilize society's political and moral resources to set sustainable transformations in motion and to build the social resilience that will be needed in a world we have permitted to warm by more than 2 degrees.

2

Capitalist modernity

Today's response to climate change is determined by social structures that have developed over the past five hundred years. Economic historians describe how these structures developed in a number of key locations from the late fifteenth century onwards, slowly at first, and then with breathtaking momentum.[1] Production, trade, and finance hubs formed, for example, in northern Italy, France, England, and the Netherlands. In many cases, these centres were globally networked from the outset, even as most people continued to live in agrarian and locally bound economies only sporadically in contact with these new global hubs.

A key aspect of this early phase of capitalism was the expansion of private property rights through so-called enclosures of large parts of the land used by peasants. This land, which had previously been cultivated collectively as common land, was then assigned to landowners as private property, turning large parts of the rural population into dependent farm labourers or vagabond day labourers. They were then available as labour for the emerging 'manufactories' and later for the urban mills and sweatshops in industrial cities.[2] The availability of wage labour is a key prerequisite for the development of the capitalist economy.

A second far-reaching development was the appropriation of land or wealth from forcibly subjugated populations in the Americas, Africa, and Asia. The spread of European-controlled slavery on the American continent, the exploitation both of natural resources and the labour force in the colonies and their use as markets for European goods fuelled the capital accumulation at home that was a prerequisite for the industrialization that began in the late eighteenth century.[3]

It was only with industrialization that the comprehensive deepening and expansion of the capitalist economy began. From this point onwards, market relations based on wage labour, colonial rule, and technological and institutional innovation spread rapidly.[4] This led in the global North to an unprecedented rise in prosperity, but also to a massive expansion in the use of fossil fuels. Somewhat earlier, a fundamental cultural transformation had begun with the Enlightenment, which gave rise to political and normative principles such as the ideas of progress, equality, and individual self-determination – principles that today still shape our understanding of nature as well.

These cultural transformations, together with the expansion of the market economy, thus define the way we interact with nature. When I speak of capitalist modernity,[5] I am referring to a model of society that is characterized both by market-based and profit-oriented economic structures and by political and cultural developments, such as a drive towards individualism and the belief in progress, which are closely interwoven with those economic structures. Both aspects are combined in today's social configurations. In order to answer the question of why modern societies are destroying the natural foundations for life, we must therefore consider not only the economic but also the political and cultural aspects of capitalist modernity.

Let's start with the economy. The spread of markets as institutions for the distribution of goods, money, and labour is central to the development of the capitalist economy.

Markets and competition as such are not inventions of modern capitalism. However, in pre-modern societies, markets were restricted to the exchange of a limited range of goods, and were highly socially regulated because they were considered a threat to the social cohesion of communities.[6] According to the sociologist Max Weber, 'the market was originally a consociation of persons who are not members of the same group and who are, therefore, "enemies"'.[7] What is new is the ubiquity of markets, their material, spatial, and temporal expansion, and in particular the widespread inclusion of money and labour into the market system. Also new is the comprehensive global networking of markets. Trade among widely separated regions took place even in the ancient world, but truly global trade networks became more and more comprehensive with the unfolding of capitalist modernity. The globalized economy penetrated the world ever deeper in the twentieth century, and with the collapse of communism and the transformation of China over the past thirty or forty years its triumph seems complete.[8]

Capitalism brings with it a specific set of mechanisms that determine economic activity. Private property rights enable individuals to appropriate profits and structure societies into classes. Company law limits investors' liability and thus the risks borne by individuals; this, along with standardization and new forms of corporate organization, encourages the expansion of economic activities.[9] At the same time, competition draws economic actors into a process of constant innovation. Entrepreneurs have to innovate to ensure that they do not fall behind their competitors. Those who do not keep up with the pressure to innovate will be wiped out on the market. The economist Joseph Schumpeter coined the term 'creative destruction' to describe this process, which is also reinforced by the financing of entrepreneurial activities through credit.[10] Credit enables the expansion of economic activities by bringing forward future profits, but at the same time requires a strategic orientation towards uninterrupted growth, since interest has to be paid on the borrowed capital. The expansion of markets thus introduces into the economic system a relentless dynamism based on innovation and expansion.

These economic mechanisms often developed through the agency of the state. In Europe, the state created the conditions for the modern capitalist economy by establishing what was initially a national economic space: building transport routes, defining weights and measures, abolishing the privileges of the guilds, and establishing a unitary monetary system.[11] At the global level, states supported the international expansion of capitalism, for instance through the rise in trade agreements and the imposition of colonial rule. The structures set up politically served to secure access to markets and resources and thus to enable economic expansion, through specialization, the sourcing of raw materials, the emergence of large-scale production facilities, and the opening up of sales markets. State oppression and gunboats facilitated and imposed modern trading networks and an international division of labour which implanted capitalism as a global economic system. State control was also vital for the emerging capitalist economies of the twentieth century, for example in Asia.[12] Alongside economic actors and the state, modern science also played its part in the development of capitalist modernity. Its beginnings date back to the sixteenth century, a time when industrial capitalism did not yet exist. Once the technological advances were applied to the production process, they accelerated and expanded the exploitation and valorization of natural resources and labour and thus became a crucial constituent of wealth creation.

The institutional structures of capitalist economies are designed for unlimited expansion. The economic model creates a dynamic mechanism for generating profits through continuous acquisitions and inventions – the inclusion of ever more new regions, new objects, additional actors, and even the future itself into the market process.[13] The result is a historically unprecedented system of unlimited growth, only interrupted occasionally by economic crises. The driving force behind the system is the subjugation of economic activity to the rationale of capital accumulation. In capitalism, economic activities are not initiated in order to meet specific needs – for example for clothing, holidays, or mobility – but because the owners of capital expect those activities to increase their wealth. Managers are constantly scouring the entire world on behalf of asset owners for new investment opportunities that promise to generate profits. Without profits, the company will eventually fail. The pressure for permanent change and ever further growth comes from the structure of the economic system.

For the generation of economic prosperity, this form of economy is a historically unprecedented success story – at least in the global North. Long-term trends in economic wealth show that societies remained virtually stagnant for centuries before a steep rise in global economic output began in the nineteenth century, continuing to this day. Societies have not always been equally prosperous; there have always been phases of greater wealth and phases of economic decline. However, these fluctuations seem almost trivial when we look at the overall trajectory of economic growth over the past two hundred years (see Figure 3). The wealth created has lifted billions of people out of poverty and given them longer and healthier lives than their ancestors, under a prosperity they could hardly have imagined. Indeed, it is unlikely that capitalism would have survived if it had not delivered these benefits.

But capitalism is not a benevolent system of charity. The exploitation of workers and their families at home, the oppression of slaves and imperial subjects abroad, and the radically unequal distribution of wealth everywhere have been subject to criticism from the start. The writings of Charles Dickens and Karl Marx and countless other authors and scientists bear

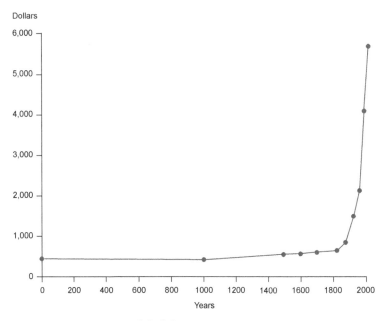

Figure 3.   Growth in global GDP per capita per year
Source: Based on Angus Maddison, *The World Economy: A Millennial Perspective*,
Paris, 2001, p. 264 (Table B-21).

witness to this to this day. But far less attention has been paid,
until recently at least, to a second form of exploitation: that of
nature.[14] Natural resources are indispensable for the production of goods, and the growing economy is devouring these
resources on an ever-increasing scale. But capitalist markets
have no in-built mechanism to take account of the ecological
damage caused by the exploitation of nature.[15]

The perpetual process of 'creative destruction' necessary for
the unending growth that produces today's wealth is accom-
panied by the utilization of resources – soil, minerals, animals,
plants, even air and water – on a scale previously unknown. In
the past thirty years alone, the 'material footprint', a measure
indicating overall resource consumption, has more than
doubled, far exceeding what scientists regard as the planetary
boundary for resource utilization.[16] With bigger, stronger, and

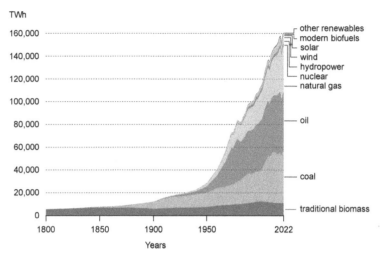

Figure 4. Global energy consumption from 1800 to 2022 in terawatt-hours

Source: Based on Our World in Data, 'Global Direct Primary Energy Consumption' (https://ourworldindata.org/grapher/global-primary-energy).

more sophisticated machines, our interventions in nature have become ever more efficient and far-reaching.

The extraordinary wealth produced under modern capitalism required an immense increase in the use of fossil fuels in particular. The large-scale mining of coal and later the extraction of oil and gas enabled the massive use of machines to manufacture and transport the goods required for the colossal increase in capital. Without coal, neither steam engines nor steamships nor the railway would have established themselves in the nineteenth century. Without oil, the triumphant advance of the car and the aeroplane in the twentieth century would not have been possible. While global consumption of fossil fuels was estimated at around 1 billion tonnes of oil equivalent in 1900, it is now fourteen times higher (see Figure 4).[17] The constant escalation of fossil fuel combustion also led to the increase in the level of carbon dioxide in the atmosphere which is heating up the planet ever further. The carbon dioxide content in the air, measured as parts per million (ppm), has risen from less than 300 ppm in pre-industrial times to over 420 ppm in 2023. To prevent escalating global environmental changes and thus ensure the maintenance of the natural preconditions for human life, scientists have specified that the maximum level should be 350 ppm. This limit was already breached in the 1990s.[18]

Our political and economic systems not only allowed but also encouraged these developments. Competition and market liberalization, an efficient financial system, mechanization, the division of labour, the mobilization of workers for the highly specialized industrial production process – all were crucial. In the capitalist world they formed, the use of fossil fuels remains profitable in spite of all the ecological damage caused as long as the costs of the destruction can be kept off companies' balance sheets. Companies base their decisions on the profit anticipated from an investment and the risks associated with it. Profit is turnover less production costs. Production costs include raw materials, intermediate products, machinery, capital, and labour, but not the costs of environmental damage. The CO_2 released into the atmosphere during the production process certainly causes damage. However, the cost of remedying that damage is not relevant to the economic calculation of the profitability of the investment. The sociologist Niklas Luhmann once summed this up by saying that markets do not inform societies about the state of their natural environment.[19] As long as the negative environmental consequences of economic activity are not reflected in prices, the economy has no sensory mechanism for the destruction it causes. Climate change – in the words of financial manager Steve Waygood – is 'the biggest market failure of all time'.[20] Individually rational behaviour based on market signals leads inexorably to the collective disaster of climate change – at least as long as companies are not effectively forced to take environmental impacts into account through regulatory intervention.

The first scientific accounts linking carbon dioxide levels with possible climate impacts appeared as early as the nineteenth century.[21] In the second half of the twentieth century, the phenomenon was increasingly well understood by scientists. And with the Club of Rome report on *The Limits to Growth* published in 1972, it became clear to a wider public that seemingly endless economic growth was coming up against a finite environment and was not compatible with the preservation of the natural foundations for life.[22] This would have been the right time to drastically reduce the use of fossil fuels. Instead, annual greenhouse gas emissions from the burning of coal, oil, and gas continued to rise. The reason is not hard to find. In capitalist economies, driven by the pressures to grow described, environmental degradation is only considered to the extent that there are economic incentives to do so, such as when energy savings reduce costs. If damage to nature is to be reduced, price signals must be introduced into the economic system from the outside, imposed by political bodies charged with taking into account more than the next quarter's corporate profits. Regulations to protect the environment, politically created quasi-markets (which enable, for example, the trading of carbon emissions), and changing consumer preferences are all examples of such signals that companies can understand and respond to.

However, all of these make climate protection into a cost factor. In an economy geared towards maximizing profits, companies will try to externalize costs as far as possible. Paying the costs would reduce profits or even make an investment unprofitable. It should be noted that evading the internalization of these environmental costs is not a reprehensible moral weakness on the part of individual entrepreneurs or managers. It is systemic. A company that incurs 'unnecessary' costs suffers competitive disadvantages and forgoes potential improvements in economic performance, thus antagonizing its owners. Nor is it realistic to expect the costs of environmental damage to be included voluntarily (except perhaps for some limited leeway that managers have in their decisions).[23] The free market pioneer Milton Friedman summarized this succinctly half a century ago in a memorable sentence: 'The social responsibility of business is to increase its profits.'[24]

However, there is more to capitalist modernity than just a market-based economic system.[25] The state and politics, on one side, and citizens and consumers, on the other, establish their own spheres of action, which interact with the economic system but are not identical to it and can prompt resistance to it. Sociologists speak of functionally differentiated societies in which subsystems develop, each of which operates according to its own principles, but all of which are interlinked and can come into conflict.[26] These subsystems are dependent on services from the other systems and can therefore exert reciprocal influence on each other.

How does this work? Both the state and private consumers need the goods and services produced in the economy and the money that flows to them in the form of tax revenues and earned income. At the same time, companies need citizens who are willing to work and consume, and who are also willing to accept the principle of private property and the prevailing economic power relations. Companies need social legitimacy. In addition, companies need the legal framework provided by the state, which helps them to coordinate their actions and determines how the wealth generated is actually distributed. The political system also shapes how society is organized. Conversely, the political system is dependent on the consent of citizens for the stable exercise of domination. In democratic societies, this legitimation is secured by linking power to the mandate delivered by elections and to broad public participation in the (rising) national income. Political scientists speak of input and output legitimation.[27] The economy and the state require social approval; its absence would lead to what sociologist Émile Durkheim called 'anomie' or to what economic historian Karl Polanyi called 'countermovements'.

In order to understand the inadequate response to greenhouse gases, it is necessary, then, to consider not only the modus operandi of the economic system itself, but also the relationships among the economy, the state, and the public. Unfortunately, these are not relationships among equals. When I speak of capitalist modernity, I refer to a world in which the economic system is dominant. Its prominence is based both on its role in creating the material wealth, which is of predominant importance for all of us, and on its global reach.[28] The state cannot do without tax revenue; citizens' earned income provides them with the means of maintaining their living standard. At the same time, the owners of capital and the financial markets decide on the investments that enable economic production. They can do this anywhere in the world, giving them a flexibility and reach that no other social system can match. In a market economy, power accumulates in the economic and financial system. This does not mean it is an absolute and untouchable power. It is subject to criticism and, in principle, also subject to constraint by the state. But the predicament we find ourselves in shows just how difficult economic powers are to manage and control for the common good.

Making these distinctions among the economy, the political sphere, and the public (in the sense of both citizens and consumers) enables us to draft a framework for understanding the network of power and incentive structures in capitalist modernity (see Figure 5) which, as I argue, are the root cause of our inadequate response to climate change.

At first glance, one might naïvely assume that the state, which is nominally committed to the common good, would simply compel companies through legal regulation either not to cause environmental damage or else to pay for it – not least

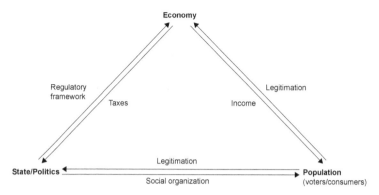

Figure 5.   Economy, state, population

because at stake is nothing less than the preservation of the natural foundations for life for future generations. The failure of the market to act certainly justifies such state intervention. However, the experience of decades of climate warming shows that political intervention in the market has never been sufficient, and indeed was never even genuinely intended to stop climate change, merely to kick the can down the road in the hope either that prophecies of disaster were exaggerated or that someone in the future would discover a painless solution.

This is why we also speak of the climate crisis as the greatest *state* failure of all time, one which has calmly and quietly run its course notwithstanding all the provisions of environmental law. I will discuss the reasons for this state failure in more detail in the chapters that follow. At this point, let me simply say that it has its roots in all three spheres: in the power of business, in the way (democratic) political processes operate, but also in the behaviour of citizens and consumers. With regard to corporate power, this means, for instance, that companies lobby against regulations that would lead to higher costs. To protect their profits, they will use their influence to avoid being forced to internalize the expenses stemming from environmental damage they cause. Where this is not possible, they will try to keep those costs low or delay them. They can do this both because of their ability to influence political decisions and because of the structural dependence of the state and the people on economic growth. Companies that feel themselves overly constrained by state regulations can make credible threats to postpone investments or to switch them to another country.[29] In this, the global nature of the economic system is of invaluable help. Companies choose to locate their operations wherever the legal framework appears most favourable. Under the globalized and liberalized economic conditions of recent decades, this has been a strategy that large companies in particular have deployed with aplomb.

Usually, however, there is no need for such direct threats because state actors, but also citizens, are well aware both of the importance of competitive economic structures and of the power wielded by companies. Greater competitiveness leads to higher tax revenues, which makes it easier for the state to fulfil its tasks, and also to more stable and higher employment, which means higher household incomes. In addition, the state needs the private investors from whom it borrows money. Politicians, who depend on elections, therefore have an incentive not to force companies to internalize the costs of environmental damage if doing so will antagonize the companies and ultimately hit voters in their wallets – especially since the increasing damage to the climate is not even visible as a reduction in gross national product.[30]

As long as the catastrophes of climate damage are seen as problems for a distant future or for other people, then there are no material incentives for effective climate protection: not for business, nor for the state, nor for citizens. This distinguishes climate protection from, for instance, the struggle of the labour movement, where conflict between capital and labour leads to negotiations in which companies have to make concessions on, say, wages or working hours. In the case of climate protection, there is no such material divergence of interests between companies, the state, and citizens. All parties can easily reach a consensus on ignoring the costs of environmental damage or postponing their settlement to an indefinite time in the future. Nature itself has no voice in the legislative process, nor can it make its voice heard by going on strike.

But what about *non-material* interests? After all, there have been significant ecological movements in many countries since the 1970s demanding an end to environmental destruction. In recent years, these movements – under such names as Fridays for Future, Last Generation, or Extinction Rebellion – have focused specifically on climate protection. On behalf of future generations, they call for tough political regulation and combine moral and practical arguments with public protests to denounce the behaviour of companies and consumers as well as the failure of states to act.

These movements are not politically powerless, and have their allies in many traditional and non-traditional parties. As legitimacy is necessary for the exercise of power, the state (in particular, but companies as well) must react to the threat of appearing illegitimate. But these social movements encounter resistance. Not only resistance from companies (which are interested in maximizing profits), but also procrastination from the state (which is dependent on economic prosperity) and a backlash from citizens (who fear for their jobs and their established consumption and lifestyle habits). As a rule, conflicts between material and non-material interests translate into political compromises. In recent decades, governments have thus intensified climate protection requirements and promoted various economic practices that seem compatible with climate protection. However, these measures are far too timid to constitute an adequate response to the 'finite calendar' of climate destruction.

As I noted, capitalist modernity is not merely an economic system mechanically interconnected with the decision-making processes of the state, citizens, and consumers. Complex cultural factors are also important, helping determine institutional structures and public behaviour, and thus, as we will see, the inadequacy of our response to climate change. The cultural identity of capitalist modernity was formed primarily during the Age of Enlightenment, but some of its roots go back to the Renaissance, and even to antiquity. I would now like to focus on three aspects of this identity, or rather on the transformations on which it is based, which were particularly consequential for the way we interact with nature. These are: a specific understanding of the relationship between human beings and nature; the idea of increasing prosperity through ever further progress in a future that is open for us to shape; and the ascendancy of a morality of individualism.

The *first* cultural transformation was recently summarized by the economic anthropologist Jason Hickel.[31] He begins by noting that many traditional societies have an understanding of nature that sees it as encompassing humankind. Nature is perceived as animate and belonging to a cosmology that comprehends humans and nature as a whole. This understanding does not preclude the utilization of natural resources by humans, but situates this within a general human duty of care and respect for the natural world, which is seen as standing in a kin relationship with humankind. Hickel paints with a broad brush, and this idyllic picture of traditional societies certainly only holds true for some of them. There are many examples of environmental destruction before capitalism. But it is fair to state that most Enlightenment thinkers from the early modern period onwards were committed to a cosmology based on the irreconcilable dualism between humankind and nature. In the early seventeenth century, the philosopher and statesman Francis Bacon enjoined his peers to achieve greater domination over nature; only a little later, the philosopher René Descartes began to treat the mind and body as separate entities and Immanuel Kant argued that human history and natural history are two different things that need to be kept apart, just as 'animality' and rationality are in humans.

This way of thinking encouraged people to see nature as an object outside the realm of morality that could be ruthlessly exploited. Certainly, there were also philosophical objections to this degradation of nature within the Enlightenment (e.g. Rousseau) and in, for example, Romanticism, but in the end the notion of a dualism between Nature and Man gained the upper hand. Thus it is hardly surprising that in later debates around the capitalist economy, its social injustices became the subject of intense dispute, but rarely its purely instrumental relationship to nature.[32]

The *second* cultural transformation is the emergence of a different understanding of the future, one expressed in the idea of progress. For most of human history, something that may seem positively outlandish today was completely normal: societies did not believe themselves to be in a process of constant change and growth, but rather in a fixed structure of repetition within constancy – determined by a seasonally and religiously defined rhythm of recurrence, in which the future is a repetition of what is already familiar from the past.[33] The historian Reinhart Koselleck has described how early modern Europeans began to portray the temporal order differently, seeing history not as cyclical repetition, but as linear progression.[34] Viewing the future as an essentially open rather than a predetermined realm of action helped pave the way for the orientation towards change and growth that characterizes capitalist modernity.[35] This transformation makes it possible to project onto the future a world that has been altered and improved by human intervention and motivates action to bring about this future state. This new idea of progress did not merely apply to the improvement of material living conditions. It also encompassed the development of art as well as the development of societies in legal and normative terms.[36]

Science and technology were relied upon to solve the problems that would arise in this process of permanent change and growth. And, certainly, technological progress has bestowed many blessings on humankind. But it is also true that without it, the tremendous environmental destruction we are confronted with today, and which has led us into the geological age of the Anthropocene, could not have happened.[37] Technological progress is a necessary component of a system which is structurally dependent on infinite growth, but which at the same time is based on a natural world with finite resources. The consequence of this internal contradiction is the accelerating ecological crisis.

The promise of infinitely increasing prosperity and rising quality of life through technological progress was also the cultural motor that drove the production of more and more things. The 'immense accumulation of commodities' of capitalist modernity has brought us countless conveniences and undoubtedly eliminated much suffering and deprivation. Economic growth has made it possible, especially in the global North, to combat poverty and disease and to contain conflicts over scarce resources. To abandon growth would mean abandoning this successful model for social integration in complex societies. However, this harmony would be equally hard to sustain in a world of climate catastrophe. Our societies, by basing their social order on the pursuit of profit and the provision of ever more goods and services, and by simultaneously abdicating their responsibility for the damaging consequences, have in effect condoned climate change and its inevitable disruptions. This, too, is part of the cultural identity of capitalist modernity.

Finally, the *third* cultural transformation was the spread of individualist behavioural norms. Here, too, we find the same internal contradiction. The strengthening of subjective rights, the liberation from the constraining norms of collectivist social communities, the individualization of lifestyles – all this exerted a tremendous attraction and would probably still be defended by most people today as desirable, and rightly so. However, this shift in values is of course also the cultural counterpart of the growth compulsion and the externalization of environmental damage.[38] In capitalist modernity, individual identity and social status are to a large extent determined by the consumption of goods. Social recognition accrues to those who can keep up with the Joneses or, preferably, get ahead in a world where consumption can be increased indefinitely. Consumer choice becomes the realm where freedom can be exercised in a world that for most people is otherwise characterized by considerable constraints. Anyone who seeks to restrict consumption must expect resistance.[39]

We also confront the motivating power supplied by the promise of individual social advancement. In capitalist modernity, when social inequality is no longer fixed by birth, differences in status seem to arise from our own decisions and even our moral and intellectual worth. Those who have a lot, we assume, are also those who have put in a lot of effort. Status advancement, the promise goes, can be achieved through personal endeavour. The social effects of this promise contribute to the dynamic growth of the economy. It is socially stipulated that everyone is required to take part in the race for prosperity and to do their best. Attempts to restrict this competitive and growth-oriented ethos are dismissed as a betrayal of what is perhaps the core promise of capitalist modernity. Even criticism of the meritocratic principle is predominantly directed not at the principle itself, but only at the fact that it does not apply equally to everyone.[40]

The connection between individualism and the social order of capitalist modernity is illustrated most clearly in the metaphor of the invisible hand. The idea behind the metaphor was originally expressed by the philosopher Bernard Mandeville and was then developed into the fundamental principle of liberal economic theory by the Scottish Enlightenment philosopher Adam Smith.[41] The basic idea is that the maximization of economic prosperity is not – as one might have expected – rooted in virtuous behaviour that seeks the common good; rather, the self-interested behaviour of market participants produces a beneficial outcome for society as a whole. Individuals are thus freed from any obligation to reflect normatively on the consequences of their actions for the community. Any scruples they might have are swept aside by the belief that good outcomes arise automatically and in the absence of intention. Anyone who intervenes in this automatic process, so the warning goes, will only cause harm, notwithstanding their possibly good intentions. Trust in the market mechanism is all that is needed. This is the standard market-liberal justification for indifference to the social consequences of economic activity, including for the natural environment.

I am not concerned here with whether the connection between self-interest and an ethically acceptable outcome fully and therefore correctly reflects Adam Smith's thinking. It does not. But in the interpretation that was subsequently applied, there emerged a powerful ideology of belief in the market and in the ethical justification for exclusively self-interested behaviour. In addition, the rationalist model of action was thereby universalized. Contrary to all anthropological understanding, the relentless pursuit of economic self-interest is not seen for what it really is, namely – historically speaking – a limited phenomenon, but is regarded as immovable, indeed as a kind of anthropological given.[42] The practical impact of this ideology, working in conjunction with the institutions created by the market, is very considerable. Milton Friedman's dictum, quoted above, according to which the social responsibility of companies lies only in the generation of profits, simply repeats unvarnished the core conviction of capitalist modernity. There is no collective rationality to guide our actions that should set limits to the individual pursuit of advantage. This brings us to a key explanation for the helplessness of capitalist modernity in the face of climate change: individually rational behaviour is not able to protect the common good that is the natural foundations of life from the destructive activity that causes climate change.

Let me summarize. The expansion of markets, the institutionalization of competition, and credit-financed investment created powerful incentives and economic structures that both enabled a tremendous if unequal increase in prosperity and ensured that the massive damage done to the environment could be ignored. These developments were culturally underpinned by the idea that human beings and nature represent a duality; by our belief in progress; by individualism; and by the social integration of societies through the promise of individual advancement. Economic institutions and cultural identities intermesh and are mutually supportive. Together, the structures that have been so successful in economic, social, and cultural terms (at least for the global North) are preventing an adequate response to the unfolding environmental destruction that has been clear for all to see for half a century. In no industry is this so clearly demonstrated as in the fossil fuel industry.

3

Big Oil

For decades, the fossil fuel industry has used all its might to prevent, delay, water down, or evade effective climate protection. It is not alone. Downstream industries and companies which burn rather than extract fossil fuels also have a history of indifference to climate change and of delaying effective action. However, their interests are more complex, as technological change could allow most to manufacture their products without burning oil or gas, allowing them to transform themselves into 'green' companies. I will say more about this at the end of the chapter.

First, I want to explore how the structures of capitalist modernity shape the commercial strategies of fossil fuel companies. These strategies rest on a simple, if unstated, aim: to make profit regardless of the consequences, including the destruction of the natural environment. Their parasitic behaviour towards the collective goods of nature, which their products destroy, is integral to the economic system, despite an intact nature being indispensable even for the companies themselves. Of course, it is not enough to look only at corporate strategies and thus at the supply side. After all, there is a demand for all that energy, and if it weren't supplied, there would undoubtedly be severe social and political turmoil. We all contribute to this demand, a subject I will turn to in later chapters as I consider the dependence of our modern ways of life on fossil fuel.

In order to shed light on the role of the fossil fuel industry in the climate crisis, it is helpful to first grasp the dimensions of the industry. The oil and gas industry has a total global turnover of around five trillion dollars, which corresponds to almost 4 per cent of global value creation. This makes it one of the most important industries in the world. Of the ten companies in the world with the highest turnover, three are in the energy sector.[1] The industry is also highly concentrated and of enormous political importance. In many countries, the profits from oil or gas are the most important source of state revenue. Energy companies are often directly controlled by the state. In all countries, whether the companies are private or public, the energy industry is subject to strong political influence owing to the strategic importance of energy security and in turn wields great influence on politics.

The fossil fuel industry does not itself emit the 34 billion tonnes of CO_2 caused by the combustion of fossil fuels, including coal, every year.[2] It mines or otherwise extracts these fuels, converts and refines them, transports them, and sells them to companies and private consumers, who then burn the products. However, the industry's business model consists of extracting as much coal, oil, or gas as is economically viable, obviously knowing precisely how it will be used. The destructive environmental consequences of its products are for the most part not taken into account in its commercial calculations. In a 2021 study, the IEA stated that no more new oil or gas reserves could be opened up if the Paris climate target was to be met.[3] Of the reserves that have already been opened up ('committed emissions'), 40 per cent would have to remain in the ground if the door to achieving the 1.5-degree target was not to be irrevocably closed.[4] The industry, however, wants to extract and sell as much of these reserves as possible. For after all, fabulous profits lie dormant in these deposits.

On average, over the past fifty years, the fossil fuel industry has raked in profits of one trillion US dollars *per year*.[5] During energy crises, such as in 1973 or after the Russian attack on Ukraine in 2022, these profits have been even higher. According to the IEA, they are said to have totalled a scarcely believable four trillion US dollars in 2022.[6] The profits of the Saudi Arabian oil company Saudi Aramco alone amounted to an unprecedented 161 billion US dollars in 2022.[7] The company is almost entirely owned by the state of Saudi Arabia. The profits made by Equinor, BP, ExxonMobil, Shell, Petrobras, Pampa Energia, Chevron, and TotalEnergies in 2022 were in each case between USD 25 billion and roughly USD 70 billion. This places them among the most profitable companies in the world, but also gives rise to a huge problem: how do you shut down a functioning and highly profitable industry?[8]

Of course, the people at the top of this industry are also aware that the coal, oil, and gas they produce are a major cause of climate change. However, the prevailing incentive structures of capitalist modernity prevent this knowledge from being translated into action to protect the climate, which in concrete terms would mean abandoning the extraction of fossil fuels. The responsible managers in the energy multinationals focus their efforts on maximizing profits and not on reducing CO_2 emissions.

For doing exactly this, the CEO of ExxonMobil, Darren Woods, received a basic salary of USD 1.9 million in 2022; his total salary package, consisting primarily of bonuses and share awards, amounted to almost USD 36 million.[9] Bonuses and awards for the top managers of oil multinationals are contingent on the performance of the company's share price and thus create an incentive for company leaders to maximize profits. Incentive systems aimed at the enhancement of shareholder value have been introduced in companies since the

1980s to ensure that managers focus on maximizing returns. In its documentation for the annual meeting of shareholders in 2022, ExxonMobil stated that the compensation strategy 'aligns executives' pay with the results of their decisions and the returns of our shareholders over the long term', a dubious claim given what we know about demands for short-term profits.[10] Senior executives are joined in benefiting from profits by pension funds, private investors, and other shareholders, by employees, and by national governments (either through tax revenues on company profits, through income from production or extraction licences, or as owners of the companies). Fossil fuels are almost literally a gushing well of money for all concerned. The profits of the fossil fuel industry are so vast they are of geostrategic political importance, forming a significant share of the global returns generated by private financial investments, and the platform for the ascent of some top managers into the league of the super-rich. It doesn't require psychic powers to foresee that these profits will not be given up simply because the average global temperature is rising a little. Companies, governments, and even ordinary citizens as employees and investors all share the same interest: the profits must continue to gush. Fossil fuels must be extracted. But couldn't these profits simply be shifted to new business opportunities in the field of renewable energy? The answer is no, because the investments made in production fields and pipelines would turn into stranded assets. In addition, the profits from oil and gas production are significantly higher than those from investments in renewable energy. This is due to the more intense competition in renewable energy markets.[11]

Although these companies are now also facing political pressure from governments and above all from civil society, and at least some of them are preparing for an energy industry that will be partially decarbonized,[12] they are nevertheless reaping whatever profits are still possible from coal, oil, and gas extraction. This is because – so the underlying 'logic' has it – investing capital in projects with lower expected returns cannot be justified if higher returns are possible.

For companies in the fossil fuel industry, the key strategic question is therefore how their established activities can be continued and possibly even expanded *despite* the knowledge of climate change. Their initial prospects are good. The world needs a constant supply of the companies' products for its economy and its energy-intensive lifestyles. Currently, 87 per cent of the primary energy consumed worldwide is obtained from fossil fuels.[13] Economic growth, which, as we have seen, is indispensable to the system, runs at about 3 per cent annually and goes hand in hand with increased energy consumption. Owing to this increasing hunger for energy, even the rapid expansion of renewable energy is at best only partially replacing the use of fossil fuels. Just since the year 2000, global consumption of fossil fuels has risen by 45 per cent.[14]

Companies are of course aware that their business model ultimately depends on a stable natural and social environment now and in the future, and that the climate change they are driving threatens this stability. However, as the terrifying consequences will only materialize at some future point, and as any firm's individual contribution to protecting the climate would only be small, there is no incentive to stop extracting fossil fuels. The future damage is discounted. In the world of corporate logic, it can be completely rational to ignore future climate damage.[15]

If there is a threat to this business model, it is likely to come from outside. As a result of public pressure on government, regulation or global investment could boost renewable energy so fast that the extraction of oil, gas, and coal plummets and energy reserves remain in the ground for purely economic reasons. We are already seeing a power struggle today between the industry and various political forces that want to prioritize climate protection over profits. There is a lot at stake for the industry, but also for states. The potential loss of value from the capital assets of the fossil fuel industry is estimated to be between 13 and 17 trillion US dollars up to 2050, a significant proportion of which is state-owned.[16] How to prevent this gigantic sum of invested capital from turning into stranded assets is a vital question for the companies involved.

One answer is lobbying. The five largest Western oil companies alone spend around 200 million US dollars every year on targeted political lobbying,[17] in other words, on seeking to tilt political debate about the continued extraction of fossil fuels in their favour. Some of this lobbying is targeted at political regulations, such as the timing of the coal phase-out in Germany, permits for oil extraction from nature reserves in the United States and Canada, or the maintenance of indirect subsidies such as not taxing aviation fuel. Lobbyists also try to influence public opinion in order to minimize pressure on business practices and preserve their social legitimacy. The strategies oil companies have used to influence public opinion have been analysed extensively.[18] They can be divided into two phases. In the first phase, man-made climate change was simply denied; then – and to this day – the response has been stalling coupled with denial of responsibility.

It has been known for several years, for example, that ExxonMobil carried out its own studies beginning in the late 1970s which very accurately predicted climate change. In early 2023, a group of scientists from the Potsdam Institute for Climate Impact Research and Harvard University provided further detail on this by analysing Exxon's corporate documents.[19] The fact that its own scientists knew about the impact of burning fossil fuels on the climate did not stop the company from playing down the issue in public; quite the opposite, in fact. At the 1999 shareholders' meeting, the then CEO, Lee Raymond, reported that climate change projections were 'based on completely unproven climate models or, more often, on sheer speculation'.[20] This was four years after the IPCC had announced that human impact on the climate could now be proven because observable patterns differed from natural fluctuations. By denying climate change, the oil multinational was attempting to evade its share of responsibility, protecting the legitimacy of the industry in the eyes of the public and warding off effective regulation.

According to Greenpeace, Exxon alone supported think tanks engaged in climate change denial with over 30 million dollars up to 2014.[21] Various PR campaigns were also carried out using ads aimed at spreading uncertainty among the public about the causes of climate change. Exxon is far from alone in this. The Koch brothers, owners of Koch Industries, one of the biggest American oil companies, financed the lobbying organization Americans for Prosperity (among others), which also organized public disinformation campaigns on climate change and helped derail planned climate protection laws by means of so-called astroturfing campaigns.[22] Such campaigns aim at making the public think that a marketing message originates not from the company but from a grassroots movement and is therefore 'authentic'. A few years ago, one study calculated that political organizations in the United States that denied climate change or played down its consequences had an annual budget of 900 million dollars at their disposal.[23] The oil industry is frequently compared to the tobacco industry, which hid its knowledge of the dangerous nature of its product from the public for decades. Incidentally, ExxonMobil is defending itself against the accusation of deliberate misinformation. This is understandable, as the company now has a lot at stake. The city of New York, for example, sued ExxonMobil, Shell, and BP in 2021, alleging that they had systematically and deliberately misled the public and investors about the climate impact of their products.[24] The state of California also recently launched a lawsuit against the oil companies. If they lose, the companies may face huge claims for compensation for the climate damage their products have caused.

Thus, further investment in fossil fuel extraction harbours the risk not only of increasing public criticism and a loss of political standing for the energy companies, but also increasing legal risks. These are not trivial matters. The desired prolongation of their business model therefore has to be defended against both the state and the wider society. Again, their weapon of choice for this purpose is sophisticated public relations work. As already mentioned, one rhetorical strategy used by companies is to shift the responsibility for climate change onto consumers. The oil companies, so the narrative goes, are merely supplying the products that consumers want and are thus responding to their needs. This argument is readily believed because the lifestyles that consumers want are indeed based on ever-increasing energy consumption. The oil multinationals, in an almost patronizing manner, then make suggestions as to how consumers can reduce their individual CO_2 emissions. Few of those consumers are probably aware that the idea of calculating individual carbon footprints was popularized in the early 2000s by the international advertising agency Ogilvy & Mather, working on behalf of BP,[25] with the aim of making responsibility for the increase in emissions a problem for each individual consumer and, above all, a problem to be tackled individually.[26] In 2004, BP offered the first carbon footprint calculator, with which we could all calculate the emissions associated with our own consumption. There are now a large number of apps available for calculating your carbon footprint, and you can atone immediately for your sins by making donations to offset your emissions. Such individualization strategies resonate in the individualist culture of capitalist modernity and demonstrate the close link between the economic system and the cultural identity of society. In developing such PR strategies, companies are seeking covert influence over the public. This demonstrates how ruthless is the defence of profit interests. At the same time, those interests always have to be concealed to preserve social legitimation, which is in danger of becoming more precarious in the face of climate change.

To this end, the advertising industry creates a green façade for its clients' products in order to hide their negative impact on the environment. A study examining the rhetorical strategies used by the energy companies BP, Chevron, ExxonMobil, and Shell found that the use of terms such as 'climate', 'transformation', and 'low CO_2' increased significantly between 2009 and 2020. However, little has changed in terms of actual business practices.[27] According to the 'impact investing' platform Inyova, the proportion of the investments made in renewable energy by TotalEnergies was 30 per cent in 2022. The company's main focus is on oil and gas production. However, if you look at the group's marketing, the advertising 'almost exclusively shows green technologies and conveys vague plans to reduce CO_2 emissions from the business'.[28] This – false – impression is also conveyed by the websites of other companies in the gas and oil industry, as anyone with internet access can easily see for themselves. In this way, a completely distorted picture of their actual business activities is created in the public eye.

Another marketing strategy is to publicize plans for a future change in behaviour. Such promises are loudly communicated with the aim of reducing public criticism and regulatory pressure. Whether they will be honoured is written in the stars. If they are not honoured, which would come as no surprise, then this is simply hypocrisy. ExxonMobil, for example, like many energy companies, promised to be climate-neutral by 2050, but by this it does not mean stopping oil production: it refers only to emissions from its oil, gas, and chemical production and the power its own business processes consume.[29] In May 2022, the oil multinational's shareholders voted against proposals to reduce emissions via new targets for reduced oil sales and to publish medium- and long-term targets for reducing greenhouse gases from fossil fuel production.[30] For a while, the British energy multinational BP wanted the two letters of its brand name to be understood as an abbreviation for 'Beyond Petroleum'.[31] On its website, the company describes its own transformation in a coded way as 'making strides' in various renewable energies but continuing 'to deliver the oil and gas the world depends on today, while aiming to cut emissions'.[32] BP is also a self-declared 'net zero 2050' company.[33] In 2022, however, 'Beyond Petroleum' generated 91 per cent of its revenues from fossil fuels. The fact that the oil multinationals' climate promises are more or less a façade presented to the public is also evident from statements made by former workers in the industry, who report that the climate friendliness presented to the outside world is reflected neither in the internal corporate culture nor in the actual business plans. For some employees, this was reason enough to quit.[34] Governments also use this 'politics of expectations'.[35] It provides short-term relief from the pressure to take action, because checking whether a target has been met can only happen ten, twenty, or thirty years later. In business and politics alike, that is an eternity. As the target date draws closer and it becomes clear that it can or should no longer be met, it is simply postponed or redefined. Such promises should therefore only be taken seriously if they contain immediate measures, list the steps that are to be taken to achieve the target in a verifiable format year by year, and are then actually verified. Otherwise, the announcement of climate targets is little more than distraction and PR – with the purpose of supporting the corporations' battle in defence of their future profits from selling fossil energy.

While the companies are creating a green image for themselves, they continue their investments in the extraction of fossil fuels. Despite climate change, their goal remains unchanged: to stabilize profits and retain strategic control over their market sectors.[36] Sure enough, some investments also go into green energies. The markets for renewable energy are growing. Over the past ten years, the amount of renewable energy available globally has increased, primarily owing to new solar and wind power plants.[37] Around 2 per cent of the global primary energy consumption of around 168,000 TWh is currently met by wind or solar energy.[38] However, looking at this growth in relation to the development of fossil fuels is revealing: since 2000, oil, gas, and coal production has also continued to increase, and hundreds of billions of dollars are still being spent annually on new infrastructure for fossil fuels.[39] In other words: in a world of increasing energy demand, despite the significant expansion of renewable energy, more oil, gas, and coal is being burnt, not less – in spite of all the climate warnings and public relations campaigning.

If we take a look at the energy companies' current and planned investments in the continued extraction of fossil fuels, a frightening picture emerges. In a piece of investigative journalism published in 2022, the British newspaper *The Guardian* found that oil and gas companies want to launch new extraction projects by the end of the decade that would release over their lifetime an additional 97 billion tonnes of CO_2.[40] This is equivalent to three years' worth of the global CO_2 emissions from burning fossil fuels. The majority of these new projects already have financial backing in place. A study focusing on so-called CO_2 bombs (i.e., extraction projects that will emit more than one billion tonnes of CO_2 over their lifetime) identified 425 such projects worldwide, with potential total emissions of 646 billion tonnes of CO_2.[41] Around 40 per cent of these projects have not yet begun production, but are planned. If all these projects go ahead, the emissions would be double the amount that would allow us to keep the temperature increase to merely 1.5 degrees.

Conservation concerns are frequently ignored when such projects are approved. In March 2023, for example, the US President authorized the company ConocoPhillips to proceed with drilling in Alaska for what is known as the 'Willow Project', which is expected to pump 600 million barrels of crude oil over the next thirty years. The pumping will take place on the largest contiguous area of pristine land in the United States still in public ownership, an area of great ecological importance. And it will lead to 280 million tonnes of CO_2 emissions. At an average oil price of 70 US dollars per barrel, the project will generate annual revenues of USD 1.4 billion for the company. The state expects a total of USD 17 billion in tax revenue, and 2,500 new jobs are predicted.[42] Residents of Alaska will also receive a direct share of the tax revenue via a state fund. They will receive annual cheques. A genuine win-win situation for investors, the state, residents, and employees – at the expense of the voiceless natural world and our own future.

Such investment decisions show how tomorrow's quality of life is sold for today's profit. Companies, the state, and citizens all work hand in hand in this. The energy multinationals have no intention of withdrawing from the fossil fuel business any time soon.[43] Even reductions in the production of fossil fuels that have already been promised are being cancelled. Under its former CEO, Ben van Beurden, Shell had announced that it would reduce its oil and gas production by 1 to 2 per cent every year up to 2030.[44] Given the urgency of global warming, this is a laughably meagre amount. However, even this is too much for his successor, Wael Sawan, who took over the group at the beginning of 2023. He announced that he would concentrate on the core business with the highest returns – which is fossil fuels – as the world 'still urgently needs oil and gas'.[45] Shell is by no means alone in backtracking in this way. BP, to take another example, had come up with a plan to reduce its oil and gas production by 2030 in such a way that CO_2 emissions would be reduced by 35 to 40 per cent. After the publication of the company's financial results for 2022, the best in its history, then CEO Bernard Looney announced that the aim was now to reduce CO_2 emissions in the oil and gas business by 2030 by only 20 to 30 per cent.[46] There was a global demand for fossil fuels, he said. BP's share price shot up after the announcement. The decisions by Shell and BP show the hypocrisy of emissions reduction targets. The investments made by the oil and gas industry in new extraction projects – despite all the warnings from experts and all the advertisements that suggest otherwise – do not suggest that fossil fuels are being phased out.[47] Given that in a capitalist economy, investment is determined by expected returns, this is hardly a surprise. What would really call for an explanation would be if companies were to voluntarily forgo potential billions in profits.

The energy multinationals' fossil fuel projects are made possible in part by loans from banks. For the financial industry, this is a lucrative business. The same applies to private investors, who achieve high returns on their investments in the relevant companies. Between 2016 and 2022, the sixty largest banks in the world financed the fossil fuel operations of the leading energy companies with a total of USD 5.5 trillion, of which USD 669 billion was in 2022 alone.[48] The banks' investment strategy is based on their expectations of continuing demand for fossil fuels even in the long term. But the more investment goes into new extraction projects, and the longer the relevant energy infrastructure is subsidized, the more difficult and protracted the exit from fossil fuels will be. Those investments would then have to be written off as stranded assets, resulting in major losses for the companies and their shareholders. Today's investments entrench the business model for decades to come.

At the same time, investment in renewable energy falls far short of what is needed for an effective response to climate change, as the IEA drily noted in 2023:

Investment to bring more clean and affordable energy into the system is rising, but not yet quickly enough to forge a path out of today's crisis or to bring emissions down to net zero by mid-century – a critical but formidable challenge that the world needs to overcome if it is to have any chance of limiting global warming to 1.5°C. Without a massive surge in spending on efficiency, electrification and low-carbon supply, rising global demand for energy services will simply not be met in a sustainable way.[49]

Energy companies are by no means alone in defending their well-functioning, fossil fuel-based business models. They are just a particularly outstanding example because they are at the beginning of the fossil energy value chain and are so rich and powerful. One only has to look at the chemicals industry, the aviation industry, or the automotive industry to discover similar strategies. At the same time, however, the picture becomes more complicated. After all, it is quite conceivable that industries that currently use fossil fuels could switch over their production and the goods and services they provide to renewable energy sources. The steel and chemicals industries, for example, will in the future be able to use green hydrogen and electricity generated from renewable energy sources instead of gas and oil for much of their production. The same applies to cruise tourism, air travel, and, of course, the automotive sector. If this were to happen, it would also have an impact on the oil and gas industry, as demand for these fuels would fall. This brings us to the prospects for a green transformation of the economy, which I will discuss in detail in Chapter 7. Nevertheless, I would like to make a few comments here that illustrate the powerful inertia of industrial structures far beyond the oil and gas industry.

First, even in those downstream industries that 'only' utilize oil and gas, the move away from existing business models will not take place in a straightforward manner. In part this is due to the principle of profit maximization, which sidelines ecological concerns. But another factor here is path dependency, getting stuck in established ways of doing business, which stems from organizational structures, existing capital investments, as well as the qualifications and mindsets of managers and employees.

A switch to 'green' business models requires above all significant technological changes which are expensive, take a long time to implement, and are often economically unprofitable, at least in the short term. They therefore lack an economic rationale. Companies invest large sums in technological pathways, capital assets, and energy supply infrastructures which are calculated to pay off over long stretches of time. If these assets have to be written off prematurely, huge losses are incurred. Companies understandably resist this. Those companies that have committed themselves to technologies that use fossil fuels have good economic and organizational reasons to hold on to the existing structures, at least for the time being, and to use whatever political power they have to defend their choices. A faster switch to renewable energies could only be enforced politically, and achieved with massive state aid. There are also material shortages that cannot all be overcome quickly, even with state aid. We don't, for example, have enough green electricity, a network of pipelines suitable for hydrogen, nor aeroplanes with hydrogen-powered engines. It will take decades before some of these infrastructures and technologies are ready to be deployed – far too long, in other words, to effectively combat climate change.

However, we are now seeing intense market competition in a number of industries between the current heavyweights, which are following established paths, and new companies which are challenging them with more climate-friendly technologies and new organizational structures. Path dependency is not a problem for these new firms. The prime example is the automotive industry, which over ten years ago saw a competitor emerge in the form of Tesla which is now exerting enormous pressure on the established companies in the sector.

How this market struggle will pan out remains to be seen, but it seems entirely possible that old companies that have dominated the market will lose a great deal of power and influence. And this is the essence of the principle of 'creative destruction', which gives the capitalist economy its dynamism. But this principle is far too weak when it comes to the climate. Incumbent companies usually pursuing the logic of economic advantage seek to hold on to their established technologies for as long as possible. To achieve this, they utilize their market power and political influence. The heavyweights of the automotive industry demonstrated this in textbook fashion by delaying the switch to new business models, bitterly resisting stricter emission standards and attempts to phase out the combustion engine. They defend tooth and nail the things they do particularly well – indeed, better than anyone else. One may well ask why the German car industry, among others, has focused its energy for so long on maintaining the status quo instead of channelling it into the development of electromobility. In addition to the path dependencies referred to earlier, it may be that Big Oil is also playing a role here. The sovereign wealth fund of Kuwait, for example, is the third largest single shareholder in Mercedes-Benz, and has a seat on the supervisory board; in 2023, Saudi Aramco invested in a joint venture between Renault and the Chinese car manufacturer Geely to develop new combustion engines.[50] However, the industry can also rely on car drivers, who are similarly often sceptical about electric cars. And of course the employees in the factories of the car makers and their suppliers fear that their jobs may be under threat.

Expectations regarding future market developments are also relevant. The companies want to position themselves as advantageously as possible. And this includes extending the production of combustion engine cars well into the future. Although the EU is banning the registration of new combustion engine vehicles from 2035 – with exceptions! – neither the United States nor China, the two largest car markets in the world, is joining this ban. The head of Renault, Luca de Meo, assumes that more than half of the world's cars will still be powered by combustion engines in 2040.[51] In Latin America, it is estimated that the proportion of electric vehicles will still be less than 10 per cent in the 2030s.[52] It is quite possible, owing to the growing number of new registrations in the car market, that the number of combustion engines in the world will still be almost as high in 2040 as it is today. From the perspective of those car companies operating globally, this means that there will still be money to be made from combustion engines in the future – so let's do it.[53] From a climate perspective, it means that without additional measures, global emissions from the transport sector will be higher in 2050 than they are today.[54] The sober conclusion of a recent large-scale study on the behaviour of companies in the climate crisis is therefore that 'the majority of companies still do not engage in practices that would signal a significant move toward deep decarbonization'.[55] If electromobility is to establish itself quickly, it cannot be left to the market, but requires regulatory intervention and large state subsidies. In the rich industrialized countries, the state is trying to overcome consumer scepticism towards electric vehicles by offering hefty subsidies to buyers. In addition, there is now – finally – a commitment in many countries to building the necessary charging infrastructure by setting standards and providing subsidies. The richer the country, the greater the likelihood that it will be able to afford the infrastructure investments and state aid required for the switch to electromobility. All of this is progressing too slowly, and of course not all countries are rich. As a result, the green transformation is much too gradual and is being only patchily implemented.

Let me summarize. In a capitalist economy, the behaviour of companies is driven by profit interests. To paraphrase Niklas Luhmann: the economic system only understands the 'language of prices',[56] everything else is just 'noise'. As long as enormous profits are made from the production of fossil fuels and combustion engines, the relevant companies will do everything they can to defend those profits. They have the structural and instrumental power to obstruct, delay, and water down climate protection regulations. In order not to lose their legitimation, they deploy strategies to cover up the detrimental impacts of their business practices and to deflect responsibility. Public relations plays a central role here. A capitalist economy is deaf to any ethical appeals to avoid ecological damage as long as those appeals have no price tag. However, the price tag can only ever originate from outside – from the state and civil society.

4

The hesitant state

It may be no surprise that corporations chasing profit have a structural hearing impairment when it comes to the requirements for an environmentally friendly economy. If they perceive these requirements at all, it's as 'background noise'. But what about politicians? Duty-bound to serve the common good not profit, politicians should in principle be expected to take the necessary measures decisively and swiftly, especially with so much at stake for the citizens in whose name they act. Theoretically, politicians have the necessary instruments at their disposal to address climate change, as they set the framework for all economic activity and determine how we interact with nature in energy policy, environmental policy, housing and urban planning policy, agricultural policy, transport policy, and, last but not least, economic policy. In practice, however, political regulation falls far short of what is required. Why is this so?

I have already given one important part of the answer in describing the power relationship between the economy and the state. This is one of mutual dependency, in which the state controls the economic framework in which companies operate but depends on those companies prospering. Most tax revenues come either directly from companies as corporation tax or from employees as income and consumption taxes. Without them, the state could not fund schools, buy defence equipment, or organize welfare provisions. It is not possible for governments to fund their priorities and extremely difficult for them to win elections if corporations and the economy are suffering. Companies are thus in an ideal position to insist on rules that promise them high and secure profits.[1]

To defend itself against unfavourable political regulations, business can credibly threaten to reduce its investments or to migrate to other countries that offer more favourable conditions. In view of this structural corporate power, the government, even assuming it wanted to, cannot simply issue companies with orders, even on existential issues such as climate protection. Politicians know this. And if they forget, they are reminded. Companies start to talk about the country's lack of competitiveness and the relative merits of other jurisdictions. Former German Chancellor Angela Merkel succinctly acknowledged the dependence of politics on the economy when she said at a press conference in 2011 that the German government would 'find ways to shape parliamentary co-decision making in such a way that it is nevertheless also market-conforming'.[2] At the time, she was talking about policies to solve the European sovereign debt crisis. But it is no less true that climate policy is determined by a contest between economic interests, on the one side, and potentially divergent social goals, on the other. The growth rationale of the capitalist economy and the dependence of the state on the private sector lead almost inevitably to inadequate environmental regulation. Might this change under a 'green growth' regime in which companies shift their profit expectations onto green investments? I will turn to this in Chapter 7.

Economic influence is also exercised in a direct way. Political scientists speak of instrumental power when referring to the use of lobbying to influence political decisions. In principle, of course, lobbying is as open to environmentalists as it is to the fossil fuel industry, the automotive industry, the chemicals industry, or the tourism industry.[3] And business associations working for green energy do indeed lobby, as do organizations such as Greenpeace and WWF. In reality, however, their power is limited. While the lobby groups of the German gas industry, for example, have annual budgets totalling around 40 million euros at their disposal, environmental associations concerned about gas have to make do with only 1.5 million.[4] In what some political scientists have dubbed 'the association state' ('*Verbändestaat*'), some associations are more equal than others.

Despite the large sums of money involved, the influence exerted by lobbyists is often invisible to the public. Contacts with politicians or ministry officials are not always disclosed. Many of these contacts are informal and what is agreed in discussions often remains confidential. A cosy chat at a reception is not subject to public scrutiny. The instrumental power of companies becomes even more obvious when political decision-makers link their private financial interests with those of climate-damaging industries. Such crony capitalism is by no means limited to authoritarian regimes but can also be observed in parliamentary democracies. US Senator Joe Manchin from West Virginia, for example, effectively vetoed President Biden's climate protection bill in 2022. Manchin's political action committee (PAC) has received substantial donations from the fossil fuel industry to support his election campaigns.[5] Before entering politics, the senator was the founder of Enersystems, a coal trading company owned by his family and managed by his son.[6] Manchin also joined other senators in ensuring that fossil fuel industry interests were taken into account in the bill passed in 2023 to raise the US debt ceiling. A rider was added to the bill to provide for a new gas pipeline to be built through West Virginia to transport fracked gas from Senator Manchin's home state.[7]

The revolving door between business and politics is another mechanism that facilitates influence, as it makes it possible for interested parties to penetrate deep into political and economic decision-making networks. For example, the CEO of ExxonMobil, Rex Tillerson, became US Secretary of State in 2017, much as Dick Cheney, former US Secretary of Defense and subsequently CEO of the oil services company Halliburton, became Vice President in 2001. Former German Foreign Minister Sigmar Gabriel is on the Supervisory Board of Siemens Energy and Chair of the Supervisory Board of Thyssenkrupp Steel Europe. Most dramatically, perhaps, former German Chancellor Gerhard Schröder became a lobbyist for a Russian gas company in the years before Russia's invasion of Ukraine.

Even the United Nations conferences on climate protection are heavily influenced by the interests of the global oil and gas lobby. The President of the UN Climate Change Conference COP28, which was held in Dubai at the end of 2023, was the Minister of Industry of the United Arab Emirates, Sultan Ahmed al-Jaber, who is also the head of the Abu Dhabi National Oil Company. One journalist commented: 'It's like hiring Pablo Escobar to fight the cocaine trade.'[8] At the climate conference in Sharm el-Sheikh, Egypt, a year earlier, more than 600 lobbyists from the gas and oil industry were registered attendees.[9] In Dubai, this number quadrupled to over 2,400 representatives from the fossil fuel industry, all joining a conference tasked with negotiating climate protection.[10] Similar lists detailing linkages between politics and business interests could be extended almost indefinitely. The connections do not violate any laws, but illustrate how powerful economic interests and government activity are intertwined and how corporate interests are pursued through the instrumentalization of politics. Any attempt to explain why the political response to climate change has been inadequate must not overlook the structural and instrumental power that economic interests are able to exert on politics. In itself, however, this is not a sufficient explanation.

The work of the sociologist Wolfgang Streeck has shed light on the Janus-faced character of state behaviour.[11] On the one hand, the state must maintain an efficient economy to preserve social stability and the standard of living. But the state cannot limit itself to satisfying economic interests alone. After all, economic wellbeing is only one of the pillars of social order. As Streeck emphasizes, societies are not driven exclusively by economic motives. In social disputes, for example, norms of justice play a central role, helping to determine the distribution of wealth and how we protect people against the vicissitudes of the market and such life risks as illness and old age. There are many other social problems and public concerns that are not directly economic but do extend into the economic sphere. The problem of climate protection is certainly one of these.

Opinion polls regularly show that large majorities of the population in many countries regard climate protection as an important political objective; many of them even regard it as the *most* important.[12] Even in dictatorships, politicians need to take account of citizens' preferences, and in parliamentary democracies, election outcomes depend on doing so. In view of this, and even if the value of such polls may be questionable (who is not in favour of environmental protection?), it is surprising, at least at first glance, that politicians find climate protection so difficult. If you take a second glance and look at the considerable gap between our general awareness of the problem and our actual willingness to support specific climate protection measures, things start to look different.[13] Of course, there are many people who demand effective climate protection measures and also support them politically, and even set an example in their own behaviour. This is perhaps most clearly reflected in participation in social movements for climate protection. There are also many citizens who support strong environmental measures when voting in elections. Nevertheless, concrete political steps in favour of climate protection receive far less support from the population than might be expected given the findings of opinion polls. Ultimately, however, this also creates incentive structures for politicians that stand in the way of an adequate response to climate change.

In this chapter, I want to explain – beyond the direct influence of companies – the reasons behind the hesitancy when it comes to political action. I will start by outlining the sheer scale of the transformation required for climate protection and then go into greater detail on its social and cultural implications for the population at large. Finally, I will look at the decision-making structures of the political system, where the relevant competences for climate protection are located at very different levels. These levels have to cooperate, but are often pursuing different goals. The result is sluggish political action and watered-down or stalled decisions. Most of the examples in this chapter come from Germany, but they could just as easily come from other countries in the global North where there is a pluralistic political order and a general awareness of the political urgency of climate protection. The situation is different, however, in the global South, and especially in countries dependent on the export of fossil energy and raw materials. This will be discussed in Chapter 5.

Let's start with the scale of the transformation required. One thing is clear: in order to implement effective climate protection, large parts of the existing, *functioning* infrastructures in the areas of energy generation, industrial production, agriculture, construction, and transport must be completely rebuilt or at least significantly remodelled. This restructuring involves enormous costs, poses a huge logistical challenge, and requires significant changes to established ways of life. But the alternative is also costly. Studies estimate the costs of climate change for Germany alone at several hundred billion euros over the next few decades. The costs of climate adaptation, repairing environmental damage, and cancelled economic activity (e.g. owing to extreme weather events or increasing drought) will have to be paid.[14] These costs, however, are easy to ignore if they are seen as lying in the distant future or as only affecting some regions and groups, but not oneself. They are more abstract and hypothetical than the immediate and concrete costs and planning challenges of installing new heating systems or building tens of thousands of wind turbines across Europe. In their accounting, businesses, politicians, and the public discount future losses, meaning climate change does not carry enough weight in the present to prompt effective action. This is short-sightedness.

Nobody knows exactly how much investment is required to meet the climate targets. However, calculations are available that at least indicate the dimensions.[15] The management consultancy McKinsey presented a simulation study in 2022 according to which USD 9.2 trillion would have to be invested globally in property, plant, and equipment each year up until 2050 in order to achieve the 2050 net-zero target.[16] This represents between 7 and 8 per cent of global GDP. In 'developing' countries, the share of economic output would be even higher. From a global perspective, investment in climate protection would have to more than double its current level. In the European Union, more than 300 billion euros would have to be invested annually in energy and transport infrastructure alone to achieve the net-zero targets in 2050, and almost 400 billion euros from the 2030s onwards.[17]

These costs would have to be borne by citizens even though the measures would not lead to a tangible improvement in the quality of life. Quite the opposite: as public expenditure, they would lead to budget restructuring, meaning that funds would no longer be available to address other important social goals. After all, public money is also needed for social services, culture, education, and defence. Tax increases might help but these are mostly blocked by party politics. Another option would be to incur greater public debt – but this route is largely blocked by major ideological reservations in most countries. In view of the scale of the climate protection challenge, the state's capacity to sufficiently reorganize infrastructures is therefore reaching its limits, even in the rich countries of the global North. Not because the money is not there in principle, but because it cannot be mobilized politically to the required extent. If private households instead tried to fund the restructuring, the expense would force citizens to cut back on consumption or on savings, perhaps for retirement provision or the purchase of a home. There would be considerable opportunity costs. In plain language: the standard of living would fall.

A couple of examples will serve to illustrate the scale of the task. To achieve climate neutrality in the building sector in Germany, 40 million buildings need to be renovated to improve their energy efficiency and 20 million oil and gas heating systems need to be replaced. How are the owners or tenants supposed to finance this? Installing a heat pump in a one-family house costs between 20,000 and 40,000 euros; the cost of a complete energy retrofit for a forty-year-old building quickly climbs to 200,000 euros. In a recent survey in Germany, over 40 per cent of property owners questioned stated that they could not afford to invest in the energy transition.[18] In transportation, price hikes for petrol and diesel as a result of the carbon tax are already raising the cost of living. But electric vehicles are significantly more expensive than combustion-powered cars; if people buy them, they need to cut their spending elsewhere. What's more, the transformation to electromobility will incur high infrastructure costs. The electricity grid has to be expanded to meet the increased demand and a nationwide charging infrastructure is needed. The expansion of the grid in Germany alone is expected to cost around 500 billion euros over the next twenty-five years.[19] These costs will either have to be borne by the state, which will then have to take on more debt, increase taxes, or make savings elsewhere, or else they will be borne by the companies involved, which will then pass on the costs to the consumer by charging higher prices for electricity.

A similar set of challenges arises in the industrial sector. The conversion of the German steel industry away from using coke to using hydrogen is expected to cost 30 billion euros, with production costs afterwards expected to be 30 to 40 per cent higher in the long term.[20] From an environmental perspective, though, this restructuring is urgently needed: Thyssenkrupp's blast furnaces alone emit 20 million tonnes of CO_2 per year, which corresponds to 2.5 per cent of Germany's total carbon dioxide emissions.[21] However, the transition to hydrogen can only be implemented with the aid of billions in subsidies, as the transformation would not be commercially viable otherwise. The German government is thus reimbursing companies for the conversion of industrial production processes and the associated operating costs for up to fifteen years through so-called climate protection contracts. A total of 68 billion euros in state aid has been earmarked for this up to 2040.[22] This is controversial not only as a departure from traditional German economic regulatory policy, but also owing to the sheer scale of the costs. After all, how do you explain to voters that public money is being passed on to the industry in the form of permanent subsidies? Where will public spending be reduced as a result? Is this really a sensible strategy? If steel can be produced up to one-third cheaper internationally, what exactly is the future business model for the German steel industry? On the other hand, without such subsidies, how can we prevent climate protection leading to the deindustrialization of the country and at the same time simply shifting greenhouse gas emissions to countries that are still willing to use fossil fuels? What would happen to a place like Duisburg, where the loss of the steel industry would completely destroy the city's social fabric?

The conversion of industrial infrastructure is not only a cost issue, but also an enormous logistical challenge, with shortages of materials repeatedly posing problems. There is currently not enough electricity to convert industrial production to green energy, nor are there enough power lines or hydrogen pipelines to transport the energy to the production sites. If energy-intensive large-scale industries in southern Germany wanted to switch to electricity as an energy source, there would not be enough available at present. As green electricity is primarily generated in northern Germany, power lines have to be built to bring the energy south. The construction of these lines is taking a long time. Complex planning procedures and, not least, protests from local residents are causing delays. Completion of the important 'electricity motorway' *Südlink* is not expected until the end of 2028. It will then have taken sixteen years from the first plans to the transmission of the first electricity. The sheer scale of the necessary transformation of infrastructures that have been built up over decades makes decarbonization a highly complex and controversial project. It is no wonder that political decision-making is making very slow progress. In planning and technological terms, the transformation is a Herculean task. What is more, the cutting back of the administrative capacity of the state in recent decades – aiming at the so-called slim state – has removed much of the state planning capacity that is essential today for the green transformation.

The necessary changes are not only expensive and wideranging, but also entail so many implications and personal impositions that many measures are controversial even among those who want to protect the climate. In order both to adapt to climate change and to protect the climate in the future, for example, livestock farming must be curtailed. But how can evolving conflicts with farmers and local residents be resolved politically? In the Netherlands, farmers have been protesting for several years against government plans to reduce livestock numbers in the country by a third in order to bring greenhouse gas emissions from the agricultural sector into line with

EU regulations and the requirements of the Dutch Supreme Administrative Court. In the spring of 2023, the dispute escalated, with farmers setting hay bales on fire and blocking roads and government buildings in The Hague. The farmers' party BoerBurgerBeweging, which was only founded in 2019, opposed the government's plans and won the regional elections in 2023, becoming the strongest parliamentary group in the Lower Chamber.[23] In Belgium, there were similar protests against plans to reduce agricultural emissions. Existing arrangements are being defended by a politically influential agricultural lobby – as well as people who are simply attached to their accustomed way of life – even if they run counter to climate protection goals.

But this is about more than just animal husbandry and farmers. Climate adaptation requires, among other things, restoring wetlands and floodplains. Many previously built-up areas would then no longer be suitable for housing, bringing the requirements of climate adaptation and the preservation of established ways of life into conflict with one another. What will happen to my house? Decarbonizing energy production will also require the installation of thousands more wind turbines and solar panels, and pipelines will have to be laid to transport hydrogen. But why does this have to happen in my community, in my constituency, or through our vineyards? Cities would have to limit their growth in order to reduce soil sealing; they would have to be greened in order to reduce heat build-up in summer; they would have to introduce different water management systems in order to secure the water supply in the face of increasing shortages. But how can this be reconciled with cities' economic growth targets and booming immigration? In order to reduce car traffic in cities, cycle paths would have to be created and traffic calming measures introduced. But how can drivers who are worried about additional traffic jams be brought on board? Here, too, we are talking about ways of life that come into conflict with each other.

Every measure is an imposition, either on people's wallets, their lifestyles, or their personal convenience, and all of them provoke political resistance from the social groups affected. The southern German states are delaying the allocation of areas for wind turbines because they are unpopular with the public. The motoring lobby blocks the introduction of speed limits. People in rural areas protest against rising petrol prices. And on top of all that, effective climate protection is a global task. All the necessary changes that can be imagined for one country must ultimately be implemented in all countries. But this is entirely beyond the remit of national politics. And who seriously believes that sacrifices made in one country will bring other countries round?

The impositions on the public and the fear of possible costs lead to political dissatisfaction, which is mobilized by opposition parties for electoral purposes. Cognitive psychologists have shown that people find it particularly difficult to cope with expected losses and adapt their behaviour to avoid them.[24] As a result, the political projects essential for the protection of the climate fail. In political science, the median voter theorem suggests that political positioning follows the interests of the voter group in the middle of the political spectrum.[25] As the burdens of effective climate protection policy affect large sections of the population in precisely this middle area, political majorities cannot be found for it. The political system lacks the strength to undertake and see through the necessary reforms. Plans are deferred, watered down, or cancelled. Subsidies continue for diesel and company cars, e-mobility is abandoned in favour of e-fuels. I have already hinted at the underlying problem: the internalization of previously externalized environmental costs leads to restrictions in personal freedom and to financial burdens, but not to any tangible gain in prosperity in the sense of more holidays, better schools, or fancier cars. The undeniable long-term benefits of climate protection investments remain unrealized because they 'merely' ensure the prolongation of existing living conditions, and anyway lie in the future. It is one thing to speak out in favour of climate protection in general. It is another to support it politically given its concrete consequences for living standards and personal comfort.[26]

An important aspect of all this is the distributional impact of climate protection. Politically, climate policy cannot be separated from issues of social justice. A prominent example is the environmentally motivated increase in petrol prices in France, which triggered the so-called 'yellow vest' protests led by less prosperous voters outside the major cities in 2019.[27] Many climate protection measures place a disproportionate burden on lower-income households. The renewable energy levy, which was introduced in Germany as a percentage surcharge on electricity costs up until 2022, represented an annual burden of up to 30 billion euros for private households. Electricity-intensive companies were exempt from the levy to help them stay internationally competitive. As a consumption tax, the levy placed a particular burden on those on lower incomes. At the same time, new subsidies such as feed-in tariffs for electricity generated by photovoltaic systems or allowances for electric cars benefit higher earners, as poorer people can't afford either even with the subsidies.[28] It is no coincidence that opinion polls show that wealthy people support the energy transition more than people from lower social classes.[29] They have good reason to do so.

The redistributive effects of a climate policy that has not been adjusted to ensure fairness increase political resistance and undermine the government's commitment to its proudly proclaimed climate targets. As a result, political decisions that have already been taken are difficult to uphold. In the Netherlands, for example, following the farmers' protests, the established political parties, above all the Christian Democrats, now want to abandon or at least scale back their plans to reduce livestock numbers. In the summer of 2023, the British government decided to postpone the ban on new registrations of combustion cars from 2030 to 2035 and to water down other climate protection measures that had already been agreed. The reason was electoral: fear of less prosperous Conservative voters, with whom the measures are often unpopular.[30] In Germany, the original plan was to further increase the cost of CO_2 emissions in the building and transport sectors in 2023. However, in view of exploding energy prices, this plan was postponed in 2022, while petrol and electricity consumption received even higher state subsidies. The additional burden on households from higher energy prices had to be offset politically. In order to at least contain the rise in energy prices and to ensure that energy was available, coal-fired power plants that had already been shut down were also brought back online. And 2022 was then the year when global coal production reached a new high.[31] All this leads to a sobering conclusion: nature loses out in situations of political stress.

Climate policy increases the need for redistribution of income and wealth so poorer citizens can afford necessary changes. Politically, however, such redistribution comes up against tight limits. Politicians who believe in free markets find it difficult to introduce redistribution programmes, even if the aim is not to reduce social inequality but to stabilize the global climate. In Germany, what is called climate money (*Klimageld*), and which is more properly known in English as a carbon fee and dividend, was to be introduced under the current government. The intention is to reduce the burden of the energy transition on citizens. But the government is hesitating, and *Klimageld* will not be paid out before 2025, and most likely not before 2027 – if at all.[32] The revenue from carbon pricing has already been allocated for other purposes, such as state aid for the transformation of large-scale industry or urgent repair work on railway tracks that has been postponed for decades. Only some private households will receive money back, for example those who can afford to install a new heating system. However, such broken promises galvanize political resistance to climate protection, which in turn dilutes and delays it.

Questions of redistribution are an issue not only at the household level.[33] Other related sources of conflict involve shifts in the balance of political and regional power. In Germany, for example, the energy transition is shifting energy production to the wind-rich northern states, while at the same time Bavaria and Baden-Württemberg in the south are losing their nuclear production due to the phase-out of nuclear power.[34] As a result, the north is becoming more attractive than the south as a location for industry. Coal mining areas in the Rhineland and Lusatia or in Poland are similarly losing their long-established economic structure together with the associated jobs and lifestyles as a result of the energy transition. All of this leads to political controversy.

Another associated line of conflict runs along generational lines. Those who are old will be less affected by climate change; those who are young have a greater interest in climate protection. As the population ages, approval of climate policy measures therefore declines.[35] Work to protect the climate will take generations. But which generation should pay for it? Climate protection policy also intersects with cultural power shifts. The transformation of societies in response to climate change strengthens political groups associated with certain socio-cultural milieus. In Germany, this can be seen very clearly in the rise of the Green Party, whose voters are urban and culturally liberal, have high incomes, and are proponents of climate protection.[36] Climate change thus becomes part of a wider culture war, which makes political action even more difficult.

Ideologically, climate policy also shifts the balance from a laissez-faire, free market approach to a more state-centred economic policy. Although large-scale private investment is required, the necessary transformations to infrastructure cannot be financed and coordinated by companies or households alone.[37] At the same time, proponents of free market ideology are resisting the growing power accruing to the state as a result of climate policy. In Germany, for example, many economists preach the doctrine of the 'black zero' (meaning a balanced national budget) as if it were holy writ.[38] In the United States, the political ideology of the Republican Party obstructs government action with its insistence that, if there is a climate problem, the market will find a solution if left to its own devices. These beliefs, however, effectively amount to climate change denial. Markets don't preserve common goods because there are no incentives for individual companies to do so. The establishment of climate-friendly infrastructures, moreover, needs coordination, which does not happen via the market, but – if at all – with the help of incentives stemming from state regulation and funding.[39] If reaction against comprehensive climate policy is becoming an ideological and electoral rallying cry, producing not only material but also political winners and losers, it is not surprising that we are making such slow progress. It does not help, in short, that climate change is becoming a new cultural and social faultline in politics.

As we have seen, another political stumbling block in the way of a vigorous and proactive climate policy is that it interferes with established lifestyles and consumer desires. We see the cultural resistance in, for example, discussions on reducing flying or introducing speed limits – measures that are rejected as trespassing on long-established freedoms. Making meat more expensive, or reducing the size of apartments or houses classified – by whom? – as 'oversized' meets with a level of resistance that politicians try their best to avoid.

Since the Enlightenment, and massively more so over the past fifty years, traditional ways of life with their associated restrictive norms have been increasingly called into question and replaced by unbounded individualist lifestyles. In a culture where many rules seem like obstacles in the way of individual freedom, it is difficult to enforce precepts of moderation and ways of life that are more strongly oriented towards the common good.[40] Liberation from obligations and the convenience that comes with the new freedom are felt to be entitlements and contribute to our ignoring the ecological consequences of our way of life.[41] This is especially the case since excess is the ultimate principle behind economic activity under capitalist modernity. 'Doing without doesn't make the world a better place,' the boss of a German cruise company was quoted as saying in an interview, encapsulating the essence of capitalist modernity.[42] Unbounded individualism sells the future for the next quarterly figures, the next election result, or today's passing pleasure.

Former US President George H. W. Bush's famous (or infamous) statement at the 1992 climate summit in Rio de Janeiro that the American way of life was non-negotiable encapsulates resistance to the changes that a climate-neutral economy would require. To this day, the CO_2 emissions of the average US citizen are twice as high as those of Europeans. Donald Trump won over his voters in 2016 in part by declaring his intention to withdraw from the Paris Climate Agreement, which was seen as unnecessary and an interference in the American way of life. Trump created the political illusion that climate change could simply be ignored, or at least that climate protection was useless because human behaviour was not responsible for it. Combine this sort of political disinformation with the unchecked consumerism and the sort of corporate disinformation we saw in Chapter 3, then factor in the immense difficulty of reaching a societal consensus on what to do about climate change, and the reasons for the hesitant political reaction become obvious. Populist movements, the diminishing cohesion of political parties, and the disorientation caused by the mass dissemination of fake news in social media are gradually undermining the governability of societies. What's more, climate policy is increasingly being drawn into a culture war that is about positioning oneself in relation to 'the science' and 'the experts'. By now, climate policy can no longer be negotiated dispassionately, as some politicians and citizens perceive it as a threat from a 'system' against which the only defence is blanket rejection.

In a political order dependent on the mass loyalty of the population in elections, the implementation of effective climate protection remains so difficult that, at the very least, it will not happen soon enough to achieve the climate targets that have been set. Even measures that have already been adopted are being abandoned or watered down so as not to lose the loyalty of existing voters or else to win over new supporters. Here, too, the temporal misalignment between the short-term incentives of politics and the long-term processes of climate change comes into effect.

To reiterate: climate protection is time-critical. Postponing it means allowing *irreparable* damage to occur. However, it is routine in politics to deal with problems by kicking the can down the road. There is thus a mismatch 'between the short timescale of markets, and the political systems tied to them, and the much longer timescales that the Earth system needs to accommodate human activity'.[43] The environmental damage appears only after the politicians responsible have stepped down from their posts, indeed often after they are dead. Politically, it does not make sense to take unpopular decisions if the hoped-for positive results lie in the comparatively distant future. The logic of political time is oriented towards immediacy, meaning short-term political risks are 'dealt with' by postponement. In case of doubt, set up another commission.

Finally, the fact that many levels of government are involved in political decision-making can lead to paralysing complication and confusion. Since the 1970s, the political scientist Fritz Scharpf has analysed the difficulties of political decision-making in so-called multi-level politics especially (but not only) in federally structured systems.[44] Decisions customarily can be made at local, state, and federal levels. There are also supranational decision-making competences, such as those held by the European Union, and additional obligations arising from international law. These nested levels of governance lead to 'joint-decision traps',[45] that is, to a tussle over competences between the different levels, to lengthy planning procedures, and to policies that are generally slow and either inadequately coordinated or not coordinated at all.

Let us look at an example, again from Germany. The expansion of wind energy depends on the identification of sites where wind turbines can be erected. Although the Federal Minister of Economics can set targets for the desired expansion, the individual states have to designate the sites, and they can set the conditions, such as the distance from residential buildings or how to conserve surrounding nature. In addition, on the administrative front, planning approval procedures have to be carried out, usually involving consultation with the local community, where there is often opposition to the erection of wind turbines. The widespread distribution of competences and frequent disagreements over implementation mean that in Germany it takes almost two years between initial application and final approval for the installation of a wind turbine. A spokesperson for the German Wind Energy Association estimated that it takes in fact between five and seven years 'from the moment a decision is made to submit an application until the wind turbine is actually connected to the grid'.[46]

Even if there is now a clear consensus in many countries (i.e., political agreement in principle) on the need for climate protection, a corresponding consensus on the action to be taken is largely absent.[47] There is simply no general understanding on the appropriate measures. More wind turbines? Should we continue with nuclear power? E-fuels after all? Only heat pumps? Wood-burning stoves as well? Every single measure offers plenty of fuel for debate. Almost everything that needs to be decided – from procedures and competences to instruments, tax regimes, technical standards, and building regulations – is controversial and has to be negotiated at multiple political levels. There are of course good reasons for dispersing political authority and insisting on processes of consultation. But without an overarching sense of emergency, what inevitably gets caught and ground up in the traps of joint decision-making and diffuse power-sharing is any hope of a swift and effective response to climate change.

Finally, another distinctive feature of climate policy plays a role: nature itself, which ultimately is what is at stake here, has no political voice. This distinguishes it from, for example, the working men and women who in the twentieth century fought for their rights and for social redistribution. Nature cannot speak for itself, but needs representatives. This is why nature could be ignored for so long by politics and business, as well as by consumers and citizens. It was simply taken for granted as given and freely available. Only the destabilization of natural conditions creates ripples in the social systems, meaning nature now appears as a passive-aggressive object which it is feared will no longer function as we have always presumed. Nature, however, can only be given a voice in political debate through representation: that is, civil society, legal, or political actors who speak 'in the name' of nature. But given the strength of conflicting interests and the multitude of decision-making levels, this will not be enough. To extend the comparison with the labour movement: although there is now a trade union office, there are no workers to demonstrate and strike. And if they did exist, they wouldn't know to whom to address their demands.

Overall, it seems the scope for political action is much more limited than it appears at first glance. How do politicians accused of being obstructionist or of sticking their head in the sand react to this? Two defence strategies can be identified here. The first strategy is to vilify those social movements that call for radical climate protection measures to be implemented rigorously and immediately. Some politicians even try to liken them to terrorist organizations; individual activists are labelled as pathological; and many politicians deny that social movements can make any productive contribution at all to solving the problem.[48] This is despite the fact that experts on social movements do not consider the climate movements to be particularly militant.[49] For politicians, discrediting the campaigners is a strategy of 'communicative denial of knowledge',[50] one which serves to divert attention from their inability to solve the problem.

The second strategy entails making political promises in order to create the illusion of effective climate protection. Europe is supposed to be climate-neutral by 2050. At the same time, it is clear that investments are currently falling far short of what would be required to achieve this goal. The apparent resolution of this contradiction is communicated by promises that shift the solution into the future.[51] This can be seen to particularly grotesque effect in the European Union's 'Forest Strategy 2030'. In 2020, the Commission promised that three billion new trees would be planted within ten years. The trees are supposed to improve the greenhouse gas balance by storing CO_2, which in terms of immediate CO_2 reduction is already seriously flawed because young trees hardly store any CO_2 at all. The strategy becomes completely absurd when one looks at the figures. The EU set up a tree planting counter, which showed that 20,964,975 additional trees had been planted by 3 July 2024[52] – less than three-quarters of 1 per cent of the target. At the current rate, the tree planting goal will not be met in six years, but in around six hundred years.

Let me summarize. The combination of political dependence on both economic interests and popular legitimation, the paralysing complexity of planning and financial requirements, and the structure of administrative decision-making means that politicians fail to make adequate use of the legal options available to them to protect the climate. This inescapably raises the question: can democracy save the climate? Some climate activists, but also some business representatives and scientists, are now responding to the diagnosis of the inadequacy of state regulation in the climate crisis – in other words, to political failure – by calling for the suspension of democratic decision-making processes and the establishment of a 'climate dictatorship', or government by ecological elites.[53] They argue that if, under democratic rules, changes take so long that it becomes 'too late', then those rules should be put on hold – at least until the climate crisis is resolved. The emergence of such voices suggests that the state, which is already losing 'output' legitimation owing to its failure to achieve climate targets, will also lose 'input' legitimation – belief in the system – as a result. Pluralistic democratic procedures will be called into question. 'They're not up to it!' will be the cry. This turn towards authoritarianism is misguided in many respects. What would happen if a political grouping were to seriously attempt to establish such a climate dictatorship? There would certainly be enormous resistance in society. And without either participation or checks and balances, how could it be guaranteed in the long term that the 'climate dictator' would actually protect the climate as required or desired? The social complexity of the problem and its conflictual nature (as described above) also speak against such a solution.

Despite all the shortcomings of climate policy in liberal democracies, it remains the case that the nature of the climate crisis as a multi-layered conflict means that it can only be dealt with effectively, if at all, in democratic structures: that is, with the help of constitutional procedures and political negotiation between the various interest groups. Pluralistically structured societies routinely have to deal with conflict between diverse interests. The competence of democratic structures, however, is contingent on certain prerequisites. It requires a political public sphere that is committed to the common good. In addition, the political process must enable a range of different voices to be heard, and decisions must be understood as being political in nature, not as the purely technical implementation of the views of supposedly objective experts. Finally, a state with sufficient capacity for political action is required, one equipped with the power and financial resources to resolutely implement decisions on processes of transformation, to compensate companies and households for (temporary) economic disadvantage, and to ensure proper coordination. Successful climate policy in liberal democracies requires the state to play an active role in planning the future rather than relying primarily on markets to determine how our society will develop.

Legitimation via elections as a fundamental democratic principle at least increases the chances of differing preferences being represented in the political system and of decisions being accepted. It can safely be assumed that the over-simplification of conflict perspectives into good and evil that characterizes authoritarian regimes would further intensify intra-societal clashes over climate protection and would thus make effective policy even more difficult to achieve. Conversely, however, it might also be true that flawed climate policy would encourage political authoritarianism. This would apply if climate policy or its failure were to accelerate the social, political, or cultural polarization of societies.[54] In fact, this can already be seen in some of the political controversies surrounding climate protection measures. It is instructive in this context to consider what happened during the coronavirus pandemic: the politically imposed restrictions on personal freedoms during the pandemic led to populist countermovements that questioned the legitimacy of the decision-making structures. Such a loss of input legitimacy for the institutions of democracy could recur to an even greater extent as a response to climate policy.

5

Global prosperity

Defenders of capitalist modernity treat it as the universal destination for humanity. Yes, the story goes, economic growth and prosperity may have emerged first in Europe and North America, but the lead was only temporary. Others have caught up and in time all regions of the world will embrace the system and reap its rewards. This imagined future of continuous and expansive prosperity is the great material promise on which capitalist modernity's claim to universal validity rests. Faith in 'Western universalism'[1] was expressed with particular conviction in the development theories of the post-war period. These assumed that economic 'take-off' – the catchy term coined by the American economist Walt Rostow in the late 1950s – would in the not too distant future also draw the so-called developing countries into the rising spiral of growth and economic prosperity.[2]

More than sixty years after this prediction, there are differing opinions as to the validity of Rostow's theory. On the one hand, hundreds of millions of people still live in absolute poverty. Many countries have only been able to increase their economic prosperity slightly, while many others are caught in what is known as the middle-income trap. On the other hand, billions of people have at least been able to escape the most extreme poverty, and some countries that were still poor in the 1950s have now achieved sensational levels of prosperity.

The most impressive example of improvement is undoubtedly China. One consequence of the phenomenal development of this huge country has been that an estimated 850 million Chinese have escaped poverty. Another, however, is that greenhouse gas emissions in China have more than tripled over the past thirty years, making it the world's largest emitter of greenhouse gases every year since 2008. India, which is also developing rapidly, is in third place on this ignominious list, and is also still increasing its CO_2 emissions at a very high rate.[3] Both countries are relying on fossil fuels, mainly domestic coal, to drive their development, although China in particular is also investing heavily in renewable energy.

This is not good news when it comes to limiting the rise in temperature, as climate protection can only be achieved by reducing the use of fossil fuels on a global scale. Expanding the use of renewable energy, obviously, does not equate to a reduction in the use of fossil fuels. And lower consumption of oil and gas in such industrialized countries as the United Kingdom and Japan does not mean that consumption will also fall *worldwide*. Today, consumption is determined more and more by economic and population growth in the countries of the global South, where 80 per cent of the world's population lives. Emerging market countries are developing rapidly, and it is predicted that the population of the African continent in particular will continue to show significant growth. It is expected to triple by the end of the century. However, 600 million people living in Africa even now have no electricity, meaning that there is still a huge backlog in terms of energy supply. If we want to see why the response to climate change remains inadequate, it is therefore essential to also look at the global South and its place in the structures of the global economic system.

The countries of the global South have to strengthen their economies to lift people out of poverty and build lasting prosperity. This will only happen if they consume more energy. However, if these countries, which have historically emitted hardly any CO_2, become increasingly significant emitters themselves, then greenhouse gas emissions will continue to rise steadily whatever happens in developed countries.[4] Global CO_2 emissions would quadruple if the standard of living enjoyed in the industrialized countries were to spread to the whole world.[5]

Poorer countries are unlikely to attain the same living standards as rich countries in the foreseeable future, given the unbalanced structure of the global economic system. But they are certainly going to grow, driven by the same mechanisms of capitalist modernity that operate elsewhere. Companies in the global South are on the lookout for new fields of business, politicians are trying to solve the problems of poverty through growth, and local populations are dreaming of catching up with the consumer paradises of the rich North. In addition, many foreign companies earn their profits from the extraction of natural resources or from selling their products in the developing world. The drive for growth does not halt at any corner of the planet if an opportunity for profitable investment arises. Such growth might be worth celebrating but it's a grim truth that the more countries succeed in raising their prosperity, the more the world is united on the path to ecological catastrophe. The only way this would not apply is if the global South were somehow to find pathways to economic development that did not involve burning coal, oil, and gas to the extent practised in the global North.

As I noted, many countries in the global South will probably remain poor anyway because their marginalized position within the global economic system prevents them from developing. A cynic might say that this is at least good news for the climate. But this is not the case. For one thing, poverty – for a variety of reasons – is associated with high birth rates, and a growing population utilizes more resources. For another, even if the countries of the global South remain poor, companies will exploit the natural resources, such as oil, gas, metals, and fertile agricultural land, that can be found in many of them. These resources are often the countries' most important economic assets. In Congo or Ecuador, for example, oil production generates a large proportion of state revenues. Chile similarly relies on the mining of metals such as copper and lithium. Indonesia has significant nickel deposits, but also has agricultural land created by the deforestation of tropical rainforests where palm trees are planted to produce the oil for, among other things, the chocolate cream that Europeans spread on their breakfast rolls. In the absence of alternatives, resource-rich countries will continue to mine their treasures with the help of multinational corporations and sell them to wealthier countries, even if this does not lead to any kind of sustainable development for local citizens. In the worst cases, the exploitation of resources takes place against a background of collapsing state structures and under the control of warlords or foreign mercenaries.

But of course, the majority of the remaining fossil fuels should not be extracted at all if the Earth is not to heat up further. And the ecosystems that we use and often destroy for raw materials are crucial for the containment of climate change, the preservation of biodiversity, and the fight against environmental pollution, and should be protected at all costs. The tropical rainforests in South America, the Congo Basin, and South Asia are huge carbon dioxide sinks. Further deforestation of the Amazon tropical rainforest is considered a potential tipping point for the global climate; at the extreme, these areas could turn into barren steppes. Despite this, deforestation is continuing at an alarming rate. In 2022 alone, across the globe a forest area the size of Switzerland was cleared.[6] Sadly, from an ecological perspective, forests are a huge economic resource. They contain wood, valuable metals, and other raw materials, and their logging opens up new areas for agricultural production. The extracted raw materials and the agricultural products are often exported to the global North or to China, raising the standard of living there more than in the export-ing countries. It is estimated that around 17 per cent of the Amazon rainforest has been cut down to date. Some scientists believe that deforestation of just another 5 per cent of the area will cause the Amazon climate system to collapse.[7]

If we want to prevent the continued sacrifice of nature on the altar of economic growth, global coordination must be enhanced and countries in the global South must be given ambitious support. Climate change is a problem of the global commons. But we lack the political governance mechanisms that could be used to counteract the incentives and the interests behind the exploitation of resources. The development models of the countries affected often rely on income from resource extraction. Owing to their poverty and the difficulties of diver-sifying economies on the global margins, they have no other choice. This could only be altered if the global North decided to make extensive transfer payments to compensate for the income lost when resource businesses close or if the global economic system was fundamentally restructured. Despite all the rhetoric about such measures at international climate conferences, the necessary policies are not being introduced. Nor is the global economic system being restructured; it is still predicated, as it has been for centuries, on the exploitation of resources from countries that were initially colonized, as I described in Chapter 2. The international division of labour is based on extracting natural resources from the global South and transporting them to the North for further processing and consumption, which is where the wealth-producing value addi-tion takes place. This is currently changing to some degree, as emerging economies, above all China, also become significant importers of raw materials. However, this widening of global economic prosperity to new countries only further increases the world's hunger for energy and raw materials, even if it's welcome for geographically broadening the economic structures of capitalist modernity that have emerged over the last five hundred years.

An example from the Democratic Republic of the Congo (DRC) shows what resource extraction means for the environment. In 2022, the country's government offered for sale rights to oil production in the Mpeka region. According to the information provided, up to 1 million barrels of crude oil per day could be extracted from the area. It is estimated that this would generate annual revenues of 32 billion dollars, which would benefit the state and account for more than half of its current gross domestic product.[8] However, the rainforest and peatlands in Mpeka are huge CO_2 reservoirs. The ecological impact of oil production would be massive. Not only would the rainforest ecosystem be polluted by the chemical processes involved in oil production, but it would also continuously shrink as a result of settlement and construction, causing further CO_2 to escape into the atmosphere. The emissions produced by the combustion of all the oil would come on top of all that.

The government in Kinshasa is well aware of the serious ecological impact of oil production in the tropical rainforest, but is resisting the resultant pressure from the global North. When the then US Climate Envoy, John Kerry, called on it in autumn 2022 to refrain from auctioning at least some of the extraction licences, the Environment Minister, Ève Bazaiba, rejected this suggestion, as it might hinder the country's economic development.[9] It was the global North, she said, that was responsible for climate change. To prevent the extraction of oil would be to deny the DRC its right to prosper. According to another government representative, the country's priority is to reduce poverty through economic development: 'Our priority is not to save the planet.'[10]

This example shows how the extremely inequitable global economic system is ultimately stacked against the protection of ecosystems that are vital for the entire world. The only viable way for the DRC to bring financial resources into the country is to extract its own natural resources. Ecological considerations have to take a back seat because reducing poverty takes precedence over protecting the climate. In the poorest countries, the extraction and utilization of fossil fuels bring greater security for the livelihoods of more people than could be achieved by reducing greenhouse gas emissions.

But anyone who thinks that the environmentally destructive exploitation of resources in the global South is taking place against the unified will of the global North is very much mistaken. The protests from John Kerry were hypocritical through and through. He did not offer American funds to make up for potential lost revenue. He also did not mention that the United States is the world's largest oil producer. Moreover, the resources of the developing world are not only extracted with the help of Western and, increasingly, Chinese companies, but most are also processed and consumed in the global North. The oil from the Congo is refined into the petrol that takes European or Asian holidaymakers to their summer vacation resorts. Congolese cobalt, which is also mined at considerable environmental and social cost, is used in the batteries of the electric cars that are helping the energy transition in Europe and America.

The imbalances in the global division of labour lead to an outrageous level of dishonesty in the climate debate: the countries of the global South are held responsible for the overexploitation of their natural resources, even though the benefits largely accrue to the global North, which also makes the extraction possible in the first place with its technology and financial capital. While the German government promotes heat pumps and wind turbines at home, it is also involved in the expansion of fossil fuel extraction in distant countries. In order to secure alternatives to Russian gas, for example, Germany is supporting Senegal and Mauritania in the development of new gas fields. Senegal is to supply up to 10 million tonnes of liquefied natural gas to Germany annually.[11] The colonialist forked tongue is also apparent when it comes to protecting tropical rainforests. Agricultural land in the tropics is increasingly exploited by multinational corporations, with forests cleared for investors in search of returns on their capital. The countries concerned allow these investments because they promise income. But a large proportion of the profits goes to the owners of capital in the global North. Here, too, the colonial pattern continues of destroying nature through land grabs in order to increase the wealth of global investors.[12]

The sale of raw materials and the expansion of farmland provide the countries of the global South with urgently needed income. Whether the extraction of resources actually brings the desired benefits in the fight against poverty is another matter. In most cases, the profits generated are distributed between the multinational corporations and a local elite, without the general population benefiting[13] – a phenomenon known in economics as the 'resource curse'.[14] A textbook example of this is the Nigerian oil boom since the 1960s, which has not led the country out of poverty, but has instead caused enormous environmental destruction in the Niger Delta and entrenched corrupt political structures in the country.[15] However, such a thoroughly paternalistic objection will not stop the plans of the government in Kinshasa either.

Nor are the DRC and Nigeria alone in exploiting fossil fuels. Other African countries – such as Algeria, Namibia, Mozambique, Uganda, Ghana, and Tanzania – also foresee billions in state revenue from the sale of gas and oil. A good example is a new project currently being developed in Uganda and Tanzania which involves pumping oil from Uganda through a pipeline almost 1,500 kilometres long to the Indian Ocean, from where it will be shipped all around the world

– with a considerable impact on the environment and high social costs owing to the displacement of local populations. The project is expected to generate two billion US dollars a year for the national budget. The Tanzanian government defends itself with the same arguments used by the DRC. According to the Tanzanian Energy Minister, Doto Biteko, those who criticize the oil project are contributing to the global hypocrisy on energy consumption: 'It's like they are saying, "Let the addiction to hydrocarbons be our exclusive right."'[16] The African Union also counters climate protection appeals from the global North by arguing that Africa needs the expansion of gas production to enable a socially acceptable transition to a climate-friendly economy.[17] Africa's contribution to global greenhouse gases, it notes, is less than 4 per cent. The income from exports provides the financial basis for its own energy transition.

It is possible that one important motive for the current expansion of oil and gas production is that in African countries, too, it is expected that demand for fossil fuels in the global North will decline in the medium term. Africa's own resources would then be devalued as a source of export revenues. Here again, the question arises as to how profits can continue to be maximized. It might require the rapid exploration and extraction of deposits – a 'rush to burn'.[18] The paradox of the energy transition in the global North might then lie in how it intensifies the consumption of fossil fuel in the short term by creating expectations of a future with less of it.[19]

Unsurprisingly, African countries saw the energy crisis caused by the war in Ukraine in 2022 as an opportunity, and offered to help meet global demand. Owing to the huge price increases for liquefied natural gas, Egypt, for example, sought to export more gas to Europe. It was responding to the price signals from the market, which promised higher revenues. And with the help of these gas imports, Europe was able to avert a prolonged energy crisis after the Russian pipeline gas dried up, thereby calming a tense political situation. For Egypt, on the other hand, the exports led to energy shortages. To enable the export of liquefied natural gas, the government encouraged the population to economize on gas, and in its own power plants the country replaced gas with heavy fuel oil, which emits particularly high levels of CO_2 when burned.[20] As a result, Egypt's greenhouse gas emissions rose sharply. This can be seen as a paradigmatic example of the concrete effects of global power inequality and of its impact on the climate.[21] Or of the effects of price signals and how they lead to a shift in greenhouse gas emissions to the global South.

Even if the consumption of fossil fuels in highly industrialized countries declines in the future, that won't necessarily reduce coal, oil, and gas production worldwide. If poor and developing countries want to expand, they need to use more energy, which means burning rather than exporting domestic fossil fuels. China and India, for example, burn huge amounts of coal mined at home to satisfy their growing domestic hunger for energy. The same thing applies to Africa as to India and China and, before them, Europe and North America: development needs energy. Only an increase in the energy supply can provide electricity to the 600 million Africans who still have none today. And the demand is constantly growing, not least owing to the high population growth on the continent. In Egypt, for example, the population is growing by 2 million people a year. This is one of the reasons why the country's energy demand has risen by over a third since 2015.[22]

This increasing demand for energy is also fuelled by climate change itself. Many of the hottest zones on Earth are in the global South, where more and more air conditioning units are being installed to protect against extremes of heat. In Asia alone, it is expected that 1 billion(!) additional air conditioning units will be sold by the end of this decade. Empirical observations from Asia suggest that if average income in a country rises to around 10,000 US dollars per capita, there will be an explosion in demand for air conditioning systems.

The IEA estimates that global electricity consumption from cooling units will triple by the middle of the century.[23] In countries severely affected by long periods of heat, such as India, Vietnam, or Thailand, electricity is often generated from coal, which is particularly harmful to the climate, and the refrigerants used in air conditioning systems cause additional harm to the atmosphere on release. Although the quantities are comparatively small, the gases are much more harmful to the climate than CO_2. The result is a vicious circle in which the effect of individuals protecting themselves from the consequences of climate change is to further exacerbate it.

If global warming is not to be further fuelled by population development and economic growth in the global South, these countries would have to base their development on renewable energy. The record on this has been very mixed so far. On the one hand, China is the country with the most advanced renewable energy programme in the world, while at the same time it continues to increase its consumption of fossil fuels. Some African countries, such as Morocco and Kenya, are also investing heavily in renewable energy, while in others, such as Ghana, it plays almost no role. Overall, it is estimated that only 2 per cent of global investments in renewable energy are made in Africa.

Where renewable energy is being expanded in developing countries, it is often designated for export, meaning it will have little or no impact on domestic patterns of consumption. Morocco, for example, received 38 million euros from Germany for the construction of a pilot plant that will produce around 10,000 tonnes of green hydrogen planned for export from 2025. Namibia similarly received 30 million euros from Germany for four hydrogen and ammonia projects, with further private investments totalling billions planned, which will help make it a leading hydrogen exporter in Africa. This energy will not benefit the local population. In Namibia, where only slightly more than half of the population has access to electricity at all,[24] there is no domestic demand for hydrogen. Here, as in many other places, a neo-colonial policy of resource extraction is apparent, one that will extend global inequalities into the future while helping the global North alone meet climate targets.[25] With regard to electricity consumption on the African continent itself, it is assumed that solar and wind energy will still account for less than 10 per cent of the electricity mix in 2030, this on a continent with no lack of sun.[26] Far greater investments are being made in electricity generation using fossil fuels. Because of the long lifetimes of power plants, this will lock many African countries – and also the Asian countries following the same path – into coal, oil, and gas for the very long term.

We can see all this by returning to the example of Egypt. Despite optimal production conditions, solar and wind power contributed less than 5 per cent to the country's electricity generation in 2022. The target was once 20 per cent. And although renewable energy is meant to become a greater priority in the future (for 2030, the ambitious goal is now set at 60 per cent), it is unclear when or if it will replace fossil fuels. This is because Egypt is also expected to produce green hydrogen for Europe through various energy partnerships.[27] The country, moreover, is basing its own energy supply plans also heavily on gas found in the Mediterranean.[28] At the end of 2022, the discovery of another huge gas field off the Sinai Peninsula was announced.[29] This will set Egypt even more firmly on the fossil fuel pathway.

One of the reasons why the transformation to green energy is at best sluggish in most countries of the global South is the enormous investment required to build the necessary infrastructure. It's not just about installing wind turbines and solar panels, but also about creating an efficient electricity grid and maintaining storage capacity for periods with neither sun nor wind. Countries that already have weak or underdeveloped infrastructure do not have the resources to put in place a completely new energy system. In many areas, there are no power lines at all, and those who need electricity and can afford it have to use diesel generators.

In 2023, the IEA offered a sober assessment of the relevant progress in developing countries:

> More than 90% of the increase in clean energy investment since 2021 has taken place in advanced economies and China. [. . .] Higher interest rates, unclear policy frameworks and market designs, financially-strained utilities and a high cost of capital are holding back investment in many other countries. Remarkably, the increases in clean energy investment in advanced economies and China since 2021 exceed total clean energy investment in the rest of the world.[30]

In order for global climate neutrality to be achieved by 2050, investment in renewable energy in developing countries would have to increase sevenfold in the current decade.[31] This is completely unrealistic, not least because – with the exception of China – they lack the necessary capital. Real change would require a reversal of the flow of resources and capital from South to North that has prevailed for hundreds of years. But there are no signs that this is happening. The social inequality between centre and periphery that has been reproduced over centuries of capitalist modernity is turning into a boomerang in the fight against climate change.

In order to prevent the energy transition in the global North from simply leading to the geographical relocation of combustion of fossil fuels, oil and gas would have to remain in the ground. It would require that we stop treating certain resources as commodities so that they could instead contribute – as common goods – to the preservation of the natural foundations for life. One obvious way to do this is to compensate the countries of the global South for not extracting their oil and gas resources but instead preserving them as CO_2 reservoirs. The same applies to the protection of natural habitats such

as tropical rainforests, which store CO_2 and are home to high
levels of biodiversity.

But under what conditions could this succeed? It would
require global cooperation. Over ten years ago, there was an
interesting experiment in this direction in Ecuador – which
failed. In 2007, the then Ecuadorian President, Rafael Correa,
proposed to forgo production from an oil field estimated to
contain 1 billion barrels in the Yasuní National Park – one of
the world's most biodiverse regions. The condition stipulated
by Ecuador was that the international community pay a total
of 3.6 billion US dollars into a trust fund to compensate the
country for half of the lost revenue. In other words, the costs
of not extracting were to be split between Ecuador and the
international community. To prevent corruption affecting the
use of the money in Ecuador, the fund was to be adminis-
tered by the United Nations. By 2013, pledges of just 13 million
US dollars had been received by the trust fund – less than
half of 1 per cent of the agreed amount. Ecuador accordingly
decided to authorize production, and the first oil flowed in
2016. Ecuador is a poor and highly indebted country in urgent
need of revenues.[32] The failure of this experiment points to a
systematic problem in our capitalist economic system when
it comes to climate protection: money can be made from the
extraction of raw materials, but not from preserving them as
commons.[33]

The fact that promises to support the global South in
climate protection and adaptation are being broken is accordingly not a phenomenon limited to Ecuador. At the Paris
Climate Conference in 2015, industrialized countries pledged
to mobilize 100 billion US dollars annually to support climate
measures in developing countries. This amount falls far short
of the support deemed necessary, as ten times this amount (i.e.,
1 trillion US dollars) would be needed each year.[34] However,
not even the original inadequate promise was kept, as the
average amount made available in the five years up to 2020

was less than 75 billion US dollars. And the majority of this was provided in the form of loans, which further increased the indebtedness of the countries involved.[35]

All of this is happening against the backdrop of the global South being disproportionately affected by the consequences of climate change. In India, rising temperatures are expected to lead to significantly lower crop yields in the future and, as a result, to rising prices for staple foods, which will increase hunger among the poor. In central Africa, brutal clashes are taking place between different ethnic groups competing for increasingly scarce economic resources. Owing to the increasing desertification of their traditional grazing grounds, cattle herders in Nigeria are moving further south, where they encounter farmers who have always grown crops on the land. According to some estimates, this conflict has led to the violent deaths of up to 100,000 people over the past twenty years, largely unnoticed by the global public.[36] This is just one of many examples of increased distributional conflicts over scarce economic resources. And we should expect more as climate change increases social polarization and strains solidarity within societies. Even in the global North, the consequences will not simply remain distant media events. Climate migration, through which people try to free themselves from situations of extreme desperation, will not stop at the external frontiers of the planet's wealthy countries.[37]

All of this is well known. Nevertheless, support from the global North falls so far short of what is needed that it can only be described as scandalous. This has continued with the 'Loss and Damage Fund' agreed at the climate conference in Sharm el-Sheikh, Egypt, in 2022. The fund, created under strong pressure from developing countries, is intended to act as insurance against losses and to help poor countries repair acute climate damage, such as that caused by floods or hurricanes. The annual global costs of climate change were already estimated in 2010 at over 500 billion US dollars, with over 80 per cent of this being incurred in the global South. These costs are expected to almost double by 2030.[38] But, bizarrely, the level of financial support for the new fund was left open. The countries in the global South fear, not without good reason, that wealthy countries will eventually do no more than reallocate money from existing funds. The unequal power relations between the global North and the developing countries mean that the countries of the South are in this and other matters merely poor supplicants whose demands can largely be ignored. And this is despite the fact that the historical responsibility for climate change lies with the industrialized countries. The international order of states does not easily respond to moral appeals. This reduces the scope for climate protection and climate adaptation measures in the countries of the South. The consequences are global.

An international aid package put together for South Africa in 2021 also shows just how inadequate the support is.[39] The United States and Europe have agreed to provide 8.5 billion US dollars to assist the transition to cleaner energy in South Africa, which currently generates 70 per cent of its electricity from outdated coal-fired power plants, making it a significant CO_2 emitter. Switching to renewable energy would make an important contribution to the fight against global warming. It might also address chronic energy shortages in the country, which regularly faces energy rationing and power cuts. But will it happen? Not if it depends on the present funding, which is once again far too low. On the current energy transition timetable for South Africa, even with the support of the international funds provided, the country will still emit 3.9 billion tonnes of CO_2 between now and 2050. In order to accelerate the transition and meet reasonable climate goals, it is calculated that the country would need almost 100 billion US dollars in international support up until 2028.[40] This money is simply not being made available, mainly because rich countries don't take the problem seriously enough to commit such vast sums, but partly also owing to problems with the corporate management of South African energy companies. Ultimately, the financial resources needed for climate-friendly energy production are not there.

Just how difficult it is to finance the energy transition in the global South can be seen from the way the South African support package was put together. Only 4 per cent of the 8.5 billion US dollars consists of grants; the plan is designed to enable South Africa to borrow the rest from international financial backers.[41] Unsurprisingly, in the global South, financing costs are a major obstacle to investment in renewable energy. Countries and companies there typically have poor credit ratings owing to their high levels of debt and various country-specific risks and therefore often have to pay much higher interest rates for loans.[42] They cannot provide the collateral that international lenders demand and often have to pay interest rates of around 15 per cent. How would it be possible for companies in the DRC to guarantee their lenders politically and economically stable conditions? The nature and decision-making processes of the financial markets thus also work against climate protection.

This situation could be alleviated by comprehensive debt cancellation for poorer countries. But who will bear the costs of this? Despite ongoing political debates over debt relief, there is nothing to suggest that this is going to happen to any relevant extent; on the contrary, the financial burden on the global South continues to grow. Today's dominant development strategy requires private investment in infrastructure projects. However, in order for private investors to get involved at all, they demand to be contractually indemnified against the associated risks, an approach known as de-risking. In other words, private capital is happy to enrich itself in the area of climate protection without bearing any risk at all. The risks have to be borne by the recipient countries. And if those risks materialize, their indebtedness increases even further.[43] The state-backed private investments thus turn out to be time bombs buried in the public budgets, some of which have already gone off. In Ghana, for example, the state's assumption of risk related to private gas extraction investments has resulted in annual budget burdens equivalent to half of the country's healthcare budget.[44]

The fact is that the climate crisis is inextricably linked to geopolitical power structures. The poverty and indebtedness of the countries of the South means that they can neither invest adequately in climate protection nor adequately protect their populations from the consequences of global warming. They simply lack the financial resources. In this way, the international financial system, which is controlled by the global North, actively works against climate protection. When the majority of Ecuadorians decided in a referendum in 2023 to cease extraction from one of the drilling fields in Yasuní National Park, the rating agency Fitch further downgraded the country's credit rating a few days before the vote on the grounds that there was an 'increase in political risks'.[45] Clearly, Fitch was thinking about the referendum. In future, this already highly indebted country will thus have to pay even higher interest rates on its loans; it is in effect being penalized for its decision to take urgently needed climate protection measures. This is entirely in line with the operating principles of the global financial system, according to which loan interest rates are set taking risks into account. The sole concern of the rating agency, whose job it is to assess risks, is that Ecuador's ability to service its debt will continue to deteriorate owing to lower future revenues from oil sales. Cancelling the servicing of the debt is not an option for Ecuador, as this would mean being excluded from the global financial markets.

However, even if a country like South Africa were to greatly expand its renewable energy output with the help of international aid, this would not necessarily mean a reduction in CO_2 emissions. This is because the growth imperative of capitalist modernity naturally also applies to South Africa. In view of the energy shortage in the country, South African politicians have already made it clear that they are not prepared to sacrifice growth by shutting down coal-fired power plants. Abandoning coal would cost jobs and set the economy back. This is certainly not the unanimous political view; there is also significant environmental opposition to new coal mines and power plants.[46] However, there are also many advocates for the protection of the coal industry. Behind this lie the interests of the companies involved, but also experience of colonialism and the fear that a future energy industry which is to a greater extent in the hands of the private sector will primarily benefit Western energy companies.[47] CO_2 emissions will continue to rise in the global South, and natural resources will continue to be destroyed, not least because the developing countries do not want to be told they have to remain in poverty and because the industrialized countries are not prepared to pay for the energy transition there.

6

Consumption without limits

When asked recently about the possibility of a rapid end to investments in fossil fuels, the CEO of the energy company RWE responded in no uncertain terms: 'If we were to stop using oil, gas, and coal today, the consequences could not be justified. Civilization would collapse.'[1] We might be inclined to interpret this merely as a self-interested defence of the company's profitable extraction of fossil fuels. But he was not wrong: it is hard to escape the conclusion that societies would indeed break down if their energy supply was seriously compromised. Over the course of the past two centuries, we have become energy junkies. The fact that no adequate response to climate change has been forthcoming cannot be understood without taking into account the dependence of modern ways of life on our historically unprecedented energy consumption.

Let's take a look at some figures. In 1820, global energy consumption was an estimated 364 million tonnes of oil equivalent; by 1900, this had tripled; in 1950, it was over 2 billion; and in 2021, it was almost 14 billion tonnes.[2] So today the world consumes forty times as much energy as it did two hundred years ago, with a global population that has grown approximately eightfold over the same period. Of course, this increase

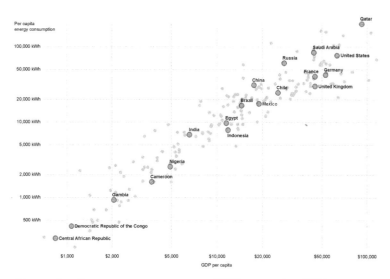

Figure 6. Energy use per person vs GDP per capita, 2021
(Note: Energy refers to primary energy, measured in kilowatt-hours per person, using the substitution method. Gross domestic product [GDP] is adjusted for inflation and differences in the cost of living between countries. GDP data is expressed in international dollars at 2017 prices.)
Source: Based on Our World in Data, 'Energy Use per Person vs GDP per Capita, 2021' (https://ourworldindata.org/grapher/energy-use-per-person-vs-gdp-per-capita?time=2021).

in energy consumption is not evenly distributed, but instead is mainly concentrated in the highly developed countries. In Western Europe, for example, energy consumption per person has increased around tenfold over the same period.[3] Clearly, energy consumption is closely linked to economic prosperity: the more prosperous a society is, the higher the energy consumption per capita (see Figure 6).

This increase in energy use is linked to high growth rates, driven to a large extent by the spread of mass consumption. Although affluence is a phenomenon that goes back a long way, it was restricted to a small social elite. Apart from this elite, people mostly lived in what we would today consider poverty, with very low consumption levels and correspondingly low energy requirements. The spread of high levels of consumption to broad segments of the population did not take off until the end of the nineteenth century, with America leading the way. The Roaring Twenties then gave a foretaste of the emerging era of consumerism, which came to full bloom in the period after the Second World War.

These post-war decades are often referred to in the social sciences as the *trente glorieuses*, the 'thirty glorious' years from 1945 to 1975. In Europe and also in the United States, these were decades of steady economic growth following the destruction and privations of the war; decades in which large sections of the population were given access to the amenities of a modern affluent society for the first time. A car of one's own, holidays in faraway destinations, washing machines, refrigerators, electric cookers, bigger modern homes with central heating – all this gradually became affordable and part of the common standard of living. Although the post-war decades were later criticized for their inequality, racial discrimination, and cultural narrowness, they were certainly an exceptional period in terms of the spread of prosperity.

In the global North, a broad middle class emerged whose consumption needs were met to an unprecedented degree. Continuous economic growth and an increase in purchasing power also made it seem realistic for those who had not yet enjoyed the same uplift in prosperity to aspire to climb the social ladder in the foreseeable future. This expansion of consumerism had a significance that went far beyond the amenities enjoyed: the realistic hope of upward social mobility supported social integration and political stability after the Second World War. In this, people also benefited from a more potent state that invested heavily in infrastructures, education, healthcare, and a general safety net protecting the weaker members of society. The increase in living standards owing to high economic growth elevated people out of poverty and led to healthier and more comfortable lives, and thereby also had a significant positive impact on life expectancy. The extension of prosperity to large sections of the population served to pacify the class conflicts of the nineteenth and early twentieth centuries and thus to stabilize the social order. Politically and economically, this was a remarkable success story.[4]

If we look at this period from an ecological perspective, the judgement has to be quite different. The newly created wealth and the consumerist lifestyles associated with it caused energy consumption to explode. The American Way of Life and the oil boom are two sides of the same coin.[5] This trend was only briefly interrupted by the oil crises of the 1970s and 1980s. Economic growth – and with it the use of fossil fuels – knew only one direction: upwards. From the 1990s onwards, climate change was stoked further when China in particular, but also other emerging economies, succeeded in significantly increasing their national incomes. For them too, growth and increased prosperity are a balm for social and political conflicts. But consumption is also indispensable for companies in their quest for profits. Just how important private consumption is can be seen from its share in the economy. In Germany, it accounts for just over half of economic output; in the United States, over two-thirds.[6] Reduced consumer demand would mean lower economic national income.

The growth of consumption, however, is not just the result of the state seeking legitimation and companies seeking returns; we cannot understand it without taking into account consumers themselves. At first glance, it may seem obvious that people want to consume more and more. Upon closer inspection, however, it becomes clear that the increasing desire to consume is not something that comes naturally.[7] Rather, historical studies show that during the emergence of capitalist modernity, people only slowly learnt to abandon their traditional lifestyle, based as it was on a fixed level of consumption, and to strive to maximize both income and consumption.[8] In the early phase of industrialization, higher incomes often did not lead to longer working hours; instead, people worked less once a desired income target was reached.[9] It was only after the cultural foundations of capitalist modernity had become more widely established that the urge to increase consumption became the norm. A conception of individualism and progress emerged in which consumption was equated with the exercise of freedom, with people comparing themselves against each other on the basis of what they could buy and picturing a never-ending improvement in their standard of living.

To this day, however, 'consumers do not automatically use surplus income to satisfy new wants'.[10] Even in modern capitalism, consumption must continue to be 'stimulated' by the state and companies. The state promotes consumption through regulation that organizes borrowing and lending and maintains consumer protection. Companies stimulate consumption by constantly offering and heavily advertising new and tempting products. Marketing arouses, reinforces, and directs consumer demand and thus drives company sales. For the state, consumption translates into tax revenue and thus helps to finance the work of government. Societies as a whole, meanwhile, benefit from the pacifying effect of increasing prosperity. The sale of more and more goods is ultimately the basis of the capitalist economy, state finances, and the social fabric of capitalist modernity.[11]

To illustrate the importance of consumption, it is worth returning to Walt Rostow. In his best-known book, *The Stages of Economic Growth*, published in 1960, Rostow developed a theory of social development in stages.[12] For him, the highest stage of evolution is a fully fledged consumer society in which high levels of consumption are possible for broad sections of the population. He obviously had in mind the America of his day. He saw this stage not only as superior in the provision of material goods, but also as fulfilling a promise of freedom in the opportunities for consumption it offered. Excess consumption, it seems, also plays a crucial role in culture. Rostow draws on the concept of consumer sovereignty, which was introduced to economics in the 1930s. As Philipp Lepenies has recently shown,[13] this is closely related to the notion of freedom as employed by neoliberal thinkers such as Friedrich August von Hayek and Milton Friedman. The ability to make 'sovereign' (i.e., unrestricted) consumer choices is at the heart of these economists' market-centred concept of freedom, which holds that nowhere else can preferences be realized as fully as on the market. It follows that regulatory intervention in private consumption should be rejected not only for reasons of economic efficiency, but also because it would compromise the desirable political good that is freedom. In other words, those who cannot consume unhindered are unjustly restricted in their personal liberty.[14]

Interestingly, corporate leaders and industry lobbyists repeatedly fall back on this cultural argument when it comes to the environmental impact of their products. When asked about the sale of large SUVs, the former CEO of Audi, Markus Duesmann, replied laconically, 'Our customers decide what they want to buy. [...] In a free market, demand determines supply.'[15] The CO_2 emissions associated with such products are thus defined as a by-product of consumers exercising their freedom and are therefore beyond questioning. Companies speak as if they have no choice but to provide products that destroy the environment. They receive support in this from some political quarters: 'It is the citizens who are failing to reach the climate targets, because people simply want to be mobile,' the German Finance Minister stated on a talk show in 2023.[16] The significance of such statements should not be underestimated. Indeed, the liberation from obligations and the comfort and convenience made possible by lavish consumption are an essential part of the appeal of capitalist modernity.

In the fight against climate change, the dilemma here is obvious. On the one hand, consumption in an economy dependent on fossil fuels increases CO_2 emissions and also causes other environmental damage, such as biodiversity loss. The more people consume, the greater the impact on the environment. On the other hand, the social system is based – economically, politically, and culturally – precisely on this consumption and its continued growth. So once again there is a tension between nature and the mechanisms by which capitalist modernity operates. Must nature always be the loser in this conflict?

To answer this question, it is helpful to first consider the two basic alternatives that could reduce the impact of mass consumption on the climate. One is for individuals to limit their consumption. The other is to alter consumption to lower CO_2 emissions. But what are the power and incentive structures that might lead to such changes? In this chapter, I will focus on those relevant to reducing personal consumption. I will then turn to the climate-neutral transformation of consumption and production in the following chapter.

In principle, every individual with a sufficient standard of living can decide to consume less. And some of course do. Every now and then, one reads about people who choose to live in conditions of extreme asceticism in order to minimize their personal CO_2 emissions. And more decide to contribute on a small scale, for example by reducing meat consumption, leaving the car at home, taking the train instead of flying, or taking 'staycations' instead of holidays abroad. Such changes in consumer behaviour are due partly to growing weary of ever more stuff, partly to changing lifestyles, and partly to environmental idealism.

However, there is no mass movement calling for people to reject consumerism. This undoubtedly has something to do with the existing infrastructures of everyday life. Work, shopping, leisure, and housing are organized in such a way that vast amounts of fossil fuel have to be used, and products are manufactured in energy-intensive value chains over which the individual has no influence.[17] Even with the best will in the world, the fight against climate change cannot be won on the battlefield of personal lifestyles. 'Every individual effort towards ecological sustainability [is] simply cancelled out by the existing infrastructures.'[18]

But this is only one reason for the relentless expansion of consumption in spite of our awareness of climate change. As important is the central cultural position of consumption in modern societies. Sociologists have described with great precision the importance of consumption styles for people's social identity and the formation of social milieus.[19] Consumption is never just about satisfying material needs, but always also about status. As we noted, the same dynamic existed in earlier societies among elites but never on a mass scale.

What has been added in capitalist modernity, however, is not only the spread of consumption as a marker of an individual's social position in all social classes; it is also that positions in the social hierarchy are formally open.[20] What does this mean? In feudal and estates-based societies, social positions were fixed at birth: people were born as serfs, nobles, or free citizens and rarely changed classes. The emerging liberal regimes of capitalist modernity took a stand precisely against this type of social order. They established class structures that are at least nominally permeable. In principle, anyone who starts as a pot-washer can become a millionaire. This formal opening up of the social structure unleashes great forces in individuals striving to climb the social ladder. The entrepreneurial energies generated are a central source of the growth dynamic of capitalist economies. This dynamic is not, however, limited to entrepreneurs, as vast numbers of wage earners also pursue ambitious careers in search of social advancement and respectability. While competition for social position is limited in an estates-based society by predetermined membership of one's estate or class, this competition becomes universal and ceaseless in modern liberal society.

This is where consumption comes into play. One's position in society is largely communicated by individual consumption practices and the associated lifestyle made possible by one's income or wealth. Owning a car and a comfortable home and taking interesting holidays identify a person as belonging to the middle class. At the same time, increasing consumption represents a relative downgrading of all those who cannot keep up. This creates a theoretically unlimited momentum towards consumption irrespective of material needs. The drive to consume is the social counterpart to the economic growth compulsion driving entrepreneurial competition on the market. Breaking out of this not only lowers one's status and conventionally measured living standards but also creates considerable social pressure to justify one's actions, a pressure most people do not want to face. Those who nevertheless do so risk social marginalization, much like the entrepreneur who does not recognize market developments and loses out on profit.

The power of consumption thus arises out of the deep structures of capitalist modernity. And importantly, not only from the apparently bloodless rationale that guides the behaviour of businesses and the state, both of which need consumption to generate profits and tax revenues, but also from the emotional forces driving society itself. Competition in status hierarchies churns away with further advancement always possible, at least on paper. It's a logic that, at the pinnacle of the hierarchy, produces a market for yachts 100 metres long, each of which emits 10,000 tonnes of greenhouse gases per year.

Given these social mechanisms, it is not surprising that demand is not moderated. Business, the state, and citizens play into each other's hands. Companies, for example, promote consumption through a gigantic marketing industry, against which there is barely any protest from either state or citizens. It is estimated that in 2023, more than 800 billion US dollars were spent worldwide on advertising alone – which is just one form of corporate marketing activity.[21] We are talking about a staggering amount of money being spent on repeatedly arousing customers' interest in products. Digital advertising now accounts for 75 per cent of the advertising market because it is particularly effective at stimulating new demand.[22] With one click you see the ad; with the next you can buy the product. Social media such as Facebook and TikTok are economically important because they enable other companies to advertise their goods and services in a precisely targeted manner. In doing so, marketing pulls out all the psychological stops. Any attempt to reduce one's own consumption faces the challenge of resisting these tailor-made temptations.

In view of the dangers of climate change, expending all this effort in order to increase consumption would probably seem a little peculiar to any dispassionate observer. How can we reconcile the fact that consumption demonstrably contributes to climate change with the huge sums spent on inciting people to consume more and more? Yet in the context of capitalist modernity, it seems completely normal to encourage consumers to engage in behaviour that is obviously harmful to the foundations of their own existence. An outsider would perhaps be moved to suggest that advertising should be severely restricted. A good model to follow here might be the fight against tobacco consumption, where advertising bans and drastic references to the health hazards of the product are used to reduce demand. However, it is highly unlikely that bans on the general promotion of goods will be extended to reduce overall consumption. This is because, as has already been pointed out, companies need demand in order to make profits, the state needs consumption in order to collect taxes, and consumers form their social identity through their consumption choices. Thus, hardly anyone ventures to disagree with the CEO of the car maker Audi when he says that SUVs are 'not bulky, but beautiful'.[23] He thereby reflects what his customers genuinely think about the product and at the same time promotes the economic interests of his company. The climate literally falls by the roadside.

For the same reasons, we ignore other potential options for restricting consumption. For example, consumption that is not necessary in any narrow sense could be taxed more heavily, weakening demand. There are in fact a few examples of countries levying additional taxes on luxury goods. However, these are rare and somewhat curious exceptions. Focusing more closely on climate protection, special CO_2 taxes could be used to draw a connection between the environmental impact of the product and its price. Although this has certainly been discussed, so far it has only been implemented as a weak price signal in the CO_2 tax on fossil fuels. This tax is so low, limited to so few countries, and has so many exceptions that it does not even come close to covering the environmental costs of the emissions caused and fails to effectively steer consumption to any degree. Moreover, the aim is not to reduce consumption, just to shift it over to other products.

In view of the importance of consumption in capitalist modernity, it is not surprising that there is no serious intervention through taxes. Making consumption more expensive would hinder consumers in their pursuit of social status. Raising prices to limit consumption would also introduce a new arena for social conflict. The wealthy are only marginally affected by higher prices. The consequences would be felt by people who are already short of money and whose ambitions for social advancement are already precarious. If the environmental costs of meat consumption were priced in, for example, beef would have to cost almost 10 euros more per kilogram.[24] Higher petrol prices affect the rural population far more than the urban population. People who live in the countryside are usually unable to switch to a bus, and cannot simply move to the city owing to higher housing costs and ties to their community. Under capitalist modernity, moreover, tax-based increases in consumer costs are consistently stigmatized as interfering with consumer freedom and the competition for social recognition, and are therefore at odds with prevailing economic and cultural mores.

Politically, climate-related price increases could probably only be implemented if the perceived loss of freedom was compensated for by transfer payments to the poorest. Although this has been considered, it has not been introduced. Even a per capita 'climate money', as proposed in Germany (but not yet enacted), would not compensate for the increased burden on lower-income groups. What is really needed is income-based compensation that also takes into account individual circumstances, such as the differences between urban and rural lifestyles. When the Social Democratic Labour Minister of the Federal Republic of Germany proposed such a model in 2022, the Liberal Finance Minister replied curtly that he was 'looking forward to the funding proposals'. The idea was effectively buried.[25] In a society that relies politically on the market as the chief instrument of governance, state redistribution aimed at making necessary climate protection measures politically acceptable to the majority through socio-political levelling measures is clearly not feasible.

Consumption might also be reduced by cutting waste – by making products more durable and also reparable, so that broken ones are not immediately replaced. The EU is planning new legislation to tighten the obligations on manufacturers to make their products reparable. This has not been finalized, though, and the initiative is of course meeting with resistance from industry. Money is made through the rapid turnover of goods and not through durability and reparability. The initiative, if put into law at all, will barely make any contribution to the reduction of European greenhouse gas emissions.[26]

But once again, it would be too easy to blame the relevant industries alone. 'Durability' as an element of a sustainable economy not only contradicts the economic logic of profit. It also contradicts the social logic of consumerism, according to which the desire for goods is not aimed at their long-term use, but at constantly buying new products with which to score points in the competition for social status.[27] The most striking example of this is undoubtedly the fashion industry: it is well established that its business model of disposable fashion is ecologically disastrous. One need only think of the environmental damage caused by cotton production, or the mountains of barely worn textiles that are thrown away and usually incinerated.[28] Furthermore, an estimated 30 per cent of textiles produced worldwide are simply overproduction. This business model, cynical as it may seem, has a commercial rationale. However, its success cannot be understood without taking into account consumers, who define their social position by wearing the latest trends. Hardly anyone chooses a pair of trousers just because they happen to cover their legs. Finally, consumption could be restricted by prohibitions or restrictions. 'Consumption quotas' could be issued to put a cap on individual purchases. Even just in theory, such a proposal sounds so far-fetched that there is no point thinking about how exactly it could be implemented politically. This kind of measure always fails. Think about the relatively trifling case of a general speed limit on German motorways. When asked about the idea, former Audi boss Markus Duesmann simply dismissed it: 'The whole world knows that Germany has no maximum speed limit, it's a symbol of our freedom here.'[29] The ban on the registration of new combustion engine cars in the EU from 2035 met with protests not only from parts of the car industry, but also from political parties who knew they had a significant proportion of car drivers (i.e., voters!) on their side. The Greens in Germany have had to pay a hefty political price for many years following their 2013 proposal to introduce a 'Veggie Day' in public canteens. On one day each week, canteens were to offer only vegetarian meals. Nothing seems further removed from the ideal of consumer sovereignty than a policy of limiting consumption through coercion and monitoring.[30] For business lobbyists, it is easy to vilify any proposal for the mandatory regulation of consumption as a 'slippery slope to authoritarianism' at the end of which lurks the 'eco-nanny state' – and thus to politically derail it.[31]

It is worth taking a closer look at the link between consumption and social inequality. I have already mentioned that proposals to restrict consumption are politically unenforceable in part because they are inextricably linked to inequality. In order to better understand this, it helps to look at the distribution of greenhouse gas emissions both between different countries and within societies. The average global citizen emits 4.7 tonnes of CO_2 per year. In the United States, it is 16 tonnes per inhabitant; in the EU, it is close to 8 tonnes; in Nigeria, it is a little more than half a tonne.[32] These differences reflect global power relations: that is, the relations that have produced the highly unequal distribution of wealth in the global state system. However, wealth disparities are also evident in the distribution of CO_2 emissions within societies. In the EU, the CO_2 emissions of the poorer half of the population are less than 5 tonnes per year. For the top 1 per cent, on the other hand, the figure is 24 tonnes.[33] As a rule, the higher a person's level of prosperity, the higher their CO_2 emissions. According to the 2022 UN IPCC report, the richest tenth of the world's population is responsible for between 36 and 45 per cent of global emissions. Each of the twenty richest people on *Forbes* magazine's global rich list emits a staggering 8,200 tonnes of CO_2 per year on average.[34] These greenhouse gas emissions caused by the excessive consumption of luxury goods are certainly significant for the climate. There are, for example, an estimated 10,000 private superyachts (ships over 24 metres in length) worldwide that emit thousands of tonnes of CO_2 per year during normal use. The ever-growing fleet of private aircraft is adding a further 37 million tonnes of CO_2.[35]

The United Nations has specified 2.5 tonnes of CO_2 emissions per person per year as the upper limit if the global temperature rise is to remain below 2 degrees. Emissions from the poorer half of the world's population remain below this limit. It is the rich countries, and in particular the very wealthy in those countries, whose way of life is destroying the climate. The consumption of the upper strata of the population therefore needs to fall. But this will not happen. This is because the climate-destroying 'conspicuous consumption'[36] of the elites is not simply selfish behaviour, but part of the social order. Persuading the wealthy and the super-rich to make drastic changes to their lifestyles and thereby to join the rest of the population on an equal footing would mean abandoning these social structures.

How should the most powerful members of society, of all people, be politically induced to stop making their exalted position visible through their consumption practices? That they should is obvious – especially as they are and will continue to be far less affected by the damage caused by climate change than the poor.[37] But who could make a serious attempt to prohibit private aeroplanes, yachts, or globally mobile lifestyles? The proposal to reduce the harmful impact of certain forms of consumption on the climate through a punitive CO_2 tax, for example, is not a bad idea, but it is completely unrealistic politically. The situation is no different to the long-standing call for a redistributive wealth tax to curb rampant social inequality.[38] This, too, fails owing to resistance from those who would be taxed. It is almost ironic that the reductions in CO_2 emissions that have been achieved in a number of countries in recent decades can be attributed primarily to savings among the lower and middle social classes, while the CO_2 emissions of the wealthy have continued to rise unimpeded.[39]

The enormous CO_2 emissions of the rich also have a knock-on effect on the actions of everyone else, impeding the necessary global coordination of climate policy. As mentioned, the poorer countries point out that they cannot possibly be the intended targets of appeals for climate action. In view of their low emissions and their poverty, they claim the right to continue their development and to increase living standards, even at the cost of higher emissions. And in richer societies that cherish the illusion of unlimited upward mobility, people see the consumption practices and lifestyles of the rich as a part of their own hoped-for future. The (upper) middle classes can certainly afford some elements of this lifestyle. Perhaps the big car, or the long-distance travel. Instead of owning their own yacht, they may only take a cruise, but, still, it's a taste of the high life, and might make you wish you were on board with the super-rich yourself. There is no clash of morally opposed lifestyles here, but, rather, fluid transitions that effectively make practically everyone an accomplice. As for those who genuinely want to play their part in protecting the climate, it saps their morale when one social group obstinately insists on freeloading in the wider struggle to preserve the climate as a collective good.[40] How are those with only a modest standard of living supposed to remain morally steadfast in their struggles to save gas, install heat pumps, and consume less meat when others are simultaneously demonstrating with their superyachts and oversized SUVs that global warming is not their concern?

Given the importance of consumption *not only* for the capitalist growth engine *but also* for the display of social status, it is no wonder that business leaders repeatedly argue that self-denial is not a good way to combat climate change.[41] And politics willingly follows suit: 'Not travelling less, but travelling differently' is the title of an information page on sustainable mobility published by the German government.[42]

As restrictions on consumption are not actually being pursued owing to their unwanted consequences, business and politics are focusing instead on a strategy of promises, and consumers on symbolic surrogate actions. The promises amount to using new technologies to reorganize production and consumption in such a way that ecologically acceptable climate budgets might be met in the future. However, this is based less on prescient forward thinking and more on the desire to avoid short-term political risks through assurances of results at a later date: the targets contained in these plans are set many years ahead. What will actually happen over these years cannot be predicted, but will in any case no longer be the responsibility of today's decision-makers. As I outlined in Chapter 2, this shifty temporal logic characterizes both political and corporate behaviour in the climate crisis and acts as a shield to safeguard the model of unrestricted growth.

How quickly such promises prove untenable is shown by the example of the technological dream of hydrogen-powered aircraft. At the end of 2022, Airbus Group CEO Guillaume Faury announced that the first prototype of such an aircraft would be available by 2029 at the latest, with flight authorization and the start of scheduled operations planned for 2035. Just six months later, this plan had more or less vanished into thin air. The company now saw hydrogen technology as just 'one way' to reduce CO_2 emissions from aviation. In reality, the detailed technological challenges involved in building such an aircraft are enormous, and, moreover, the infrastructure at airports for the use of the technology will not be available for a long time.[43]

In the light of such rapidly evaporating technological dreams, it becomes clear just how dangerous it is to reject calls for a reduction in consumption. The equation is simple: the more we consume, the more greenhouse gas emissions we produce. This equation could only be broken by a deep decarbonization of production and consumption. However, in view of the far-reaching changes to socio-technical infrastructures this would require across the globe, and in light of the technological improvements and innovations still needed and the 'finite calendars'[44] available, it is not likely to happen fast enough. It's important to remember, too, that the ecological crisis is not just a matter of global warming, but also of environmental pollution, the loss of biodiversity, and other ecological harms.

These crises within the crisis will not be solved by switching over to a new energy supply, but only by reducing resource use overall.

The experts are unanimous that energy use has to fall if the climate targets are to be met. And this will only happen if overall consumption also declines. Again, Germany can serve as an example. If, as planned by the government, energy demand is to be reduced by almost 25 per cent by 2030, energy efficiency will have to increase by 3.2 per cent every year.[45] However, over the past fifteen years, the actual annual increase has only been 1.4 per cent.[46] Only if demand is reduced will the targets for renewable energy uptake and increased efficiency also be reduced.[47] The order of the day is therefore: fewer cars, fewer cruises, and smaller homes. But this will not happen. Since economic growth and consumerism are built into the DNA of the system, a politically prescribed contraction of the economy is simply not feasible.

So that leaves consumers themselves. After all, people could voluntarily switch their demand to products that are less harmful simply because they are concerned about the dangers of climate change. If this were to happen, companies would be incentivized to make rapid changes to their product range. Their current business model would become obsolete, and the climate would be helped. Changing consumption practices would be a thoroughly 'market-conforming' mechanism, as the market system doesn't give a hoot about the moral qualities of the goods sold. What kind of products or services are used to generate the essential growth and profits is irrelevant. If consumers focus their demand on products that do less damage, and if they are prepared to pay a premium for them, companies will offer products that are classified as sustainable. Markets are 'moralized' when, on the demand side, not only are products evaluated according to costs and benefits but criteria such as climate protection or social justice are also taken into account.[48] Such ethical markets have attracted a great deal of attention in the media and the social sciences in recent decades.

The findings, however, are sobering. Ultimately, ethical markets are probably no more than symbolic substitutes that concerned citizens use to hide from themselves that social forces are far too strong for the climate to be saved through individual action. There are, of course, people who adapt their consumption to the ecological requirements, at least in part. But studies repeatedly show a large gap between what people aspire to do and what they actually do.[49] They find that actual spending on environmentally friendly products is only a tenth of what consumers had previously stated they were willing to spend on them.[50] In reality, the change in consumer demand triggered by such shifts in preference is far too small to have a significant positive impact on the environment. The market for ethically produced clothing, for example, makes up no more than 0.4 per cent of the global apparel market.[51] And this despite the fact that the fashion industry emits more CO_2 than the aviation and shipping industries combined.

Psychologists and behavioural economists have good explanations for the gap between intentions and behaviour. For example, we may behave sustainably in one area, but ignore the climate impact of the rest of our behaviour because we tell ourselves that we have already done something positive for the climate. Our environmentally harmful behaviour is mentally 'offset' by the one good deed.[52] Overall, it seems that 'green behaviour' can be expected when the associated costs and the resulting inconvenience are low.[53] However, this brings with it the risk that cheap but ineffective climate action will displace more effective options that come at greater personal cost.[54] Strategies to reduce cognitive dissonance can be used to bridge the gap between green awareness and green action. For example, people justify their adherence to their own lifestyle by saying that they cannot save the climate on their own anyway, or by pointing to others whose behaviour is even more harmful to the environment: the rich, the Chinese, long-haul holidaymakers, SUV drivers, or simply 'the others' in general.

Another reason for the failure to create moralized markets is a lack of transparency. What exactly does 'organic' mean in relation to food? What is a pair of jeans produced in accordance with climate criteria? Scandals concerning so-called greenwashing have also shown that it remains unclear to buyers what the conditions of production actually are at the distant ends of supply chains. The many different labels intended to provide information about the environmental friendliness of products do not really help because their information content is opaque. The production conditions are sometimes not even clear to the companies involved in the supply chains, perhaps because they buy intermediate products whose origin they know little about. Sometimes the labels themselves are simply fraudulent. Journalists then find out, for example, that bags supposedly made from 100 per cent marine plastic are actually only made from 59 per cent of it.[55] Too often the premium paid by morally concerned consumers is skimmed off as further profit. The profit motive does not disappear when confronted with consumers' moral scruples. Labels certifying sustainability or climate neutrality are hence often suspected of being nothing more than misleading advertising. According to a study conducted by the European Union in 2020, more than half of the advertising claims for environmental or climate friendliness in the EU were 'vague, misleading, or unfounded', and a further 40 per cent were simply 'untenable'.[56] Many consumers and even some companies are already turning their backs on environmental labelling, and not without good reason.[57]

The individualization strategies aimed at supporting climate-friendly behaviour also include programmes in which people can pay to offset the emissions they have caused personally. Modelled on the Kyoto Protocol, which came into force in 2005, these schemes allow people to buy special certificates, the cost of which is then used to fund climate protection measures.

The individual carbon footprint caused by the consumption or production of goods is thereby supposedly 'offset' by activities that lead to a reduction in CO_2 emissions elsewhere. Many of the voluntary offsetting certificates support reforestation projects, others dam projects, and yet others the purchase of electric vehicles. In the case of forest-planting certificates, the CO_2 released by climate-damaging production is supposed to be absorbed again by new forests, or to remain absorbed by the protection of existing ones. Buying such certificates soothes the consumer's guilty conscience about the climate, while enabling companies to advertise themselves as 'climate-neutral'.

Numerous studies, however, have shown that the climate impact of such schemes is low to non-existent. Moreover, there are allegations of negative social impacts and human rights violations linked to many of them.[58] The certificates are primarily about applying a coat of magical green paint. And this can be substantiated using quantitative data. A study conducted for the EU in 2016 by the Freiburg Institute for Applied Ecology came to the conclusion that in 85 per cent of the projects examined there was a high probability either that they would lead to no actual CO_2 savings or that more certificates would be issued than the CO_2 savings achieved.[59] This does not seem to concern the 'impact investors' who run this trade. For them, the certificates represent a lucrative business.[60] The market is now worth an estimated USD 2 billion and is expected to increase fivefold by 2030. The companies that buy the certificates can greenwash existing fossil fuel business models while at the same time soothing consumers' guilty consciences. A win-win situation for everyone – except the climate.

We cannot expect a sustainable shift away from climate-damaging production methods to be achieved by imposing ethical market behaviour on private individuals.[61] And yet businesses and politicians, themselves trapped in the dilemmas of capitalist modernity, are trying to convince people that this is the way forward. This is supported by an individualistic ideology conveyed through measures designed by behavioural psychologists and aimed at guiding consumers in their decision-making. Labels or green shopping assistants on smartphones inform customers in real time what their personal ecological footprint is and thus 'nudge' them towards the 'correct' choices. However, as consumer decisions are embedded in a political economy of growth, within the existing infrastructures and routines and the social dynamics of status competition, what we have here are gimmicks rather than solutions to the climate problem.[62]

It is telling that the consumption of products classified as climate-friendly is most likely to take off where it is used by buyers as a status marker and thus itself becomes a symbol of social superiority. Sustainable consumption then becomes a means of demonstrating moral superiority and social distinction. Be it organic food, a vegan diet, a specific coffee mug, cargo bikes, or electric cars, environmentally conscious consumption is now dividing societies along what sociologists call the 'cultural axis'. This is because the moral convictions behind an ecological lifestyle are not shared across all socio-cultural milieus. Not everyone thinks that eating a lot of meat is a problem, or that cycling is the better mode of transport. Such ecological lifestyle norms alienate traditional social milieus, leading to political conflicts which are fought out with judgements about moral superiority and thus provoke a populist backlash.[63]

However, the fact that the idea of climate-friendly consumption is so politically charged is not just a matter of cultural differences. These conflicts are also linked to social inequalities. Even in rich societies, many people live in modest or precarious circumstances and struggle to shoulder the additional burden of higher prices for sustainable products. Electric cars may well be more climate-friendly, but they are most certainly more expensive.[64] Owning one therefore signals both environmental awareness and economic strength. Anyone who drives a Tesla not only has a lot of money, but in addition deserves to be recognized as a better person because they are protecting the climate. For the others, there is only shame or anger.

7

Green growth

How to combat climate change? There are two basic positions: de-growth and green growth. Those who argue for an end to growth want to ensure that fewer resources are consumed, primarily by reducing consumption and strengthening a circular economy of reuse, sharing, and recycling, which would both lower greenhouse gas emissions and protect the environment.[1] Those who argue for green growth, on the other hand, maintain that the mechanisms of the capitalist economy will in future be able to reconcile growth with climate protection. Technological progress and changes to the structure of the economy, they say, will allow societies to prosper without damaging the climate. There will be more economic activity but fewer emissions. Although this would require radical technological shifts which would initially entail high costs, the long-term benefits of effective climate protection justify a basic optimism. A path to economic growth can be found that is compatible with a stable climate.

In a widely acclaimed book, the journalist Ulrike Herrmann recently rejected this optimism about green growth and outlined the idea of a radically shrunken economy as the *only* possible response to the climate crisis.[2] In doing so, she was able to draw on calculations made by the United Nations. If the temperature rise is not to exceed the 1.5 degree mark, greenhouse gas emissions must be reduced by a further 45 per cent by 2030 over and above what has already been agreed.[3] Herrmann argues that such a dramatic reversal means green growth is out of the question, because the energy necessary to maintain current consumption patterns in the global North cannot be provided in the foreseeable future without coal, oil, and gas. Others argue that *every* increase in economic growth is associated with an increase in energy use and resource consumption, and thus only further increases ecological destruction.[4] This argument becomes particularly persuasive if the additional ecological damage of economic activity beyond CO_2 emissions is taken into account.

According to Herrmann, people would unavoidably have to consume less and industry would have to produce less for our lifestyles to align with what is ecologically required. We would have to abandon private cars and air travel. We would have to take up significantly less living space. The chemical industry would have to shrink by half. In addition, products would have to be recycled after use and defective goods would have to be repaired instead of being replaced with new ones.

I believe that the arguments put forward here are worth considering in many respects. There are pressing environmental and cultural arguments for shrinking the economy. There is plenty of robust evidence as to why more is not necessarily better. And there are examples on a small scale that show what social life could look like in a society not geared towards constant growth and increased consumption. Transition Towns, Slow Cities, and Economy for the Common Good are movements that advocate organizing social coexistence in ways which run counter to the growth imperative in capitalist modernity and which could have great appeal. However, it's unclear if these models could be extended to entire societies. And when criticizing consumption, it must always be borne in mind that even in the rich industrialized countries there are many people who enjoy only a modest standard of living – not to mention the hundreds of millions of people around the world who live in poverty and for whom abandoning growth would mean remaining poor. An economy that ended overall growth would need to be one redistributing wealth on a massive scale from the wealthier parts of the world to the poor.[5] This, once more, brings up the issue of feasibility: can the idea of a fundamental change of course towards a shrunken economy be anything other than a 'regressive utopia'?[6]

I don't think so. My scepticism stems first from the fact that the growth imperative is a *structural* part of the system of competitive markets and private property rights. I have already outlined how this works: the owners of capital drive forward the dynamic processes of constant innovation and growth to increase their wealth. In order to halt this process, it would be necessary to abolish private property rights to capital itself and thus to draw a line under capitalism.[7] Nowhere is this a realistic political prospect, and it remains open to question whether the consequences of such a system change would actually benefit even the environment. Yes, technological progress would then – as intended – slow down dramatically, but this would possibly also close the door to new technologies that might have helped the fight against climate change. In addition, the normative consequences of economic contraction, as outlined in the previous chapter, would also have to be considered.

Second, I believe that a programme of targeted reductions in living standards in the industrialized countries and the renunciation of the right to economic development in the global South is simply politically impossible because the existing power and incentive structures block the implementation of any strategy for shrinking the economy. This is due of course to the profit motives of companies, but also to the consumer demands of citizens. As explained above, the pacification of conflicts over the distribution of wealth in modern societies depends on increasing prosperity. Even if the economy were only to stagnate, distributional conflicts would explode because struggles between groups would focus on securing a larger piece of the unchanging pie for themselves. Above all, a larger slice would need to go to the global South to enable the reduction of global poverty. As economist Branko Milanovic has calculated, in a no-growth world, this would demand drastic reductions in living standards in the global North.[8] It would be delusional to think this could happen. And then there's geopolitics: countries that abandon the path of growth and innovation would sooner or later fall behind economically and technologically and thus lose international influence. Growth also serves to confer superiority in key industries over one's geopolitical adversaries.[9]

In order to grasp the futility of a policy of deliberate economic contraction, it is worth briefly taking a closer look at Ulrike Herrmann's book. Herrmann cites in support the British war economy of 1940, when the state ordered a drastic reduction in general consumption in order to free up scarce resources for the defence of the country against Hitler's Germany. However, this historical analogy is flawed: the concrete existential threat of war effectively bonded the population of the United Kingdom together in 1940, and it is doubtful whether the ecological threat will have a similar effect. Unlike the threat of war, the ecological threat and the measures it demands often remain distant; the consequences of climate change will only materialize to their full dramatic extent in the future, and climate protection is a global problem, one that lacks a single political body with control over the measures to be taken.

But there are also differences in society. Back then, the British people had not (yet) heard a forty-year eulogy to individualism and consumerism. Rather, they lived in an organized society that could be politically regulated by state intervention in a way that is no longer conceivable today – and this applies not only to Great Britain. The question for us today is therefore: where and how would it be possible to make a political decision to ban private cars, to compel people to live in smaller homes, or to lay up private superyachts in dock? There are no majorities for such measures, so there will be no policy of deliberate economic contraction. Proclamations along the lines of 'We have to do *x*' are no more than cheap talk as long as the political conditions for *x* have not been created.

But what are the chances of addressing climate change through green growth? Even if it sometimes seems that way in political debate, just because one option is not feasible does not mean that the alternative necessarily will be. Green growth in essence means leaving the growth-based social model of capitalist modernity intact, but at the same time decarbonizing production and consumption with innovative technologies that do less damage. In a nutshell: value creation per tonne of CO_2 emitted increases[10] – ideally, to the point where value creation and greenhouse gas emissions are completely decoupled. Wind turbines and electromobility, the direct reduction process in steel production, heat pumps and low-energy houses are all part of this transformation towards decoupling economic growth from climate pollution. Advocates of green growth also recommend structural economic change, in particular the expansion of the service sector, where value creation is expected to be less CO_2-intensive.[11]

In order to integrate climate protection into the operational infrastructure of capitalist modernity, a fundamental technological reorganization of the economy is required. For this to happen, companies, the state, and citizens have to believe that investments in climate-friendly products will pay off in economic terms, if not immediately then at least in the near future. At the same time, the conviction has to grow that fossil fuel business models are financially high-risk and should therefore be abandoned soon. Climate protection must be translated into the 'language of prices'.

For a long time, it looked as if this transformation would not get off the ground at all. However, this has changed in recent years, at least in some countries. The deployment of renewable energy is on the rise, electric vehicle registrations are increasing, and more and more homeowners are using heat pumps to warm their properties. Many companies appear to be adapting to this transformation, as demonstrated by the incipient reorganization of the steel industry, the planned phase-out of coal-fired power generation in several countries, and the cement industry's search for technology to capture and store the CO_2 that it unavoidably produces. And indeed, greenhouse gas emissions are falling in many countries, despite economic growth. So can we be optimistic after all?

Probably not. It can be assumed that the transition to technologies hailed as climate-neutral will be driven forward globally over the next few decades by many trillions of dollars in investment and will bring about a significant transformation in many economies. However, these investments will fall far short of what is actually needed to achieve the climate targets and will also take far too long. It is also questionable whether the expansion of technologies touted as climate-friendly is actually capable of stopping climate change and the ecological crisis. We have to take into account that renewable energy will not simply replace fossil fuels but will to a significant degree fuel additional energy consumption. After all, green capitalism is not only intended to revolutionize energy production. It is also intended to bring about further growth, which will increase energy consumption and produce collateral ecological damage. The overexploitation of resources and the resultant ecological crisis will intensify in a number of areas – caused by the very transformations that are supposed to rescue us. I will seek to justify my scepticism in this and the following chapter. Next, I will focus on the financial and material conditions for the green transformation before addressing the question of planetary boundaries in Chapter 8.

The historical development of capitalism can be analysed as a sequence of regimes of economic governance. These regimes regulate decision-making behaviour and are based on expectations expressed in narratives about future development paths. These narratives, which are neither fictional nor based on perfect, complete knowledge, are supported by institutional structures.[12] Expectations regarding future socio-economic developments, in conjunction with institutional regulation, reduce uncertainty for business and politics. They create a framework that helps to coordinate and steer strategic decision-making. Such 'grand narratives'[13] manifest themselves in the business plans of companies, in macroeconomic growth models, and also in social utopias such as that of 'prosperity for all'. They guide private and public investment as well as research programmes into technological advances; they shape political decisions on the regulation of the financial industry; they inform party political programmes; and they influence the behaviour of consumers and voters.

In the nineteenth century, for example, the narratives of free trade, European power, and imperial expansion produced expectations about where and how economic agents could safely invest. In the twentieth century, Fordism was the most important of these socio-economic regimes. Economic structures were organized, with considerable state involvement, around industrial mass production and the strengthening of private consumer demand through rising wages.[14] This regime entered a crisis in the 1970s and was replaced by the liberal market regime that still dominates today. Despite the major differences between the three regimes, they share one feature: they are blind to the ecological consequences of economic growth.

'Green growth' can be understood as a shift to a new socio-economic regime. We are witnessing the capitalist economy shedding its skin once again and, under the label 'green', directing a considerable proportion of investment flows, technological innovation, and consumption towards climate neutrality. In line with a narrative of decarbonization, state and private resources are being channelled into new technologies and business models that at least hold out the promise of a possible answer to climate change. In the jargon of corporate leadership: green growth is a 'mega-topic'. Or, in the words of Larry Fink, CEO of US asset management company BlackRock: climate change opens up 'historic investment opportunities'.[15]

Green growth is attractive for business not because it preserves the natural foundations of life, but because it may prove to be a new source of profits and because it reinforces the social legitimation of companies. The scale of green investment will therefore ultimately depend on the expected return on capital for investors as well as on political majorities and consumer preferences. Growth rates have been declining in the wealthy economies over the past few decades. In fact, it has become increasingly difficult for investors to find opportunities that are both low-risk and lucrative for the now enormously expanded pool of private assets.[16] There is a surplus of private capital seeking new investment opportunities.

Given the sheer scale of the investment required, green growth could be an answer to this macroeconomic problem. As already mentioned in Chapter 4, the investment required for climate protection is estimated by the consulting firm McKinsey at USD 9.2 trillion per year up to 2050, or 7 to 8 per cent of global value creation.[17] According to the IEA, investment in the energy transition would have to triple by 2030 if the Paris climate targets are to be met.[18] Other estimates are even higher. As a citizen, you might well ask: who is going to pay for all this? However, companies look at these sums in a completely different way: some of the largest markets of the coming decades are currently emerging in the area of green growth, and with them gigantic business opportunities. Companies are rushing into the starting blocks to secure a slice of this pie.

However, these business opportunities only arise thanks to government intervention. This is because green investments are often economically unviable when the market is left to itself: for example, hydrogen-based steel production is more expensive than conventional steel production. The new business models are in competition with the old fossil fuel models.[19] Only if the state subsidizes green technologies, makes fossil fuel business models more expensive, and creates stable long-term framework conditions for green technologies can the engine of private investment get going. The public 'de-risking' of new business models is required: that is, the assumption of risks and the creation of favourable rules for private investors by the state.[20] Taxes, subsidies, and regulation need to be used in such a way that the most powerful possible coalitions of support for the green transformation can come together. In addition, the state needs to create the regulatory conditions for the actual implementation of investment decisions. In plain language: the state needs to speed up approval procedures, shorten planning procedures, fast-track construction permits, and ensure that sufficient raw materials and labour are available. In consumer goods markets, suitable developments must also be supported by consumers with a preference for 'green' products, whether owing to ethical convictions or government incentives. The question is: are there mechanisms by which financial flows can be channelled towards green investments at sufficient scale and speed?

For most economists, the holy grail for the decarbonization of the economy is the taxation of CO_2 emissions, or, more specifically, the introduction of emissions trading systems. The idea for this regulatory mechanism was developed back in the 1970s, chiefly by the American economist William Nordhaus.[21] The basic principle is simple. The emission of CO_2 is only allowed if the emitter has previously acquired a permit that authorizes them to pollute in this way. The number of permits is in turn limited so that only as much greenhouse gas can be emitted as is compatible with the existing climate targets. The permits are bought and sold on a trading floor; the fewer there are, the higher their price, and the less profitable the use of fossil fuels becomes. Owing to the price signals, rational economic actors will then invest in climate-neutral business models and reduce investments in CO_2-intensive technologies. Consumers will also adjust their consumption decisions and, as a result, a green transformation of the economy will occur.[22] That at least is the theory.

The European Union in particular has committed to the climate policy instrument that is emissions trading, also known as cap-and-trade. Since 2005, the European Emissions Trading System (ETS) has included emissions from the energy sector and from most energy-intensive industries and, since 2012, from European aviation. The road transport and building sectors have been exempt so far but are due to be included in the system from 2027. Emissions trading is the key lever for achieving the goal of reducing emissions in the EU by 55 per cent by 2030 compared to 1990 levels.

Notwithstanding the lofty theory, the results of the ETS have been modest in practice.[23] The actual reduction in greenhouse gas emissions prompted by the system has fallen far short of the targets. There are many reasons for this. First and foremost is an obvious one: for the effective control of CO_2 emissions through permits, *all* emissions would have to be included. However, they are not.[24] Even in the European Union, only 45 per cent of greenhouse gases are covered by carbon pricing, and worldwide just 23 per cent.[25] This means that over three-quarters of global emissions remain outside permit systems, and it does not look as if other countries are going to follow the path of carbon taxation in the future. The United States, for example, opted in its most ambitious green transformation legislation, the Inflation Reduction Act of 2022, for subsidizing climate-friendly technologies rather than an emissions trading system.

In the European Union and in Germany, there are also many exceptions, even in those areas covered in principle by the ETS, which reduces its effectiveness. This applies in particular to energy-intensive manufacturing industry, which until recently was allocated almost all permits free of charge to help with competitiveness. As noted, key CO_2-emitting sectors in the EU – road transport and buildings – will remain completely exempt until 2027. Moreover, so many allowances have been allocated that their trading price has mostly remained far below the threshold at which significant economic incentives to reduce emissions kick in. And in addition, as the certificates have no expiry date, companies have been able to buy them on a speculative basis. Some thus bought up permits early on when they were cheap and will hence be able to extend their existing business models well into the future, even if the price of permits rises, without CO_2 costs becoming a significant factor. RWE, for example, one of the largest energy companies in Europe, purchased permits to enable the continuing combustion of its Rhineland lignite years ago. Thanks to this clever hedging, it can continue to burn lignite for many years to come without significant additional CO_2 costs.[26]

But that's not all. Until 2021, European companies were also allowed to use international credits from climate protection projects (mostly in developing countries) as permits, which further increased the scale of their emission allowances while lowering their price.[27] RWE also purchased some of these credits to 'offset' the burning of lignite. Among other things, the credits RWE bought related to huge dams built by the Chinese government to generate electricity in the Bala Valley in Guizhou province.[28] Because dams cause lower CO_2 emissions than coal-fired power plants, CO_2 offsetting credits could be issued. The government in Beijing was able to use the revenue from these credits to help finance the dams. But the dams would have been built anyway, even without the support. The credits were therefore completely useless in reducing greenhouse gases, but allowed RWE to continue burning lignite in Germany at a profit.

Permits have been and remain a blunt instrument. In the German case, this is also because emission prices are set at the political level. Outside the scope of the European scheme, Germany introduced a carbon tax for the building and transport sectors. But the price – currently 45 euros per tonne of CO_2 – is much too low to incentivize consumers to use less fossil fuel. Economists estimate that even prices of 180 euros per tonne of CO_2 in the building and transport sectors would not have a sufficient steering effect for the statutory climate targets to be met.[29] This is a failure in market design, one that reflects the perverse power and incentive structures in the economy, state, and society. Both the interests of companies in suppressing the cost of environmental pollution and the resistance from consumers affected by cost increases lead to political opportunism. We can conclude that market design is inevitably geared towards what is politically feasible rather than what is ecologically necessary.

Furthermore, for the effective countering of climate change, the European system is of course insufficient because it is limited to carbon emissions in the European Union. The failure to include global emissions could in principle be compensated for by means of a carbon tax on imports into the EU, which is something the Commission is planning for several especially energy-hungry industrial sectors from 2026. This would protect domestic industry, but would increase prices for consumers, and is also considered unfair by countries in the global South. Although these countries have no historical responsibility for climate change, they are still being asked to pay for the costs of combating it.[30] If steel from India were to become 15 per cent more expensive in Europe owing to a carbon import tax, Indian companies would be able to sell less steel to Europe. Such protectionism leads to further geopolitical tension, which is also detrimental to the absolutely essential international coordination of climate protection policy. Whether a carbon tax on imports actually materializes will therefore be determined largely by trade and foreign policy considerations, which will presumably remove any climate protection teeth from the proposed levy.

The public are also fighting back. Carbon taxes act as a tax on consumption and therefore particularly affect low-income earners,[31] even those whose per capita emissions, on account of their low standard of living, are already close to the reduction targets in the climate agreements.[32] Resistance to these taxes is growing, as one might expect. And although the European Union is planning a Social Climate Fund for the period 2026–32 to cushion the hardship caused by further carbon pricing, the sums earmarked for this are modest. A maximum of 65 billion euros is proposed for the EU as a whole over the entire seven-year period.[33] If only one in ten households in the EU were to benefit from the Social Climate Fund, each household would receive no more than 470 euros per year. The other 90 per cent would be left empty-handed. So people shouldn't hold out too much hope of a big windfall. The same sort of problem exists across the EU: in the prevailing market-liberal political culture and in view of empty budget coffers, an expansion of transfer payments to share the burden of the green transformation more evenly across society is politically unrealistic. Moreover, the EU hardly has any money at its disposal anyway.

Finally, any changes that might result from emissions trading are slow and imprecise. This is because investments are not channelled into specific new technologies and infrastructures. Instead, decisions are left to the market. As a result, there is a lack of targeted and coordinated investment in technology and infrastructure that might drive forward the effective defossilization of production and consumption. This is inadequate, given the urgency of the necessary response to climate change. How, for example, will market forces create a functioning local transport system in rural areas? How will competition alone drive the radical transformation of a complex technological system such as energy supply? Such a transformation requires coordination, and this in turn requires political management. For example, it involves creating long-term planning confidence for investment through the selection of particular technological pathways. This is another reason why the United States has taken the route of direct subsidies for technologies classified as climate-friendly.

However, as the American approach does not increase the cost of using fossil fuels, but merely introduces additional energy sources, climate-damaging technologies will not disappear from the market. As long as there is no carbon pricing in the United States, the Inflation Reduction Act will make little contribution to reducing emissions – which suits the interests of the powerful fossil fuel industry and at the same time supports the country's consumption-based growth regime, which is built on cheap energy.[34] The total amount of energy available will increase, and this will trigger further growth. This is exactly what we see in China, where renewable energy is being rapidly expanded, but at the same time more and more coal is being burnt. In the past twenty years, coal consumption in China has more than doubled.[35] It boils down to the fact that the new technologies are merely *supplementing* fossil fuels in a growing and therefore increasingly energy-hungry world, not replacing them. If this continues, climate targets cannot be met.

Carbon pricing can be seen as an (inadequate) 'stick' for the transformation to green capitalism. It makes the use of fossil fuel technologies more expensive. The 'carrot' for companies is the promotion of green investment through state subsidies and the targeted channelling of private capital. Together, these two measures are intended to incentivize companies and consumers in such a way that the energy transition succeeds and we meet our climate targets. Success requires the rapid mobilization of enormous financial resources, and the United Nations and the IEA repeatedly point out in their reports how large is the gap between the investment required and that actually made. The estimates vary from a fivefold up to a sevenfold increase worldwide by 2030.[36]

Of course, it is impossible to predict how financial investment in green technologies will develop over the next few decades. But because the gap between what is happening and what is needed is currently so large, the assumption that these investments will increase sufficiently in both scale and speed seems implausible. I have already set out in the preceding chapters why the gap is so large and will therefore only briefly repeat the reasons here. They include the market competition between fossil fuel and decarbonized business models; political resistance to the costs associated with the transformation for private households; budget constraints that limit potential government support; high financing costs, especially for the countries of the global South; the expected rates of return for private investors; and, finally, ideological and cultural objections.

Which brings us back to 'de-risking', which under these circumstances represents the best hope of mobilizing private capital: the state simply assumes the risks associated with the green investments. This hope extends precisely as far as the public budgets available and the rates of return demanded by investors.[37] De-risking also has distributional consequences. In the global North, for instance, state subsidies flow to wealthy buyers of electric vehicles, or to those who invest in photo-voltaic systems on their private roofs with guaranteed feed-in tariffs. In the global South, neo-colonial rentier incomes are generated for private investors from the North, the risks of which are borne by the public purse despite these countries already being poor.

In order to improve both the speed and the fairness of the green transformation, the financial role of the state could of course be significantly strengthened.[38] For instance, by changing the monetary policy of the central banks. Or by increasing government debt, which would also make it possible to spread the burden of the transformation over several generations. Or through a change in policy to tax great wealth more heavily, as recently proposed by the French economists Lucas Chancel and Thomas Piketty.[39] However, political support for such measures is lacking, at least in Europe. An increasingly restrictive monetary and fiscal policy as well as legal constraints such as the German debt brake stand in the way of any expansion of the state's role as financier of the green transformation. That could be changed, and relevant proposals are on the table. But there are no majorities in favour of such a policy shift. In view of high wealth inequality, demands for higher taxation of wealth or inheritance have been raised for years now without being politically implemented anywhere. There is nothing to suggest that the threat of climate change will lead to a rethink.

Of course, this does not mean that policy changes that accelerate the switch to the green economy are ruled out for the future. Political scientists have developed interesting models illustrating how they might come about. They postulate, for example, that the interdependencies between different parts of the political system could lead to reciprocal influences setting off significant changes.[40] If a change occurs in one area, it can subsequently influence existing political coalitions in other areas and bring about similar changes there. This can be pictured as a cascade in which a small initial change subsequently leads to ever-larger knock-on effects. Changes in the area of energy policy, for example, can be conceptualized using such models. The adoption of renewable energy, as is currently taking place at least in some countries, is driven by such dynamic processes of shifts in political coalitions. However, these transformations are not taking place fast enough anywhere as prevailing coalitions work against the necessary changes. There is also the risk, once again, that the process will just make additional energy available instead of putting an end to the burning of fossil fuels.

But what about the financial markets? The question arises for the simple reason that companies finance their investments by attracting private capital. Financial markets therefore have – at least potentially – a decisive influence on the green transformation. Around 450 trillion US dollars of private assets are invested in the markets, enough money to make the green transformation a reality.[41] A carrot-and-stick strategy might also be possible here. Investors could withdraw funds from companies with climate-damaging business models and instead make them available to companies driving forward the green transformation. The structural power of capital would thereby be brought to bear not only on politics but also on the distribution of capital between different sectors of the economy. For companies with climate-damaging business models, this would result in increased financing costs and thus lower profitability. The financial markets would be speaking the language of prices.

And at first glance, it looks indeed as if financial investors are aware of their responsibility and are in fact driving the green transformation forward. In recent years, investments in funds that invest their money according to so-called ESG criteria (environmental, social, and governance) have skyrocketed. According to one estimate, over 35 trillion dollars has now been invested in such funds.[42] The financing of the green transformation appears to be making good progress.

But this appearance is deceptive. A closer look reveals that this boom by no means represents the major shift in financial flows that might be assumed. Rather, studies show that investment funds that flaunt their sustainability labels are almost indistinguishable from ordinary funds.[43] The obvious reason for this is that – except in the EU – the financial markets themselves decide what is deemed sustainable. The state does not regulate what counts as a climate-friendly business model; rather, rating agencies and index providers categorize companies or funds as sustainable using various labelling and certification schemes, enabling financial companies to choose whatever categorization suits them best.[44] Fittingly, the agencies are paid by the funds and companies that use the labels. For the rating agencies and consulting firms that certify companies and funds, this is a lucrative area of business. This also applies to the asset managers, who earn money from the fees paid by investors. The greater the demand for 'sustainable' funds, the greater the incentive for asset managers to categorize their products as sustainable.[45]

The outcomes seem almost random. A comparison of the sustainability ratings of three major providers (MSCI ESG, RobecoSAM, and Sustainalytics), for example, revealed a total of 235 different companies across their combined top 100 ESG ratings. Only eleven companies were in the top 100 for all three rating firms.[46] The criteria for classification are apparently chosen to optimize investors' risk exposure, but not their impact on the climate.[47] However, political influence also plays a major role. The European Union's taxonomy of 'sustainable economic activities', which came into force in 2023, also classifies nuclear energy and natural gas as sustainable. Nuclear energy was included owing to political pressure from France, natural gas at the request of Germany. The Chinese taxonomy even categorizes 'clean coal investments' as green.[48]

If this arbitrary way of categorizing financial investments is viewed against the backdrop of the inner workings of capitalist modernity as described above, then its defects will not come as a surprise. As much as investors might like to do some good with their money, they pay even closer attention to their returns. Even green growth does not change the fact that the overriding social responsibility of companies is to generate profits. Investment decisions will always be made on the basis of estimations of risk and return. The categorization of financial investments as green serves primarily as a fig leaf of legitimacy for investors in the face of increasing public concern about climate change. In reality, however, nature continues to take a back seat.

The hypocrisy of some of the most important players in the financial markets is evident in many other ways. BlackRock, the world's largest asset management company with over USD 10 trillion in funds, declared in 2018 that it wanted in future to align its investment strategies more closely with green criteria in order to be more responsible and to take into account the ethical preferences of its clients. In a public letter, Larry Fink urged CEOs worldwide to take greater account of the social consequences of their decisions in future, including the consequences for the natural environment.[49] The CEOs, who depend on the financial markets to fund their investments, might well have understood the announcement to mean that BlackRock would provide less investment capital to companies with climate-damaging business models in future, which Fink then confirmed in another open letter to CEOs. BlackRock would no longer include companies that were not committed to sustainability in its actively managed investment funds, and in the case of passive funds would vote against the board of directors at annual general meetings if they did not adopt climate-friendly business strategies.[50] However, investigations into the voting behaviour of asset management companies at shareholder meetings of 'carbon majors' from the energy, cement, and mining sectors show no such pattern. At the annual general meetings of energy companies, asset managers from the 'big three' tended to vote against measures aimed at improving the environmental performance of the companies, and the voting behaviour for their ESG funds did not differ from that of investment funds that did not invest using sustainability criteria.[51]

Notwithstanding this, asset management firms have been criticized in the United States for their public statements on climate action. Republican representatives, mostly of conservative American states, accuse them of representing 'woke capital' and in some cases are withdrawing their state-level pension funds from their portfolio. They say it is not the job of asset managers to pursue political goals such as the decarbonization of the economy, and that making investment decisions in line with environmental and social criteria would lead to lower incomes for the pensioners on whose behalf the money is held and invested. In addition, they argue that a decline in investment in the oil industry would jeopardize tax revenues and jobs in the oil-producing states.[52] Financial decisions, they say, should be guided solely by profit expectations. Although the Republicans' accusations have little basis, given the composition of ESG funds as described and the actual voting behaviour of the major asset managers, BlackRock has rowed back with public statements on its own climate ambitions.[53] The debate shows once again that climate issues have now become part of a general culture war and that capitalist modernity is at odds with climate protection.

However, it is not only the underfunding of CO_2-saving investments that stands in the way of success for the green growth model. The necessary transformation of industry, transport, and heat generation within the time remaining faces seemingly unsurmountable practical challenges. This even applies to the rich countries of the global North. I will illustrate this with an example from Germany, but it could just as easily come from a different country.

Germany plans to generate 80 per cent of its electricity from renewable sources by 2030. In 2022, electricity consumption in the country amounted to around 550 TWh, of which slightly less than half (256 TWh) was generated from renewable sources.[54] According to the Federal German Ministry for Economic Affairs and Energy, electricity demand will increase to 750 TWh by 2030, owing in particular to the expansion of electromobility, the switch to electricity-based heating systems, and the increased use of electricity as an energy source for industry. If, as planned, 80 per cent of electricity in Germany is to be produced from renewable sources by the end of this decade, their contribution would have to more than double in the next six years (from 256 TWh to 600 TWh). In 2022, the actual increase was only 12 TWh; in 2023, it was 17.5 TWh.[55] If expansion continues at this rate and the projections for future electricity demand are correct, Germany will generate more electricity from fossil fuels in 2030 than it does today – despite the further expansion of renewables.

In order to achieve the electricity mix targets, over the next six years around twelve thousand powerful wind turbines would have to be added to the almost thirty thousand existing ones, which would double the amount of wind energy generated on land. Five new wind turbines would have to be connected to the grid every day. If we compare this to the actual expansion of wind energy in recent years, it becomes clear how far removed from reality these plans are. In 2022, 551 new wind turbines were erected in Germany, just over a quarter of what was required.[56] In 2023, 745 wind turbines were added, which is still only a third of what was specified as necessary.[57] The rate of expansion for photovoltaics would also have to be tripled.[58]

Despite the country's reputation for efficiency, change in Germany is much too slow. One might wonder whether global trends offer more room for optimism. But this is not the case. According to a study by McKinsey, global electricity consumption is set to double by 2050.[59] In 2022, solar supplied just 0.8 per cent of the primary energy consumed worldwide, while wind power contributed just over 1.3 per cent. The IEA estimates that the share of wind and solar energy in global primary energy consumption will increase to only around 6 per cent by 2030.[60] Achieving the goal of climate neutrality would require a global expansion of wind and solar energy by 1,000 gigawatts per year every year between now and 2050. This is roughly three times the global expansion rate for 2022.[61] The situation in the world as a whole is therefore no better than in Germany.

The wide gap between goal and reality in the energy transition is often due to entirely practical obstacles. The relevant industry associations say the main bottlenecks are in planning and approval procedures. In Germany, for example, the planning horizon for commissioning a new wind farm is almost six years.[62] But higher turbine prices, high costs of capital, delivery problems, and a shortage of skilled labour are all mentioned too.[63] Are enough skilled workers and engineers available? Is there sufficient production capacity, and are there enough components and raw materials? Are the supply chains stable? Can the grids cope with the increased volumes of electricity?

Moreover, the energy transition is by no means limited to the installation of wind turbines and solar panels. The major disadvantage of producing electricity from renewable energy sources rather than fossil fuels is that the former are difficult to store. In periods when neither the sun is shining nor the wind is blowing, so-called 'dark doldrums', there is no energy available without stored reserves. Electricity can be stored in batteries, but these are expensive and can only stabilize the power grid for a short time. Energy from wind and solar plants can also be stored by converting it into hydrogen or ammonia or using hydroelectric power plants. However, these all entail considerable energy losses, and transporting hydrogen requires an infrastructure that does not yet exist. If, as planned, hydrogen for Europe is to be imported from Africa on a significant scale, a huge supply chain coordinated across the two continents will have to be established, something that also harbours major geopolitical risks.

Of course, it is conceivable that the world will build up high renewable energy capacities, including storage capacities, in the long term. However, it is difficult to believe that this will happen within the limited timeframe available, or that renewable energy will actually replace fossil fuels. Green growth still lags far behind what is needed for an adequate response to climate change.[64] Ultimately, the state lacks the power to establish the incentives required for the green trans-formation. This applies to cap-and-trade systems just as much as to the assumption of risk for private investments and the targeted channelling of financial flows by classifying them as 'sustainable'. And above all, the state lacks the power and the motivation to curb economic growth and thereby reduce energy consumption.

Nevertheless, belief in the miraculous potential of techno-logical innovation and diffusion is widespread. This also applies to what is called carbon cycle management, in which carbon dioxide in the atmosphere is extracted and stored. Behind this is a Promethean will to transform nature. 'Planetary nature and biological life are understood in their entirety as a legitimate field of intervention for engineering and technological strate-gies: a mastery over nature from the atom to the atmosphere.'[65] But there seems to be no alternative. There is a consensus among experts that curbing global warming requires not only a reduction in future CO_2 emissions, but also the removal of the CO_2 that is already in the atmosphere and is still being produced. A product such as cement cannot be manufactured without CO_2 emissions, which is why climate neutrality is only possible if this carbon dioxide is captured and permanently stored or further processed. In the IPCC scenarios, which assume a maximum temperature rise of 2 degrees, the removal of this CO_2 is already firmly factored in.[66]

One option for removing CO_2 from the atmosphere is – at least technologically – very straightforward: more CO_2 can be stored in plants through planting trees, forest management, and the re-naturalization of wetlands. Around 2 billion tonnes of CO_2 is already being removed from the atmosphere today through afforestation, planting on land that has long been without forests.[67] The obvious limits to this approach lie in the availability of soil for the additional plants. It is also under-mined by continuing deforestation and large-scale forest fires. And although 2 billion tonnes sounds like a lot, it actually only corresponds to around 5 per cent of the greenhouse gases emitted annually by fossil fuels.

To achieve the much-proclaimed goal of climate neutrality by 2050, between 6 and 16 billion tonnes of CO_2 would have to be filtered out every year starting from the middle of the century. According to the IPCC special report on the 1.5-degree target, a total of 730 billion tonnes of carbon dioxide would have to be removed by 2100. This corresponds to around twenty times the amount of carbon dioxide that is currently emitted worldwide each year from the combustion of fossil fuels.[68] Other scenarios assume as much as 1,100 billion tonnes needs to be removed. Technical solutions are therefore indispensable.

CO_2 capture and storage is a green technology for which companies in the fossil fuel industry also have high hopes. Wouldn't it be fabulous if fossil fuels could continue to be burnt and somewhere in the world there were plants that filtered out, stored, or reused the CO_2 produced? It is no coincidence that the oil and gas multinationals and energy-intensive industries are promoting such innovative technologies as a miracle cure in the fight against climate change.[69] Is this a realistic scenario or pure greenwishing, nothing more than a delaying strategy? Of course, technological progress cannot be accurately predicted in this area either. And there are undoubtedly fascinating ideas around not only for CO_2 storage, but also for the further utilization of captured CO_2. However, all of these projects have so far been small-scale experiments, and it is unclear whether, when, and at what cost the technology can be scaled up. Once again, many promises are being made, but their practical implementation lags far behind. To date, CO_2 storage on a relevant scale has not been achieved. Globally, the plants operated for this purpose had a total capacity of 45 million tonnes in 2022. Based on current plans, the IEA predicts that CO_2 storage capacities in 2030 will be just 20 per cent of what would be required to achieve climate neutrality by 2050.[70] A scientific study in early 2023 found that by 2050, the capacity of the corresponding plants would have to be 1,300 times greater than in 2020.[71] The belief in successful climate mitigation requires an almost religious technological optimism. Companies in the fossil fuel industry and in energy-intensive manufacturing industries are fuelling this optimism because it reduces public pressure to phase out fossil fuel business models. In other words, it buys time for the continuation of climate-damaging business practices.[72]

Technical challenges, the uncertain risks involved in the storage of carbon dioxide, political resistance, and questions of profitability have all contributed to the sluggish development of carbon capture technologies. Technically, for example, the CO_2 must not be permitted to escape back into the atmosphere. Upscaling also presents major challenges. The current capacity of all facilities for the direct air capture of CO_2 is around 10,000 tonnes. The first commercial plant for the direct removal of CO_2 from the air in the United States opened in California at the end of 2023. It has an annual capacity of 1,000 tonnes, which corresponds to the emissions from a few hundred combustion engine cars.[73] The IEA's climate neutrality scenario requires that this capacity increase to almost 1 billion tonnes by 2050. Such targets are set in the absence of the technologies and implementation plans that might enable the target to be achieved.[74] A lack of political support must also be added. Whether with good reason or not, the technology was already abandoned in Germany around ten years ago because politicians feared the reaction from voters who did not want a CO_2 repository under their homes.[75]

High costs are a further problem. The filtering and stable chemical binding of CO_2 already requires a lot of energy. The direct removal of CO_2 from the air is currently estimated to cost between 600 and 1,000 dollars per tonne, while the IEA estimates the future costs for a large plant with a capacity of 1 million tonnes at 125 to 335 dollars per tonne. However, such a plant does not yet exist anywhere.[76] The IEA hopes that from 2030, it will be possible to filter out a tonne of CO_2 for less than USD 100 using the direct air capture process.[77] The costs of other technologies to capture and store CO_2 are also high. At the same time, there is little incentive for companies to invest in such technologies with their own money when the costs resulting from CO_2 emissions are either fully externalized or CO_2 emission permits can be bought cheaply.[78] It can only be done via public subsidies.

Even if the technology can be made to work, there are still huge structural and economic challenges. Assuming a volume of 6 billion tonnes of CO_2 needs to be removed annually and a capacity of 1 million tonnes per plant per year, six thousand such plants would be required. But where would they be located? On the very optimistic assumption that the cost per tonne would be USD 100, the annual bill would be USD 600 billion. Who will foot this bill? Perhaps one reason why there is far too little political support for the development of this technology is that few people believe that the plans can be realized anyway. In any event, it is telling that the self-imposed obligations made by governments avoid specifying the scale of the necessary CO_2 removal. One thing is clear: if green growth is to lead to climate neutrality, then the new technologies must remove massive quantities of CO_2, and quickly. In view of the technological uncertainties, the disappointing investment flows to date, and the political hesitancy, it is clear that, as a path for limiting climate change, continuing to burn fossil fuels while removing huge amounts of CO_2 from the atmosphere is nothing more than a very risky gamble.

It is now often predicted that although the Paris climate targets will be temporarily exceeded in the middle of the century, the Earth will have cooled down again by 2100. The euphemistic term for this is 'overshoot': even if no progress is being made at the moment on reducing greenhouse gases, it is no cause for alarm; in the second half of the century, the technology will be available to filter large quantities of greenhouse gases out of the atmosphere and store them. And by injecting aerosols into the stratosphere, a protective screen will be created that will reflect sunlight back into space, thereby cooling the Earth. Such hopeful and at the same time grandiose proclamations of predicted technological advances in geoengineering – despite the fact that their actual feasibility, associated risks, and financing are largely unexplored – are intended to mask both the current lack of action and the widespread feeling of impotence. Technologism aims at reassurance. At the same time, other ideas that focus on possible changes to the structural operation of capitalist modernity are being pushed out of sight. All bets are being placed on a further extension of our 'mastery over nature'.

There is no doubt that technological progress is of enormous importance for the future of climate change. However, the evolution and practicality of technology cannot be predicted, nor can it be assumed that technologically feasible solutions, if they are found, will be implemented politically. Technologism is a form of magical thinking that distracts us from the failure of the structures of capitalist modernity in the face of climate change and thus masks the need for painful decisions in the present. Technologism is part of a 'promise machine' which declares even climate change a part of the 'myth of endless progress'.[79]

8

Planetary boundaries

What if I'm being too sceptical? Let's take the optimist's viewpoint for a moment and imagine that the whole green growth thing works, that the transformation towards defossilization actually succeeds. Let's assume plans for climate neutrality are followed, if not exactly, then closely enough that, in conjunction with the removal of CO_2 from the atmosphere, it turns out to be possible to stop climate change before it gets completely out of control. Wouldn't it be a tremendous victory for humanity?

It would certainly be comforting. We pin our hopes on green growth as the ultimate solution because it's consistent with the beating heart of capitalist modernity, namely its belief in prosperity through growth and progress. On the one hand, the quest for green capitalism seems daunting, exhausting, and dangerous. On the other hand, there is also something incredibly comforting about undertaking the epic journey, because, at the end of it, a return to normality beckons. We will no longer be changing spark plugs, but we will still be travelling to work by car. The machines in the factories will continue to run, only now they will be powered by hydrogen rather than gas. We will go on holiday and dress fashionably, and above all we will continue to dream the dream of ever-increasing prosperity for all and strive to make it a reality. At this point, however, the thoughtful realist returns and wonders: could it be that this return to normality is impossible, even if we succeed in halting climate change?

In my view, the dream of green capitalism has long faded. Yes, it would be an important victory if we stopped climate change, and a necessary one. An unchecked rise in temperature would have such drastic consequences that preventing it is our most vital task. But an ecologically sustainable way of life requires much more: sufficient drinking water, fertile farmland, the pollination of plants, and stable fish stocks in the oceans.

For some years now, Earth system science has been using the concept of planetary boundaries to describe the conditions for the stable existence of human life.[1] These boundaries are metrics specifying upper limits, or thresholds, beyond which further resource depletion will cause ecological systems to become unstable. Earth system science has identified planetary boundaries in nine dimensions. In addition to the climate crisis, these are: ocean acidification, stratospheric ozone depletion, atmospheric aerosol pollution, freshwater consumption, land use, biodiversity loss, the phosphorus and nitrogen cycle, and chemical pollution from novel entities in the environment. Quantitative thresholds have been defined for each of these dimensions and have already been exceeded for six of them, including climate change (owing to the high concentration of CO_2 in the atmosphere) and biodiversity (due to the alarming rate of species extinction).

Planetary boundaries broaden the perspective beyond climate change to include the ecological impact of human activities as a whole. Earth Overshoot Day, whereby a calendar date is calculated each year on which the use of natural resources such as trees or fish exceeds the planet's capacity to restore them, is an idea along the same lines.[2] Seen from the perspective of planetary boundaries, natural resources have been overexploited since 1970, and the trend is worsening. The resources the planet can (re)generate over an entire year are now already being used up by the beginning of August. This date comes much earlier for the highly industrialized countries and much later for the poorer countries, as the latter consume only a small proportion of planetary resources. If the trend in the global use of resources were to continue unabated in this way, then in 2050 we would be consuming twice the resources that the Earth has available for the long term. We would need two Earths. This overexploitation destabilizes ecosystems and cannot be sustained. It equates to ecological collapse.

'Material footprint' is a third benchmark for the consumption and overuse of natural resources. The 'footprint' quantifies the weight of raw materials extracted in the world each year and ultimately used to satisfy consumer demand. In 1990, it was around 43 billion tonnes. By 2023, it had risen to over 100 billion tonnes, an increase of 140 per cent (Figure 7).[3] Materials extraction is increasing faster than both economic growth and population growth. In East and Southeast Asia in particular, the material footprint has grown enormously, owing both to the construction of new infrastructures in countries such as China and to the relocation of industrial production from the United States and Europe to Asian countries.

This finding is enormously significant because it shows that it has not yet been possible to decouple economic growth from damage to the natural environment. On the contrary, economic growth is actually placing an *increasing* burden on the natural environment. Scientists put the upper limit for sustainable material consumption at 50 billion tonnes per year. Yet it is estimated that it will increase to 200 billion tonnes by 2050 – four times the sustainable level.[4] More and more landscapes are being churned into cheap commodities. This has been a feature of capitalist modernity for centuries, but is now advancing ever faster and with an ever wider reach.[5]

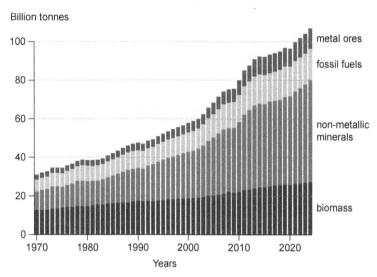

Billion tonnes

metal ores

fossil fuels

non-metallic minerals

biomass

Years

Figure 7. Global extraction of raw materials, 1970–2024, by material groups
Source: WU Vienna 2023, 'Material Flows by Material Group, 1970–2024'. Visualization based on the UNEP IRP Global Material Flows Database, Vienna University of Economics and Business (https://www.materialflows.net/global-trends-of-material-use/).

Analytical models such as planetary boundaries, Earth Overshoot Day, and material footprint demonstrate that the ecological crisis is far wider than just climate change and that the energy transition on its own will not be enough. If the climate crisis is viewed in isolation, we might think change in the way energy is produced might reconcile capitalist modernity and environmental protection. But an energy transition only goes so far. Electric cars are not built of electricity, but use all kinds of materials that need to be extracted and transformed. Every economic activity, even if it has a green dimension, has an impact on ecological systems. The expansion of renewable energy, unfortunately, is a prime example. We think of it as a simple good, limiting the burning of fossil fuels. But some severe environmental problems are actually caused by the energy transition itself.

The technologies deployed for the energy transition are often highly damaging to the environment in their manufacture, use, and disposal. The production of solar modules, for example, requires a great deal of copper. To be precise, a single solar module measuring 1.7 square metres contains around 1 kilogram of copper, primarily for cables, inverters, and transformers. Mining the ore for this quantity of metal produces around 200 kilograms of toxic mining sludge containing arsenic, cadmium, mercury, lead, and other heavy metals. Overall, the sludge from mining copper for use in photovoltaic systems is estimated to amount to 100 million tonnes per year, which has a severe impact on the environment in the mining areas.[6] While photovoltaic panels are being installed on rooftops in Europe and the United States, the resource-producing countries in the global South are choking on the toxic waste which is a by-product of this 'clean' energy. And when the solar panels are replaced after twenty years, additional huge amounts of hazardous waste are produced, as only a small proportion of the materials can be reused.

Producing the batteries for electromobility is also a dirty business. It requires large quantities of lithium, the mining of which also causes ecological damage and demands the sacrifice of ever more land to environmental pollution. Again, the resulting copious volumes of mining sludge are highly toxic, and in addition the mining consumes tremendous amounts of water: 2 million litres per tonne of lithium.[7] So one element of the global sustainability crisis (global warming) is being 'solved' at the expense of another (environmental pollution). The term 'environmental sacrifice zones' has been coined in Latin America to describe this destruction of nature for the extraction of raw materials. What's more, the environmental consequences of the mines have a profound impact on the lives of the people living nearby.[8] The countries in the global South that supply the raw materials are being asked to facilitate the energy transition in the global North at the expense of their own environment and the destruction of local cultures. In a recent interview, Mercedes boss Ola Källenius made clear just how much managers in the global North take for granted their access to these resources and how much their thinking represents a continuation of structures that resemble those from colonial times:

> Lithium, which we need in huge quantities for batteries, is the new oil. The expansion of lithium mining and processing capacities is a gigantic industrial project. Not all of these raw materials will be mined in Europe. We need trade agreements with Canada, South America, and Australia. Government support is essential for this.[9]

This continuation of the use of other countries for the supply of resources applies not only to the mining of lithium.[10] Chile, for example, is at the centre of global plans for the production of green hydrogen using wind energy. These projects are already being criticized for causing environmental damage and violating the rights of indigenous peoples. The same applies to projects in Namibia. Also in the global North wind projects cause collateral ecological damage. For example, there are plans to build huge wind farms in the North Sea with tens of thousands of turbines to supply electricity for up to 300 million households. Gigantic quantities of concrete will be used for the foundations and the turbines will have a considerable impact on the ecosystems of the surrounding seas.[11] This is not an argument for abandoning wind energy. But it does show the extent to which the growth fuelled by the energy transition is in turn causing further ecological damage and compromising the environmental bottom line of the transformation. In economic terms, achieving the goal of climate neutrality will lead to new forms of the externalization of environmental damage. A new wave of resistance is also mobilizing against this, however, and not just in the global South, where social movements are rebelling against the environmental and social damage caused by lithium mining, among other things.[12] In 2023, climate activist Greta Thunberg protested in northern Norway against the failure to dismantle the new wind farm on the Fosen peninsula off Trondheim. The Norwegian Supreme Court had previously declared the project's licence invalid because the turbines threaten the traditional way of life of the Sami people and their culture of reindeer herding.[13] Much of the electricity produced by the wind farm is used to supply energy to Germany.

It could perhaps be argued that the negative ecological consequences associated with the energy transition could be tackled by increasing the reuse of valuable materials via an expanded recycling economy. However, experts do not expect this to happen. According to the IEA, even by 2040 only 12 per cent of the source materials for battery production will be recycled.[14] There are both technical and economic reasons behind this: extracting lithium from old batteries is difficult and much more expensive than mining it. This leaves only the hope of further technological advances that would effectively reduce the need for environmentally damaging extraction. In battery production, one such hope is that some of the batteries will no longer be produced using lithium but use sodium instead.

But this will not stop the overexploitation of planetary resources either, or the externalization of environmental impacts. To maximize profits, the capitalist economy 'needs an "outside"' that it can pass the costs on to.[15] Selling the future by ignoring ecological destruction is an essential part of our economic system, one we can modify but never eliminate. And this sell-off is also part of our social system, which ensures social integration through growth. This is precisely where the limits of the model of green capitalism lie, at least if the term means the sustainable reconciliation of environmental protection and economic activity.

Against this backdrop, it is hardly surprising that even the net carbon reductions from the new technologies developed for the energy transition are less than clear-cut. The production of technologies that are greenhouse gas-neutral once they are operational often requires large CO_2 emissions. In order to calculate the net carbon footprint of electric cars, for example, the production, use, and disposal of the car all have to be taken into account. For electric vehicles, the manufacture of the battery in particular has a high environmental impact, as we have seen. The most powerful electric cars use batteries with a capacity of around 100 kilowatt hours. The production of one such battery leads to the emission of around 13 tonnes of CO_2 equivalent.[16]

Electric motors have an obvious carbon advantage in operation because they are emission-free and, unlike combustion engines, do not convert a large proportion of their energy input into heat. But the advantage may be undermined by how the electricity is generated, and also by the weight of the vehicle. If the electricity is generated using fossil fuels, then an electric vehicle is simply transferring its exhaust gases to the power station. And the more powerful and heavier the vehicle, the lower its carbon advantage, because such vehicles consume more electricity and require more powerful batteries that cause greater environmental damage. So far, however, car manufacturers have been launching mainly heavy models with particularly powerful motors onto the market. Compared to a light and less powerful combustion engine car, these 'land yachts' have no carbon advantage at all. This demonstrates an unwavering determination to adhere to the competitive rationale of modern mass consumption – even electric cars must be status symbols – during the switch to the new technology. Calculations made by the Fraunhofer-Gesellschaft, a German research organization, show that, depending on battery capacity, the carbon footprint of an electric vehicle with the current electricity mix in Germany improves on that of a comparable combustion engine only after 52,000 kilometres of driving, while in the worst cases of very large cars this benchmark is reached after 230,000 kilometres – at which point there is no longer any genuine climate benefit from electromobility.[17]

It also needs to be borne in mind that electromobility continues to have a negative impact on the climate because electric cars, no less than others, make use of the existing transport infrastructure: that is, roads, car parks, charging stations, garages, and car washes. In addition, all e-cars will have to be scrapped at some point, just like combustion engine cars. If we really wanted to reduce the overall environmental impact of transport, we would have to reduce the volume of car traffic – which is not compatible with the concept of green growth. As I noted, the German government's motto on this is 'Not travelling less, but travelling differently.'

The fact that the structures of capitalist modernity remain unchanged by the green transformation means that, despite fundamental alterations in the way energy is produced, the planetary boundaries continue to be breached, because what does not change is the mantra of growth. Environmental economists repeatedly point out that efficiency gains must also lead to actual savings in energy use in order for the climate targets to be achieved. But this is precisely what often does not happen. Instead, resources that are freed up are immediately reinvested in boosting output.[18] Climate scientists refer to this as the rebound effect. The heavy electric vehicles mentioned above are an example of this. Their powerful motors and excessive weight mean that they use no less energy than other vehicles. But saving energy is not regarded as an issue for electromobility. The energy consumption of electric vehicles is not scrutinized because it is assumed that the electric motor solves all environmental problems in that it does not emit greenhouse gases in use. The reinvestment of efficiency gains in additional consumption often occasions astonishment. Environmental activists reproach consumers for this habit, accusing them of being unwilling to make any sacrifices. This ignores the fact that such behaviour is not simply moral weakness, but a manifestation of the growth culture of capitalist modernity.[19]

The rebound effect can be observed in many areas. Better transport infrastructure makes the car an attractive means of transport for more people and thus leads to more traffic. Even non-stationary car sharing schemes in cities do not have the intended effect of reducing the number of private cars. People who do not own a car are now using these schemes to improve their mobility.[20] The electric scooters available for hire in many cities have an adverse net carbon footprint because they generally replace walking or taking the underground, not the car.[21] The fuel consumption of aeroplanes has been reduced significantly in recent decades by technological innovations, but since the 1970s, global air traffic has increased tenfold and is expected to double again by 2040, leading to ever higher emissions of greenhouse gases.[22] These are just a few examples.

Rebound effects are a significant obstacle on the path to a climate-neutral and environmentally friendly economy. However, they are completely in line with the growth rationale of capitalist modernity. In the capitalist economy, all efficiency gains are in principle translated into additional economic activity. A more efficient machine, one that can be operated by fewer workers than the previous model, does not lead to shorter working hours, but to the purchase of an additional machine where the now superfluous labour capacity is then deployed. This reinvestment of efficiency gains is the basic economic principle underlying growth and profits. It should come as no surprise that this also happens in the case of innovations that could, in principle, lead to lower environmental damage. The same applies to consumer behaviour: if the price of a consumer item falls, people do not spend less but buy something else in addition. Here, too, the prevailing ethos of ever more, ever more powerful, and ever bigger is entirely in line with the principles of capitalist modernity. It is precisely the prospect of a car with an even more powerful engine or of even more disposable energy that motivates consumers to accept the changes in the first place. The green economy prevails when it reaffirms the growth agenda of capitalist modernity. The climate and the environment fall by the wayside. In order for this to change, something would have to happen that cannot happen under the prevailing structures: a decline in economic activity.

9

What next?

The ever-expanding emission of greenhouse gases can be compared to a tanker with a braking time of many decades. The fact that it takes so long to come to a halt is not only due to its weight. The steering controls also only allow certain manoeuvres, while others are blocked. Many different people work on the bridge and in the engine room. Some of them want to brake sharply, others simply want to keep going. Others suspect that the tanker cannot be stopped at all without breaking apart.

So far, I have taken a look at the construction blueprints, the bridge, and the engine room of this tanker, to gain an understanding of the forces and mechanisms that have caused the climate crisis and block the way out. The 'considered realism' underpinning this book entails, first and foremost, understanding the forces at work in business and politics, as well as among citizens and consumers, that shape the fight against the climate crisis and prevent adequate responses.

Nobody can know with any precision what climatic conditions will prevail at the end of the twenty-first century, but this much is clear: in the coming decades, we will suffer from further significant global warming. The effects will be considerable, they will be global, and they will be unevenly distributed both among countries and within societies. Until now, societies have been able to take the continuity of the natural foundations for life for granted – even if we were occasionally rocked by passing natural disasters. Climate change, however, is creating what cultural theorist Martin Müller calls a 'new unreliability of nature'.[1]

Nature itself becomes a variable once its unreliability, its underlying fragility, becomes apparent. This presents societies with the challenge of drastically heightened complexity. So far, however, the unfolding crisis has not triggered the social forces necessary to direct existing social structures towards a realistic solution. The fight against climate change is failing owing to the power and incentive structures of a social configuration geared towards profit-making, consumption, and unlimited growth – despite our knowledge of the dangers of future climate change. Time is also running out on the political clock, as the increasingly complex dynamics of climate change make it progressively difficult to manage.

That doesn't mean that nothing is happening. But it's not enough. Nor does it mean that nobody shows any concern. There are plenty of social movements and growing numbers of climate activists drawing attention to our plight through campaigns and actions that are often quite spectacular. Scientists and the media also frequently issue warnings. And opinion polls show that the vast majority of people in many countries see climate change as a major problem – even the biggest problem – of our time. This is also true for many politicians. Company bosses, too, have families whose future lives are presumably not a matter of indifference to them. But understanding and concern are no match for the power of deeply embedded social and economic structures. Investment decisions at work will be made on the basis of profitability, regardless of what managers discussed with their families around the breakfast table that morning. Politicians have to build majorities, and to do so they make compromises.

Consumption and its escalation, the fear of losing an accustomed lifestyle or an established job, help drive the social order of modern societies. And even people with the greatest possible level of environmental awareness cannot avoid using the infrastructures that have been constructed for a life based on fossil fuels. Our responses to climate change operate within structurally determined guardrails that guide us away from the necessary changes. What we need is an emergency stop, a rapid reduction that would bring the multiple instances of resource overexploitation back within planetary boundaries. The only way to bring this about would be to nullify pressures for economic growth through politically agreed and enforced climate protection measures and a shift to lifestyles in which excessive consumption no longer takes centre stage. But none of this is happening. Instead, the burning of fossil fuels continues to increase, political decision-making remains narrowly confined within the tipping points of voter approval and the rates of return expected by private investors, and consumers continue to defend their established lifestyles.

What options remain? What should we focus on if we assume that at the end of this century the Earth may be up to 2.5 degrees warmer than in the pre-industrial age? In the final pages of this book, I will try to sketch out what it might mean to act wisely and morally in the face of this knowledge.

Ideas for political action are not easy to find under the conditions I have described. I have shown how the power and incentive structures established by capitalist modernity block an adequate response to climate change. Resignation in the face of this would be perfectly understandable. However, it is not the conclusion I draw. Regardless of the difficulties, societies have to react. Anything else would be to accept the collapse of civilization.

So if not resignation, then what? Some may be led by the preceding chapters to call for the abolition of capitalism itself. If the social system of capitalist modernity were overturned, the idea goes, space would be created for a social order free from both the growth compulsion and the consequent over-exploitation of natural resources. This is the position taken by advocates of a post-growth society. I have already mentioned the book by Jason Hickel in which he shows how capitalism is destroying the natural foundations of the planet and why the solution can only lie in reducing the consumption of resources.[2] He outlines an appealing vision of alternative post-growth society. The American philosopher Nancy Fraser recently sounded a similar note. In order to tackle the climate crisis, she states, 'what is needed, first and foremost, is to wrest the power to dictate our relation to nature away from the class that currently monopolizes it so that we can begin to reinvent that relation from the ground up'.[3]

I agree that in order to live within the planetary boundaries, there is no way around restrictions on economic growth and excessive consumption, especially in highly developed countries, and that such restrictions are not compatible with the existing structures of capitalist modernity. And yet I wonder whether there is anything more behind these eloquent demands for comprehensive system change than just a habitual radicalism.[4] Most advocates of sweeping change are completely silent on how existing societies can transform themselves into post-growth societies given the prevailing power and incentive structures. They are also silent on how a shrinking economy might be made compatible with social stability. As long as the demand for system change is unaccompanied by a viable political programme, it is nothing more than a utopian fantasy into which sympathetic readers can briefly escape. Moreover, such tales of redemption in a new and non-capitalist world inevitably generate new disappointments as it soon becomes apparent that the changes they depict will not materialize – or at least not in the foreseeable future. In any event, the fantasies are of little help in tackling the acute and immediate problem that is climate change.

Undoubtedly, capitalist modernity is merely a historical epoch that, like all historical configurations, will at some point come to an end. There is no guarantee of eternal life for capitalism. One day, a museum dedicated to the history of capitalism will be built, which visitors will walk through with a similar look of disbelief as we have today at an exhibition on ancient Rome, the Mayan civilization, or feudalism. But anyone who walks around the world today with a discerning and watchful political eye will see that capitalism remains vibrant, shaken by crises from time to time but evidently capable of adapting, chameleon-like, to changing conditions. Our actions to reduce greenhouse gas emissions so far confirm this, pointing as they do to green turbo-capitalism rather than an end to our economic system. A broad-based protest movement against capitalism, as called for by Nancy Fraser, does not currently exist, however much some would welcome it. That time may come but it is certainly not in sight.

The question 'What next?' calls for an answer that identifies *practicable* ways of taking pressure off the Earth's ecological systems. Overturning the entire economic and social order might not even get us any closer to this goal. After all, it is not something that would be agreed with a handshake and a peaceable process of dismantling, but rather via bitter political and economic conflicts, during which climate policy would presumably not be a priority. Moreover, fundamental processes of social change have historically taken place over decades or even centuries.[5] Given the unrelenting timetable dictated by climate change, we simply do not have the time to first overturn the existing social order, then build a new one, and then finally tackle the climate problem. This is quite apart from the fact that we would have to be sure that a different political and economic system would actually prioritize the natural environment and be able to enforce the priority throughout the world. All of this may be seen as adding further layers of paradox to our current situation. But these problems cannot simply be wished away.

For me, what follows from the above is the need to identify realistic approaches to climate policy, in the clear knowledge that these will not cut any Gordian knots and that further global warming must therefore be assumed. Climate policy happens within a web of complex entanglements of interests and structures, ways of life and belief systems, as well as perceived options and alternatives, which manifest themselves as dilemmas across the entire spectrum from the local to the global and sometimes encompass enormously long time horizons. This is the reason why climate change is a wicked problem, one that comes with a high degree of uncertainty as to its future course and does not allow for clear and easy solutions.[6] The best we can hope for are partial solutions – and solutions that will constantly change in the light of developments and experience and that will remain inherently controversial. Furthermore, they will take place against, and frequently disrupt, an ever-changing social and political backdrop. Wicked problems, in short, deserve their name.

At a general level, it is therefore essential to develop an approach that is politically feasible. It should buy time for societies to adapt to climate change, accelerate the defossilization of energy production, and curtail the growth of resource consumption. To repeat the point: climate change is not an either-or issue, but rather one of more-or-less. Slowing down climate change merely buys more time, but this time could provide the opportunity for social and technical developments to emerge that open up new political options. It is also possible that the increasingly dramatic effects of climate change we can now foresee could in themselves focus minds, perhaps increasing the willingness of business, politicians, and citizens to take action.[7]

In any event, the starting point has to be the reality of our situation. Climate change has arrived; it is going to intensify and to become increasingly consequential. According to experts, an increase in the global average temperature of 2.7 degrees Celsius compared to pre-industrial levels would lead to a third of the world's population falling out of the so-called climate niche.[8] This would mean that in the twenty-second century, about 3 billion people around the world would have to live in areas that are actually uninhabitable for the human organism owing to extreme heat, drought, or flooding. Recent heat-waves in India and Thailand and rising temperatures in Arab countries already serve to demonstrate what this will mean in concrete terms. And we have seen, too, in the more moderate climates of the United States and Europe harbingers of a future in which societies have to fight the causes and the conse-quences of climate change simultaneously. Climate mitigation is an epochal task as, unchecked, climate change would have consequences so devastating that in the end nothing could help. Even as we try to prevent the worst, however, it is clear that we have to take measures to adapt to those changes that are already with us or seem inevitable.

If drought becomes more widespread, for example, it will be necessary to redesign water systems to preserve and safeguard the supply for households, industry, and agriculture. How can agriculture be managed to reduce water consumption? Will tourism have to be cut where water is scarce? Clearly, many cities will need redesign. When temperatures rise to over 40 degrees Celsius in summer, urban areas must be kept habitable through, for example, greening, providing shade in public spaces, and constructing public areas for cooling down. If prolonged heatwaves become more frequent in some parts of the world, people must be protected by, for instance, the installation of air conditioning systems – whether in large cities in Asia or retirement homes in France – and through public healthcare systems that are prepared for the impact of heatwaves on health. At the same time, electricity grids must be expanded and enhanced so that they can withstand the increased energy demand. And if the sea level rises, coastal communities must be either protected or evacuated. These are just a few of the necessary adaptations that will require political decisions in a world where the consequences of climate change will increasingly move centre stage. They are already posing significant challenges today.

Climate adaptation, however, is not just a task for engineers. Social and political structures must also become more resilient as social stresses rise. In my view, this issue is still receiving far too little attention, and the social sciences need to do more to highlight the dilemmas. There can be no doubt that as the impact of climate change becomes more tangible, social and political structures will confront intensifying conflicts within and among societies. These will revolve around competition for increasingly scarce water resources, controversial but necessary changes to agriculture and construction, the extraction of resources, and unwelcome changes required to lifestyles. They will worsen as an ever-increasing proportion of the available financial resources will be needed for short-term adaptation and damage repair and will therefore not be available for other tasks. Neither for climate mitigation, nor, for that matter, for the numerous other tasks that already arise in every community and that require funds and political attention.

The increasing damage caused by climate change and the need to devote greater resources to climate protection and adaptation are leading to a potentially unstable social and political situation. Societies, especially in the global North, will need to cope with a future in which there will be ever-declining gains and ever-increasing losses to be distributed.[9] This undermines capitalist modernity's ideal of perpetually increasing prosperity, devalues the promise it holds out for the future, and fosters polarization and conflict. In addition, it will be necessary, especially on the global level, to contain conflicts exacerbated by climate change and to respond to the increasingly precarious supply of basic needs as agricultural productivity may decline and social conflicts grow. When natural disasters happen, poorer population groups generally have less protection and suffer greater harm than richer ones.[10] This will apply no less to climate change. The greatest damage is expected in the global South: that is, in the countries that have the least resources with which to protect themselves from the consequences. Maintaining an inclusive structure of social order under these circumstances will require great vigilance. Otherwise, we risk a scenario that the sociologist and historian Mike Davis described a few years ago as follows:

> Instead of galvanizing heroic innovation and international cooperation, growing environmental and socio-economic turbulence may simply drive elite publics into more frenzied attempts to wall themselves off from the rest of humanity. Global mitigation, in this unexplored but not improbable scenario, would be tacitly abandoned ... in favor of accelerated investment in selective adaptation for Earth's first-class passengers. The goal would be the creation of green and gated oases of permanent affluence on an otherwise stricken planet.[11]

So how is social stability possible under conditions which include the increasing 'unreliability' of nature and the necessity – as outlined above – for a redistribution of the available resources? To answer this question, I would like to return to the analytical model presented in Chapter 2. On the basis of a distinction between the economy, the political sphere, and the populace (citizens and consumers), I argued there that although the actors each proceed according to their own principles, they are also mutually dependent and exert influence on each other. The hypothesis that follows is that climate adaptation and climate change mitigation measures only have a realistic chance of being implemented if the steps involved are tailored to utilize the respective rationales of the various spheres of action and their reciprocal channels of influence.

This suggests concrete starting points for a realistic climate policy.

Let's look first at the economy. As argued above, it makes no difference to commercial enterprises how they make their profits. Only the prospect of profit as such motivates investments; the estimated costs and expected revenues of individual business models are the decisive factors. The mechanism for bringing about change in economic activity can therefore only be the alteration of entrepreneurial incentive structures, either through financial carrots or through regulatory sticks. The structural power of the economy (i.e., its ability to shift or refrain from investment) means that 'acceptable' profit expectations for companies must be maintained. However, the path to profit must change through the promotion and subsidization of climate-friendly business models together with systematic and stringent financial sanctions on greenhouse gas emissions through taxation and new regulations. Of course, the incumbent big hitters in the market will often resist such changes to maintain and extend their existing lucrative business models.[12] But even corporations can be steered in new directions by incentives, and policy-makers at least have a clear and capitalist-friendly means to promote economic change: designing competition policy to strengthen the position of environmentally sound challengers vis-à-vis the incumbents. This will be part of a broader challenge to foster coalitions within business and politics as well as between them to take climate protection forward.

As the rules governing business are determined in the public sphere, setting regulations to accelerate decarbonization depends on political power. In turn, the scope for political action depends on whether the ruling government has a realistic prospect of maintaining economic prosperity, tax revenues, and the loyalty of the electorate. Any political credit the regime has in the bank must be used to channel investment into climate protection and adaptation.[13] And politicians need to work at the same time to persuade people that protecting the climate is the right thing to do. The legal system can play an important role in this, as it can be used to bring the rights of future generations and the preservation of natural resources to bear more heavily on business and politics.[14]

This leads us to the second main task for policy-makers: working with the electorate to address problems rather than dictating solutions from on high or seeking votes by pretending change is unnecessary. This means increasing political support for climate protection and adaptation measures among the public, not only in the abstract sense of winning approval in opinion polls, but also in increasing understanding of measures that entail costs and significant disruptions.[15] As we have seen, climate protection measures are resisted, spark conflict, and often fail if they involve significant personal restrictions.

Research shows that voters are more likely to approve of climate adaptation measures than climate change mitigation measures.[16] This is because the former are much more likely to be experienced as a practical benefit. The adoption of flood protection measures in your own town, or the installation of air conditioning in local schools, or the planting of trees in town squares are tangible improvements in defence systems against the consequences of climate change. They amount to collective goods from which everyone benefits. The situation is often different with measures aimed at climate protection. Obliging people to install heat pumps or increasing petrol prices are burdens that bring tangible losses and only abstract benefits. The question then often asked is: what difference does my sacrifice make, given the global scale of the problem?

My suggestion would be to focus more on adaptation measures that can be experienced as practical everyday improvements, also in the hope that this will increase people's awareness of the importance of the climate problem and gradually create a social climate that strengthens a readiness to act. This presumably will be all the more true when people are directly involved in the measures to be implemented locally and can see their benefits. But beware: this does not mean that mitigation could be neglected.

Prudent political action must also take into account the fact that attitudes to climate policy differ between social groups. Urban middle-class milieus, for example, think about the climate-friendly transformation of their neighbourhoods, with bike-friendly and traffic-calmed streets, urban greening, eco-friendly development, and sustainable shopping opportunities. By contrast, as sociologist Sighard Neckel points out, traditional and less affluent social classes are less interested in a green lifestyle than in the provision of collective public services that reduce their environmental impact and enable healthier lives. So this means green recreation areas, healthy school meals, and well-functioning local transport. Neckel quotes urban researcher Miriam Greenberg: 'Whose sustainability are we talking about?'[17] This suggests that climate policy may be able to mobilize broader social support if it takes these differing interests into account by using multi-layered political measures.

Another important step to increase public support is undoubtedly to ensure that burdens are distributed fairly.[18] In this book, I have referred at various points to the distributional issues raised by climate policy. Be they carbon taxes, heat pumps, or electric vehicles: the additional burdens that are easy for the wealthy to shoulder often overtax household budgets all the way up the ladder to the upper middle class. This is especially true at a time when widespread stagnation of incomes over the past few decades has affected the middle ground of society and already put many people in a financially precarious situation. The resulting fear of slipping down the social ladder gives rise to political resentment, which bolsters precisely those political movements and groupings most opposed to climate policy. The more irrefutable and severe the damage caused by climate change and the higher the cost of effective change, the greater is the danger that climate policy will become a stark dividing line in society and will fuel authoritarian populism, which in turn will block effective policy measures.[19]

This risk could be reduced if, first, climate policy measures could be communicated without any undertone of moral superiority, reducing the perception (whether justified or not) of condescension and lack of respect among a section of the population. At the same time, financial burdens on the individual would need to be cushioned right up to the upper middle class, either by covering the costs collectively from the outset (i.e., from public budgets) or, where this is not possible, by systematically, consistently, and publicly compensating individuals for their additional costs.[20] It should be borne in mind that climate policy measures also offer political opportunities to provide targeted structural policy assistance to individual regions, thereby gaining political support from social groups that tend to be sceptical about climate policy.[21]

Resistance to the support required for the global South must also be overcome. This is no easy task: it is almost impossible to convince an electorate that scarce tax money should be spent outside one's own country. However, it may help if it can be made clear how interconnected our own living conditions are with those in poorer countries. The harmful impact of greenhouse gases is completely independent of where in the world they are emitted. In addition, climate protection measures are often particularly efficient in the global South, for example because outdated coal-fired power plants can be decommissioned there. The global South and North are also interlinked when it comes to the social consequences of climate change. Global climate policy and migration policy will be inextricably connected in the future. People will try to escape a hostile natural environment, which will lead to an increase in migration – in the first instance, within the region of origin. But sooner or later, the global North will also increasingly become a destination for climate-induced migration, something that can already be observed, for instance, at the Mexican–American border. Reducing this migratory pressure is a goal that has political appeal.

However all this is managed in detail, climate protection will not be possible without compensatory social and structural policies and without extending financial support to the global South. And this is perhaps the key political message of my book. The past forty years have seen a shift in the relationship between the state and the economy in almost all countries towards steering social development through market forces. The idea has prevailed that the state should step back and allow markets to develop freely so as not to stand in the way of achieving the maximum possible prosperity. This doctrine has led to worsening social inequality within countries and produced serious social tensions. The haemorrhaging of public budgets, especially at the local level, has also led – quite independently of climate change – to a crisis in public infrastructures. The miserable condition of public transport networks, the decaying public school and university buildings, and the underfunding of public healthcare systems in so many countries are just a few examples of this. The provision of public services, the creation and maintenance of which depend on adequate state funding, has dried up.

Climate change brings with it a huge additional task for public services: the need to set up and maintain a whole new set of public goods for mitigation and adaptation. In this situation, it becomes painfully clear how misguided the overly pro-market policies of recent decades have been. In order to preserve a stable climate as a common good, public funds must be mobilized on a dramatically larger scale than before. The scope for public investment must also be increased in order to create 'green' infrastructures that will benefit all citizens in adapting to climate change. This requires an expansion of the state's fiscal headroom through higher public debt earmarked for climate policy, differentiated interest rates, and an increase in overall tax revenue. The necessary increase in the provision of these public goods demands a fiscal and monetary policy that breaks away from fiscal austerity and requires tax increases for the wealthiest section of the population, who have been able over the last few decades to reduce their tax burden and massively increase their private wealth. Such a reversal of the prevailing economic policy dogma will meet with political resistance from all those who, because of their wealth, are able to find private alternatives to the missing public goods if necessary. However, it may be possible to mobilize political support for increasing public spending on the provision of these public goods from other social groups, as this would create a form of wealth that is available to all instead of dividing societies into rich and poor.[22]

Ultimately, climate protection policy must also be supported through the behaviour of each individual. This, too, however, is about collective change, not the manipulation of individuals through 'nudging' or through purely symbolic displacement activities such as the trade in opaque offsetting certificates. Significant changes in individual behaviour will only come about if, for one thing, the public infrastructures mentioned above are modified so that environmentally friendly behaviour is encouraged and supported. People will make more use of local public transport services if they are reliable, user-friendly, and frequent enough. Air and car traffic will be reduced if trains connect cities punctually and efficiently. Electromobility will win out if the vehicles on offer can compete with combustion engines on price and there is a nationwide charging infrastructure. This is about creating structures to which individual behaviour can adapt. What is needed are practical alternatives for which political support can be mobilized because they offer the prospect of tangible improvements in how people manage their everyday lives. It is up to the polity to create these infrastructures; we cannot expect the market to provide them. Once again, it is about the creation of collective goods and public services.

At the same time, there is a need for a stronger orientation of people's behaviour towards the common good.
Climate protection will fail if citizens' actions are guided
solely by the principle of the maximization of individual
benefit. Accordingly, it is not only prudent behaviour that is
needed, but also virtuous behaviour. Nothing illustrates this
more clearly than the problem of collective goods identified
so clearly in economic theory, according to which the creation of common goods fails because individuals refuse to share
the related costs.[23] The relevance of this problem is apparent whenever support for climate protection is refused on the
grounds that the individual's contribution is irrelevant anyway.
What is true for the individual becomes a catastrophe for the
world because the climate as a collective good is destroyed and
climate adaptation measures are not taken. The fact that this
kind of free-riding is so widespread contradicts the culturally
influential narrative of the beneficial outcomes of the invisible
hand of the market and of self-interested behaviour generally.

But this narrative has its limits anyway. It is by no means
the case that people always refuse to create or contribute to
common goods. It is rather that economic theory promotes a
narrow view of human behaviour, as people often act altruisti-
cally and in support of rules and practices that promote the
common good on account of their values and convictions. And
sometimes they act on these even when they know that this
entails personal costs and that there are other people who will
be free-riders. People can do the right thing even at a price and
when success is unlikely.[24] Consistent with this, studies show
that climate adaptation measures are particularly popular
when they are perceived as a social norm, when people see
that they are effective, and when they see how they can make a
contribution themselves.[25]

In business and politics, this kind of non-selfish behaviour
is too often blocked by systemic constraints. Market incentives

and the culture of individualism in capitalist modernity are both parasitic on and destructive towards the commons. Unselfish behaviour, however, can prosper and receive support and encouragement outside these functional systems: in close family relationships and friendships, of course, but also in the sphere of civil society. Moral resources that can nurture and support community-oriented behaviour arise and flourish in such sites of social bonding and social exchange.[26] They engender political reflection and action that take the common good as their yardstick. The various national and international climate movements are an example of this, as are the countless local initiatives in which people actively campaign for climate protection and environmental conservation.

These civil society resources cannot simply be taken for granted, but rely on established social relationships and practices that are learnt through socialization. They thrive through contact with formal and informal institutions that both support values and convictions and exert moral pressure on the actions of individuals and organizations. The ethical and behavioural orientations of the lifeworld thus become relevant for business and politics too. This is because both spheres are dependent on social legitimation and therefore cannot simply ignore citizens' values. This leads to the question of how value orientations that might lead into support for climate protection can be politically strengthened.

Climate change is unquestionably a global problem, but it does not follow that the values necessary to build political support for effective policy will emerge from pronouncements at international climate conferences. Ethical behaviour, rather, emerges locally from the social network of relationships in the community, in families and friendships, and in civic engagement. Climate protection policy should therefore build on people's immediate lifeworlds within democratic civil society.[27] This would suggest involving citizens much more closely in decisions on climate protection and adaptation measures and underlines the importance of local politics – *even though* climate change is global.

We have been witnessing the importance of local action, in fact, for a long time now, in environmental initiatives to stop coal mining in South Africa, in climate strikes by schoolchildren and students in many countries, in local initiatives in the Ahr district in Germany, where citizens are battling to ensure the restoration of their neighbourhoods following the floods in summer 2021. It is in such social projects that cultural attitudes towards environmentally friendly behaviour are formed. This is not important because these initiatives immediately lead to grand political decisions, but because insights can grow here which acknowledge that climate change is a serious problem requiring far-reaching political measures that are worth investing in. A popular climate-oriented perspective can emerge from this which business and political leaders cannot completely ignore and which also influences other levels of political action. Sighard Neckel expresses this idea succinctly, referencing the American philosopher and social reformer John Dewey:

> Actors are able . . . in a self-reflexive way to distance themselves from their own interests in order to bring them into alignment with the interests of those with whom they share the political arena. Democracy is thus deeply rooted in the co-operative character of human social coexistence.[28]

Such socially embedded initiatives can have a positive influence on cognitive and ethical frameworks in the wider society as they spread. Community-oriented behavioural resources should therefore be supported in the hope of diffusion through a kind of 'moral contagion'.[29] A widespread readiness to support measures against the overexploitation of natural resources can only be engendered, if at all, with the involvement of civil society: that is, from the bottom up, not from the top down. Of course, the implementation, financing, and coordination of climate policy measures require the legislative powers in the hands of politicians, but they in turn depend on support from citizens, in their beliefs and convictions and their willingness to support the public good.

The spread of such beliefs and convictions can also be supported politically through, for example, the funding of model projects that can serve as learning centres.[30] The sociologist Erik Olin Wright once advocated 'real utopias', locally based initiatives such as real-world laboratories that feature new social lifestyles and can win over more people by demonstrating different ways of organizing social life.[31] As noted, enabling new ways of living to be directly experienced seems to be particularly important for supporting processes of social change. In such model projects, people can gain insights that can be shared in the political arena. And if they are expanded into functioning material infrastructures, new patterns and routines of environmentally friendly behaviour can establish themselves in the new framework.[32]

Such infrastructures also include positive images of a future society that has adapted to the conditions required to preserve the natural environment.[33] What does such a society look like? What is life like in such a society? What are the gains in quality of life? The sketches of a post-growth society outlined above certainly play an important role here, because they set against the existing, unquestioned ways of life alternatives that may come to seem increasingly attractive. Visions of a possible future, some of which can already be tried out, could build popular support for change and put beneficial civil pressure on business and politics. The same is true of the public mourning of losses resulting from the climate crisis – be it the loss of one's own home to flooding or forest fires, or the loss of their livelihoods for people in distant countries owing to the melting of the Arctic ice or rising sea levels. We should also mourn the destruction of still untouched nature, as expressed in the description by Tom Kizzia with which I began this book. And also the fact that ways of life that were previously cherished and deemed valuable will simply come to an end. Such mourning testifies to the emotional attachment we feel to the natural foundations of our lives. If this grief can be expressed and heard in the public sphere, then this, too, may support a spirit of stewardship and care and encourage a greater readiness to take action.[34]

We should recall that government policy and corporate behaviour will continue to obey their systemic rationales and will only accommodate the protection of natural resources if and when it's compatible with the principles of profit and of holding on to power. But perhaps the parameters of these rationales can be shifted at least a little by the actions of citizens. That would be no small thing, even if it does not lead to a sufficient response to climate change. The consequences of climate change might at least be cushioned a little further, and a social transformation that slows the change and helps societies adapt to the new climatic conditions could gather a little more momentum than it has now. None of this is simple, and none of it is likely, because all of it has to prevail over structures that resist and oppose such changes. But even the faint hope of delaying and further mitigating climate change makes active engagement in the pursuit of this goal a rational step, and also a moral duty. The extent to which we actually succeed will determine how our children and grandchildren live, and how they judge us.

Acknowledgements

This book was first published in German in March 2024. Michael Bollig, Benjamin Braun, Christoph Deutschmann, Mark Ebers, Anita Engels, Timur Ergen, Sighard Neckel, Wolfgang Streeck, Wolfgang Vortkamp, and Leon Wansleben read earlier versions of the manuscript and offered astute comments. For this I cannot thank them enough. It is a tremendous privilege to have such colleagues and friends. I am profoundly grateful to Marion Neuland for her outstanding editorial guidance over many months, to Susanne Hilbring, Cora Molloy, and their colleagues for marvellous support in sourcing the literature, and to Thomas Pott for preparing the figures for publication and for going through the manuscript again with incredible meticulousness during the final stages. Eva Gilmer from Suhrkamp encouraged me to write the book and enriched the German manuscript with her remarkable linguistic flair. I would like to thank her and all the other staff at Suhrkamp Verlag. The manuscript was translated into English by Ray Cunningham, whom I would like to thank for his superb work and his great patience discussing detailed formulations with me. The English version of the book follows the German manuscript closely, but there are a few alterations and some updates where new data was available. All direct quotations for which no English source is cited are translations by the author and translator. I would like to thank the Goethe-Institut and the German Research Foundation (BE 2053/11-1) for supporting the translation of the manuscript. My gratitude goes to Ian Malcolm, who went over the English version with a fine-toothed comb. This is the fourth book I have published with Ian as my editor, and I thank him for his long-standing trust in my work over the last twenty-five years and his sharp intelligence and wit. Last, but certainly not least, I would like to thank my wife, Annelies Fryberger, for her support, which made it possible for me to spend so much time writing this book, for being ready and willing to discuss many of its ideas with me, and for her help in editing parts of the English translation.

Notes

Chapter 1   Knowledge without change

1 Tom Kizzia, 'End-Times Tourism in the Land of Glaciers', *The New York Times*, 22.11.2022 (https://www.nytimes.com/2022/11/22/opinion/glaciers-alaska-climate-change.html).

2 Our World in Data, 'Cumulative CO_2 Emissions' (https://our worldindata.org/grapher/cumulative-co-emissions).

3 UN Environment Programme, *Emissions Gap Report 2022: The Closing Window – Climate Crisis Calls for Rapid Transformation of Societies*, United Nations Environment Programme, Nairobi, 2022   (https://www.unep.org/resources/emissions-gap-report -2022).

4 Luke Kemp et al., 'Climate Endgame: Exploring Catastrophic Climate Change Scenarios', *Proceedings of the National Academy of Sciences* 119:34 (2022), pp. 1–9, here p. 3; Timothy M. Lenton et al., 'Quantifying the Human Cost of Global Warming', *Nature Sustainability* 6 (2023), pp. 1237–47.

5 As this indicates, I am focusing here on the democratic countries of the global North. This is justified because these countries bear almost all of the responsibility for the increase in CO_2 concentrations in the atmosphere to date and are still the largest emitters relative to their populations. Only in Chapter

5 do I address the problem from the perspective of the global South.

6 Dipesh Chakrabarty, *The Climate of History in a Planetary Age*, Chicago and London, 2021, p. 12.

7 On the problem of the short-term nature of corporate decisions, see Natalie Slawinski et al., 'The Role of Short-Termism and Uncertainty Avoidance in Organizational Inaction on Climate Change: A Multi-Level Framework', *Business & Society* 56:2 (2017), pp. 253–82. On the question of the conditions under which organizations institutionalize extremely long-term time horizons, see Frederic Hanusch and Frank Biermann, 'Deep-Time Organizations: Learning Institutional Longevity from History', *The Anthropocene Review* 7:1 (2020), pp. 19–41.

8 The temporal and spatial structures particular to climate change also go some way towards explaining why the response to climate change differs so markedly from that to other crises, such as the coronavirus pandemic or the outbreak of war in Ukraine. In both cases, radical measures were taken immediately and with the expectation of rapid impacts.

9 This is the approach taken in (and at the same time a problem with) the Dynamic Integrated Climate-Economy (DICE) model developed by William Nordhaus, which attempts to calculate economically optimal global warming: William D. Nordhaus, 'Rolling the "DICE": An Optimal Transition Path for Controlling Greenhouse Gases', *Resource and Energy Economics* 15:1 (1993), pp. 27–50.

10 Relevant academic studies: Anita Engels et al. (eds), *Hamburg Climate Futures Outlook 2023: The Plausibility of a 1.5°C Limit to Global Warming – Social Drivers and Physical Processes*, Hamburg, 2023; Joost de Moor and Jens Marquardt, 'Deciding Whether It's Too Late: How Climate Activists Coordinate Alternative Futures in a Postapocalyptic Present', *Geoforum* 138 (2023), 103666 (https://doi.org/10.1016/j.geoforum.2022.10 3666). And a journalistic article: 'Goodbye 1.5°C', *The Economist*, 5.–11.11.2022, p. 13.

11 See Climate Action Tracker (https://climateactiontracker.org/).
    The fact that climate protection targets are invariably missed and
    other political promises are also broken shows that much of the
    summit drama around climate change policy is purely symbolic.
    However, similar to the declaration of human rights in the late
    eighteenth century, climate targets create a normative basis from
    which existing practices and regulations can be criticized and
    pressure for action can be built up.

12 McKinsey & Company, 'Global Energy Perspective 2021' (https://
    www.mckinsey.com/~/media/mckinsey/industries/oil%20and
    %20gas/our%20insights/global%20energy%20perspective%2020
    21/global-energy-perspective-2021-final.pdf).

13 On the important concept of plausible climate expectations,
    see Engels et al. (eds), *Hamburg Climate Futures Outlook
    2023*.

14 IEA, *World Energy Outlook 2022*, Paris, 2022 (https://www.iea
    .org/reports/world-energy-outlook-2022/key-findings). The oil
    multinational ExxonMobil takes a similar view and in its 'Global
    Outlook' expects energy-related CO_2 emissions to fall by 25 per
    cent by 2050, which would correspond to annual emissions of
    just under 28 billion tonnes: ExxonMobil, 'ExxonMobil Global
    Outlook: Our View to 2050', 2023 (https://corporate.exxonmobil
    .com/what-we-do/energy-supply/global-outlook#Keyinsights).
    Even the most optimistic scenarios do not expect greenhouse
    gases to be removed from the atmosphere over the next twenty-
    five years on a scale that would neutralize the expected new
    emissions from the combustion of fossil fuels.

15 Even if this is successful, the emissions permitted under the
    German Climate Protection Act would not limit the rise in tem-
    perature to 1.5 degrees, but with a 67 per cent probability would
    allow it to rise to 1.75 degrees. See Mario Ragwitz et al., *Szenarien
    für ein klimaneutrales Deutschland. Technologieumbau,
    Verbrauchsreduktion und Kohlenstoffmanagement*, Munich,
    2023.

16 IEA, *World Energy Outlook 2022*.

17 Walter Benjamin, 'Surrealism: The Last Snapshot of the European Intelligentsia', in *Selected Writings*, ed. Michael W. Jennings, Vol. 2, Part 1, Cambridge, MA, and London, 1999, pp. 207–21.

18 On ecological mourning, see, for example, Rebecca Elliott, 'The Sociology of Climate Change as a Sociology of Loss', *European Journal of Sociology* 59:3 (2018), pp. 301–37; Ashlee Cunsolo and Karen Landman (eds), *Mourning Nature: Hope at the Heart of Ecological Loss and Grief*, Montreal, 2017; Carl Cassegård and Håkan Thörn, 'Toward a Postapocalyptic Environmentalism? Responses to Loss and Visions of the Future in Climate Activism', *Environment and Planning E: Nature and Space* 1:4 (2018), pp. 561–78.

19 For example, the journalist Ulrike Herrmann, *Das Ende des Kapitalismus. Warum Wachstum und Klimaschutz nicht vereinbar sind – und wie wir in Zukunft leben werden*, Cologne, 2022.

20 Reiner Grundmann, 'Climate Change as Wicked Social Problem', *Nature Geoscience* 9 (2016), pp. 562–3; Dominic Duckett et al., 'Tackling Wicked Environmental Problems: The Discourse and Its Influence on Praxis in Scotland', *Landscape and Urban Planning* 154 (2016), pp. 44–56; Peter J. Balint et al., *Wicked Environmental Problems: Managing Uncertainty and Conflict*, Washington, DC, 2011.

21 The real situation with regard to CFCs is of course more complex. Here I am concerned solely with the problem structure of the 'hole in the ozone layer'.

22 Brad Plumer and Nadja Popovich, 'Yes, There Has Been Progress on Climate. No, It's Not Nearly Enough', *The New York Times*, 25.10.2021 (https://www.nytimes.com/interactive/2021/10/25 /climate/world-climate-pledges-cop26.html).

23 David I. Armstrong McKay et al., 'Exceeding 1.5°C Global Warming Could Trigger Multiple Climate Tipping Points', *Science* 377:6611 (2022) (https://www.science.org/doi/full/10. 1126/science.abn7950).

24 In this sense, there is also no contradiction between recognizing the failure to meet published climate targets and continuing to

endeavour to mitigate climate change. See also de Moor and Marquardt, 'Deciding Whether It's Too Late'.

Chapter 2   Capitalist modernity

1 Fernand Braudel, *La dynamique du capitalisme*, Paris, 1985; Jürgen Kocka, *Capitalism: A Short History*, trans. Jeremiah Riemer, Princeton, 2016; Jason W. Moore, *Capitalism in the Web of Life: Ecology and the Accumulation of Capital*, London, 2015.

2 Karl Polanyi, *The Great Transformation: The Political and Economic Origins of Our Time*, Boston, 1957.

3 Jason Hickel, *Less Is More: How Degrowth Will Save the World*, London, 2020.

4 See also Pierre Charbonnier, *Affluence and Freedom: An Environmental History of Political Ideas*, trans. Andrew Brown, Cambridge and Medford, MA, 2021.

5 On the term 'capitalist modernity', see Paul Kennedy, *Vampire Capitalism: Fractured Societies and Alternative Futures*, London, 2017. My aim in using the term is to emphasize the connection between economic, political, and cultural developments, which are at the same time irreducible. The term 'market society' as used by Karl Polanyi, for example, harbours the risk, as does 'capitalist society', of attributing the historical developments of the last five hundred years solely to the economic system.

6 Polanyi, *The Great Transformation*, p. 43.

7 Max Weber, *Economy and Society: An Outline of Interpretative Sociology*, ed. Guenther Roth and Claus Wittich, Berkeley, 1978, p. 639.

8 Global capitalism is a hierarchical system with some countries at the centre and other countries on the periphery, included in the system but disproportionately affected by exploitation. The consequences of climate change are particularly evident in the peripheral countries of the global South, most of which are not themselves responsible for the climate crisis.

9 Katharina Pistor, *The Code of Capital: How the Law Creates Wealth and Inequality*, Princeton, 2019.

10 Joseph A. Schumpeter, *The Theory of Economic Development: An Inquiry into Profits, Capital, Credit, Interest, and the Business Cycle*, Cambridge, MA, 1934.

11 Neil Fligstein, *The Architecture of Markets: An Economic Sociology of Twenty-First-Century Capitalist Societies*, Princeton, 2001.

12 Social scientists speak of a 'developmental state', which gets a capitalist economy going in the first place through macro-economic planning and exerting influence on private companies: Peter B. Evans, *Embedded Autonomy: States and Industrial Transformation*, Princeton, 1995.

13 Christoph Deutschmann, *Disembedded Markets: Economic Theology and Global Capitalism*, London and New York, 2019.

14 For a recent example, see Nancy Fraser, *Cannibal Capitalism: How Our System Is Devouring Democracy, Care, and the Planet – and What We Can Do about It*, London, 2022.

15 This does not mean that a better approach to nature can be expected from a planned economy. The history of actually existing socialism has given ample proof of this. However, 'actually existing socialism' is no more; capitalism in its various forms is therefore the only currently relevant economic system, and its modus operandi determines how we treat the natural environment around the world.

16 See also Hickel, *Less Is More*, pp. 101f.

17 Jean-Marie Martin-Amouroux, 'World Energy Consumption 1800–2000: The Results', 14.03.2022 (https://www.encyclopedie-energie.org/en/world-energy-consumption-1800-2000-results/).

18 Will Steffen et al., 'Planetary Boundaries: Guiding Human Development on a Changing Planet', *Science* 347:6223 (2015) (https://www.science.org/doi/10.1126/science.1259855).

19 Niklas Luhmann, *Ecological Communication*, trans. John Bednarz, Cambridge, 1989, p. 62.

20 Martin Hock, 'Die Finanzbranche sollte ein Beispiel geben', *Frankfurter Allgemeine Zeitung*, 14.01.2023 (https://www.faz.net/aktuell/finanzen/fondsgesellschaft-brauchen-ein-klima-bretton-woods-18591986.html).

21 For an overview of the development of our understanding of climate change, see Marie-Luise Beck and Jochem Marotzke, 'Sehenden Auges ins Treibhaus geraten. Ein Streifzug durch die erstaunliche Geschichte der Klimaforschung', in Martin Lohse (ed.), *Wenn der Funke überspringt – 200 Jahre Gesellschaft Deutscher Naturforscher und Ärzte*, Leipzig, 2022, pp. 104–7.

22 Donella Meadows et al., *The Limits to Growth: A Report for the Club of Rome's Project on the Predicament of Mankind*, New York, 1972. Climate change as a core problem of sustainable development only entered the public consciousness around fifteen years later, above all through the testimony of Jim Hansen, a director of NASA, before the US Senate.

23 Jens Beckert, 'Sind Unternehmen sozial verantwortlich?', in Olaf J. Schumann et al. (eds), *Unternehmensethik. Forschungsperspektiven zur Verhältnisbestimmung von Unternehmen und Gesellschaft*, Marburg, 2010, pp. 109–24.

24 Milton Friedman, 'The Social Responsibility of Business Is to Increase Its Profits', *The New York Times Magazine*, 13.09.1970, p. 1.

25 Karl Polanyi (*The Great Transformation*, p. 71) speaks of a 'market society' and states that 'a market economy can exist only in a market society'. For Polanyi, a market society is characterized by the fact that the 'fictitious commodities' of labour, money, and land are institutionalized *as if* they were real commodities. According to Polanyi, however, this is only an unstable borderline case to which societies react with social countermovements. Conceptually, it seems to me to make more sense not to speak of a market society, but rather to characterize the tension between the economy, the state, and the people in terms of a typological distinction between the three spheres of action, while at the same time emphasizing the dominant role of the economic system in capitalist modernity. 'People' here refers to citizens and consumers as actors.

26 Niklas Luhmann, *Social Systems*, trans. John Bednarz, Jr with Dirk Baecker, Stanford, 1995; Talcott Parsons and Neil J. Smelser,

Economy and Society: A Study in the Integration of Economic and Social Theory, London, 1984; Jürgen Habermas, *The Theory of Communicative Action*, Vol. 2, trans. Thomas McCarthy, Boston, 1987; David Lockwood, 'Social Integration and System Integration', in George K. Zollschan and Walter Hirsch (eds), *Explorations in Social Change*, Boston, 1964, pp. 254–66.

27 Fritz W. Scharpf, 'Economic Integration, Democracy and the Welfare State', *Journal of European Public Policy* 4:1 (1997), pp. 18–36.

28 Jens Beckert, 'Wirtschaftssoziologie als Gesellschaftstheorie', *Zeitschrift für Soziologie* 38:3 (2009), pp. 182–97; Christoph Deutschmann, *Kapitalistische Dynamik. Eine gesellschafts-theoretische Perspektive*, Wiesbaden, 2008; Uwe Schimank, 'Die Moderne: eine funktional differenzierte kapitalistische Gesellschaft', *Berliner Journal für Soziologie* 19 (2009), pp. 327–51.

29 Fred Block, 'The Ruling Class Does Not Rule: Notes on the Marxist Theory of the State', in Thomas Ferguson and Joel Rogers (eds), *The Political Economy: Readings in the Politics and Economics of American Public Policy*, London, 1984, pp. 32–46; Charles E. Lindblom, 'The Market as Prison', *The Journal of Politics* 44 (1982), pp. 324–36.

30 In fact, the opposite is the case: the expenditure required to remedy climate damage makes a positive contribution to gross national product. See also Timothy Mitchell, 'Carbon Democracy', *Economy and Society* 38:3 (2009), pp. 399–432, here p. 418.

31 Hickel, *Less Is More*. But see also Dipesh Chakrabarty, *The Climate of History in a Planetary Age*, Chicago, London, 2021; Charbonnier, *Affluence and Freedom*; and Lorraine Daston, 'How Nature Became the Other: Anthropomorphism and Anthropocentrism in Early Modern Natural Philosophy', in Sabine Maasen et al. (eds), *Biology as Society, Society as Biology: Metaphors*, Dordrecht, 1995, pp. 37–56. For a comprehensive overview, see also Philippe Descola, *Beyond Nature and Culture*, trans. Janet Lloyd, Chicago, 2013.

32 For Karl Marx, too, nature is the material basis from which the transformations under the labour process begin. There is no contradiction here with the thinkers of liberalism. Later, the Frankfurt School made the critique of a purely instrumental approach to nature an important starting point for its analysis of capitalist modernity. See Max Horkheimer, *Critique of Instrumental Reason*, trans. Matthew O'Connell, London, 2013.

33 Pierre Bourdieu, *Algeria 1960*, trans. Richard Nice, Cambridge, 1979.

34 Reinhart Koselleck, *Futures Past: On the Semantics of Historical Time*, trans. Keith Tribe, New York, 2004.

35 Jens Beckert, *Imagined Futures: Fictional Expectations and Capitalist Dynamics*, Cambridge, MA, 2016.

36 Max Weber, *The Protestant Ethic and the Spirit of Capitalism*, trans. Talcott Parsons, London, 1976. On the concept of progress, see also Peter Wagner, *Progress: A Reconstruction*, Cambridge and Malden, MA, 2016.

37 The term 'Anthropocene' is widely used to describe the fact that the influence of human beings on the biological, geological, and climatic processes of planet Earth has become so significant today that we can speak of a distinct geochronological epoch. I do not use the concept of the Anthropocene in the rest of this book because, in my view, it is too unspecific with regard to the concrete social structures that characterize the relationship between humans and nature under capitalist modernity. See also Moore, *Capitalism in the Web of Life*.

38 See also Charbonnier, *Affluence and Freedom*.

39 See Philipp Lepenies, *Verbot und Verzicht. Politik aus dem Geiste des Unterlassens*, Berlin, 2022.

40 Michael J. Sandel, *The Tyranny of Merit: What's Become of the Common Good?* London, 2020.

41 See Adam Smith, *An Inquiry into the Nature and Causes of the Wealth of Nations*, originally published in 1776.

42 Polanyi, *The Great Transformation*, p. 250.

Chapter 3 Big Oil

1 Nathan Reiff, '10 Biggest Companies in the World', updated 20.06.2024 (https://www.investopedia.com/articles/active-tra ding/111115/why-all-worlds-top-10-companies-are-american .asp).

2 However, an estimated 120 million tonnes of methane is released into the atmosphere every year as a result of oil, gas, and coal extraction. Methane is considered thirty times more harmful to the climate than carbon dioxide. See IEA, *Global Methane Tracker 2024*, Paris, 2024 (https://www.iea.org/reports/global -methane-tracker-2024).

3 IEA, *Net Zero by 2050*, Paris, 2021 (https://www.iea.org/repor ts/net-zero-by-2050); Dan Welsby et al., 'Unextractable Fossil Fuels in a 1.5°C World', *Nature* 597 (2021), pp. 230–4.

4 Kelly Trout et al., 'Existing Fossil Fuel Extraction Would Warm the World Beyond 1.5°C', *Environmental Research Letters* 17:6 (2022), 064010 (https://dx.doi.org/10.1088/1748-9326/ac6228).

5 Damian Carrington, 'Revealed: Oil Sector's "Staggering" $3bn-a-day Profits for Last 50 Years', *The Guardian*, 21.07.2022 (https:// www.theguardian.com/environment/2022/jul/21/revealed-oil -sectors-staggering-profits-last-50-years).

6 IEA, 'World Energy Investment 2023: Overview and Key Findings' (https://www.iea.org/reports/world-energy-invest ment-2023/overview-and-key-findings).

7 Saudi Aramco, 'Aramco Announces Record Full-Year 2022 Results', 12.03.2023 (https://www.aramco.com/en/news-media /news/2023/aramco-announces-full-year-2022-results).

8 Timur Ergen and Luuk Schmitz, *The Sunshine Problem: Climate Change and Managed Decline in the European Union*, MPIfG Discussion Paper 23/6, Max Planck Institute for the Study of Societies, Cologne, 2023.

9 Sabrina Valle, 'Exxon CEO's Pay Rose 52% in 2022, Highest among Oil Peers', Reuters, 13.04.2023 (https://www.reuters.com /business/energy/exxon-paid-ceo-woods-359-million-2022-sec -filing-2023-04-13/).

10 ExxonMobil, 'Notice of 2022 Annual Meeting and Proxy Statement', 07.04.2022 (https://d1io3yog0oux5.cloudfront.net/_ff99020d563b1c72d677411b93e350f1/exxonmobil/db/2301/21384/proxy_statement/2022-proxy-statement.pdf). See also Rakesh Khurana, *From Higher Aims to Hired Hands: The Social Transformation of American Business Schools and the Unfulfilled Promise of Management as a Profession*, Princeton, 2007.

11 Brett Christophers, 'Fossilised Capital: Price and Profit in the Energy Transition', *New Political Economy* 27:1 (2022), pp. 146–59. The oil company ConocoPhillips also recognizes this yield gap in its 2022 'Net Zero Energy Transition' plan (https://static.conocophillips.com/files/resources/plan-for-the-net-zero-energy-transition.pdf).

12 Anita Engels et al., 'A New Energy World in the Making: Imaginary Business Futures in a Dramatically Changing World of Decarbonized Energy Production', *Energy Research & Social Science* 60 (2020), 101321 (https://doi.org/10.1016/j.erss.2019.101321).

13 OECD, 'Renewable Energy' (https://data.oecd.org/energy/renewable-energy.htm).

14 Our World in Data, 'Global Direct Primary Energy Consumption' (https://ourworldindata.org/grapher/global-primary-energy).

15 Discounting is a financial technique used for cost–benefit analyses to assess the present value of future events. The results depend on the period under consideration and the chosen discount rate. In such calculations, even dramatic future losses have almost no significance for current behaviour if they occur sufficiently far in the future and the assumed discount rate is high. See Liliana Doganova, *Discounting the Future: The Ascendancy of a Political Technology*, New York, 2024.

16 Tyler A. Hansen, 'Stranded Assets and Reduced Profits: Analyzing the Economic Underpinnings of the Fossil Fuel Industry's Resistance to Climate Stabilization', *Renewable and Sustainable Energy Reviews* 158 (2022), 112144 (https://doi.org/10.1016/j.rser.2022.112144).

17 Niall McCarthy, 'Oil and Gas Giants Spend Millions Lobbying to Block Climate Change Policies [Infographic]', *Forbes*, 25.03.2019 (https://www.forbes.com/sites/niallmccarthy/2019/03/25/oil-and-gas-giants-spend-millions-lobbying-to-block-climate-change-policies-infographic/).

18 Marco Grasso, *From Big Oil to Big Green: Holding the Oil Industry to Account for the Climate Crisis*, Cambridge, MA, 2022.

19 Geoffrey Supran et al., 'Assessing ExxonMobil's Global Warming Projections', *Science* 379:6628 (2023) (https://doi.org/10.1126/science.abk0063).

20 Hiroko Tabuchi, 'Exxon Scientists Predicted Global Warming, Even as Company Cast Doubts, Study Finds', *The New York Times*, 12.01.2023 (https://www.nytimes.com/2023/01/12/climate/exxon-mobil-global-warming-climate-change.html).

21 Greenpeace, 'Exxon's Climate Denial History: A Timeline' (https://www.greenpeace.org/usa/fighting-climate-chaos/exxon-and-the-oil-industry-knew-about-climate-crisis/exxons-climate-denial-history-a-timeline/).

22 Christopher Leonard, *Kochland: The Secret History of Koch Industries and Corporate Power in America*, New York, 2019; Campaign against Climate Change, 'The Funders of Climate Disinformation' (https://www.campaigncc.org/climate_change/sceptics/funders).

23 Robert J. Brulle, 'Institutionalizing Delay: Foundation Funding and the Creation of US Climate Change Counter-Movement Organizations', *Climatic Change* 122:4 (2014), pp. 681–94.

24 'City of New York v. Exxon Mobil Corp.', 2021 (https://climatecasechart.com/case/city-of-new-york-v-exxon-mobil-corp/).

25 Mark Kaufman, 'The Carbon Footprint Sham', *Mashable* (https://mashable.com/feature/carbon-footprint-pr-campaign-sham). The concept of the ecological footprint was devised by Mathis Wackernagel and William Rees: see Mathis Wackernagel and William E. Rees, *Our Ecological Footprint: Reducing Human Impact on the Earth*, Gabriola Island et al., 1996.

26 Viola Kiel, 'Denn sie wussten, was sie tun', *Zeit Online*, 07.12.2022 (https://www.zeit.de/green/2022-12/oelkonzern-bp-klimakrise -internationaler-strafgerichtshof-big-oil).

27 Mei Li et al., 'The Clean Energy Claims of BP, Chevron, ExxonMobil and Shell: A Mismatch between Discourse, Actions and Investments', *PLOS ONE* 17:2 (2022), e0263596 (https://doi.org/10.1371/journal.pone.0263596). See also, spe-cifically on ExxonMobil: Geoffrey Supran and Naomi Oreskes, 'Rhetoric and Frame Analysis of ExxonMobil's Climate Change Communications', *One Earth* 4:5 (2021), pp. 696–719.

28 Inyova, 'Die Werbeindustrie als Steigbügelhalter der Öl-Industrie', 2022 (https://www.altii.de/die-werbeindustrie-als-steigbugelhal ter-der-ol-industrie/).

29 Damian Carrington and Matthew Taylor, 'Revealed: The "Carbon Bombs" Set to Trigger Catastrophic Climate Breakdown', *The Guardian*, 11.05.2022 (https://www.theguardian.com/environ ment/ng-interactive/2022/may/11/fossil-fuel-carbon-bombs-climate-breakdown-oil-gas).

30 Sabrina Valle and Rithika Krishna, 'Exxon Shareholders Back Board, Vote against Faster Carbon Emission Cuts', Reuters, 25.05.2022 (https://www.reuters.com/business/energy/exxon-shareholders-back-board-vote-against-accelerating-carbon-emission-cuts-2022-05-25/).

31 BP, 'BP Brand and Logo' (https://web.archive.org/web/2014083 0080553/http:/www.bp.com/en/global/corporate/about-bp/our -history/history-of-bp/special-subject-histories/bp-brand-and -logo.html).

32 BP, 'Our Transformation' (https://www.bp.com/en/global/cor porate/what-we-do/our-transformation.html).

33 On BP's rhetorical strategy, see George Ferns and Kenneth Amaeshi, 'Fueling Climate (In)Action: How Organizations Engage in Hegemonization to Avoid Transformational Action on Climate Change', *Organization Studies* 42:7 (2021), pp. 1005–29; Philipp Krohn and Roland Lindner, 'Die Widersprüche von Shell, Exxon & Co.', *Frankfurter Allgemeine Zeitung*, 26.01.2023

(https://www.faz.net/aktuell/wirtschaft/shell-exxon-co-erdoel -und-nachhaltigkeit-vertragen-sich-schlecht-18631824.html).

34 Alex Lawson, 'Shell Consultant Quits, Accusing Firm of "Extreme Harms" to Environment', *The Guardian*, 23.05.2022 (https:// www.theguardian.com/business/2022/may/23/shell-consul tant-quits-environment-caroline-dennett); OGV Energy, 'Shell Executives Quit amid Discord over Green Push' (https://www .ogv.energy/news-item/shell-executives-quit-amid-discord-over -green-push).

35 On the term 'politics of expectations', see Jens Beckert, *Imagined Futures: Fictional Expectations and Capitalist Dynamics*, Cambridge, MA, 2016.

36 Neil Fligstein, *The Transformation of Corporate Control*, Cambridge, MA, 1990.

37 Our World in Data, 'Primary Energy Consumption' (https://our worldindata.org/grapher/primary-energy-cons?tab=table).

38 Hannah Ritchie et al., 'Renewable Energy', 17.12.2020 (https:// ourworldindata.org/renewable-energy).

39 IEA, *World Energy Investment 2022*, Paris, 2022 (https://www.iea .org/reports/world-energy-investment-2022).

40 Carrington and Taylor, 'Revealed'.

41 Kjell Kühne et al., '"Carbon Bombs" – Mapping Key Fossil Fuel Projects', *Energy Policy* 166 (2022), 112950 (https://www.science direct.com/science/article/pii/S0301421522001756?via%3 Dihub).

42 Lisa Friedman, 'Biden Administration Approves Huge Alaska Oil Project', *The New York Times*, 12.03.2023 (https://www.nytimes .com/2023/03/12/climate/biden-willow-arctic-drilling-restric tions.html).

43 Christophers, 'Fossilised Capital', p. 153.

44 Carrington and Taylor, 'Revealed'.

45 'Shell will das Solarunternehmen Sonnen schon wieder verkaufen', *Frankfurter Allgemeine Zeitung*, 09.09.2023 (https:// www.faz.net/aktuell/wirtschaft/unternehmen/shell-will-sonnen -wieder-verkaufen-19160802.html).

46 Nick Edser et al., 'BP Scales Back Climate Targets as Profits Hit Record', BBC, 07.02.2023 (https://www.bbc.com/news/business -64544110).

47 Trout et al., 'Existing Fossil Fuel Extraction Would Warm the World Beyond 1.5°C'.

48 Banking on Climate Chaos, *Fossil Fuel Finance Report 2023* (https://www.bankingonclimatechaos.org/wp-content/uploads /2023/06/BOCC_2023_06-27.pdf). On the banking sector, see Markus Frühauf et al., 'Das große Null-Versprechen der Banken', *Frankfurter Allgemeine Zeitung*, 19.11.2022 (https:// www.faz.net/aktuell/finanzen/klimaschutz-so-blauaeugig-sind-die-versprechen-von-banken-18468247.html).

49 IEA, 'World Energy Investment 2023'.

50 Markus Fasse and Franz Hubik, 'BMW will weiterhin in Verbrennungsmotor investieren', *Handelsblatt*, 13.03.2023 (https://www.handelsblatt.com/unternehmen/industrie/diesel -und-benzin-bmw-will-weiterhin-in-verbrennungsmotor-invest ieren/29020350.html).

51 Ibid.

52 Ibid.

53 Caspar Busse, 'Porsche macht weiter Stimmung für E-Fuels', *Süddeutsche Zeitung*, 13.03.2023 (https://www.sueddeutsche.de /wirtschaft/porsche-vw-e-fuels-autoindustrie-wissing-eu-1.576 7865).

54 Agora Verkehrswende and GIZ, *Towards Decarbonising Transport 2023: A Stocktake on Sectoral Ambition in the G20*, 2023 (https://www.agora-verkehrswende.de/en/publications/to wards-decarbonising-transport-2023/).

55 Anita Engels et al. (eds), *Hamburg Climate Futures Outlook 2023: The Plausibility of a 1.5°C Limit to Global Warming – Social Drivers and Physical Processes*, Hamburg, 2023, p. 115.

56 Niklas Luhmann, *Ecological Communication*, trans. John Bednarz, Cambridge, 1989, p. 62.

Chapter 4 The hesitant state

1 Charles E. Lindblom, 'The Market as Prison', *The Journal of Politics* 44 (1982), pp. 324–36.

2 Press and Information Office of the Federal German Government, 'Pressestatements von Bundeskanzlerin Angela Merkel und dem Ministerpräsidenten der Republik Portugal, Pedro Passos Coelho', 01.09.2011 (https://www.bundesregierung.de/breg-de/service/archiv/alt-inhalte/pressestatements-von-bundes kanzlerin-angela-merkel-und-dem-ministerpraesidenten-der-republik-portugal-pedro-passos-coelho-848964).

3 On behalf of Lobbycontrol e.V., Christina Deckwirth and Nina Katzemich conducted a study on the influence of the gas indus-try on German politics: *Pipelines in die Politik. Die Macht der Gaslobby in Deutschland*, Cologne, 2023.

4 Ibid., p. 43.

5 Srijita Datta and Jorja Siemons, 'Joe Manchin Cuts Climate Deal with Democrats But Remains Backed by Family Orbit of Oil and Gas', *Open Secrets*, 05.08.2022 (https://www.opensecrets.org /news/2022/08/joe-manchin-cuts-climate-deal-with-democrats -but-remains-backed-by-family-orbit-of-oil-and-gas).

6 Scott Waldman, 'How Manchin Used Politics to Protect His Family Coal Company', *Politico*, 02.08.2022 (https://www.polit ico.com/news/2022/02/08/manchin-family-coal-company-0000 3218).

7 Jonathan Mingle, 'Congress is Turning Climate Gaslighting into Law', *The New York Times*, 01.06.2023 (https://www.nytimes .com/2023/06/01/opinion/debt-ceiling-mountain-valley-pipe line-joe-manchin.html).

8 Christian Stöcker, 'Warum RWE jeden Argwohn verdient hat', *Der Spiegel*, 15.01.2023 (https://www.spiegel.de/wissenschaft /mensch/luetzerath-warum-rwe-nicht-zu-trauen-ist-kolumne-a -5e8e3254-1665-4bc3-8d84-d402901d89ee).

9 Sam Meredith, '"A Twisted Joke": UN's Flagship Climate Summit Sees Sharp Jump in Fossil Fuel Industry Delegates', CNBC, 10.11.2022 (https://www.cnbc.com/2022/11/10/cop27-

sharp-jump-in-fossil-fuel-delegates-at-un-climate-talks.html). The participation of the fossil fuel industry in international climate negotiations has a long and inglorious history: see Marten Boon, 'A Climate of Change? The Oil Industry and Decarbonisation in Historical Perspective', *Business History Review* 93:1 (2019), pp. 101–25.

10 Kick Big Polluters Out Coalition, 'Record Number of Fossil Fuel Lobbyists at COP28' (https://kickbigpollutersout.org/articles/ release-record-number-fossil-fuel-lobbyists-attend-cop28).

11 Wolfgang Streeck, *Buying Time: The Delayed Crisis of Democratic Capitalism*, trans. Patrick Camiller, London, 2014.

12 Sebastian Levi et al., *Geographische und zeitliche Unterschiede in der Zustimmung zu Klimaschutzpolitik in Deutschland im Zeitverlauf*, Potsdam, 2023; European Commission, 'New Eurobarometer Survey: Protecting the Environment and Climate Is Important for over 90% of European Citizens', press release, 03.03.2020 (https://ec.europa.eu/commission/presscorner/detail/ en/ip_20_331). However, there are considerable differences between the supporters of different parties. In the United States, for example, 63 per cent of Democratic Party voters describe climate change as an important issue. In contrast, only 16 per cent of Republican voters share this view: Lisa Friedman and Jonathan Weisman, 'Delay as the New Denial: The Latest Republican Tactic to Block Climate Action', *The New York Times*, 20.07.2022 (https://www.nytimes.com/2022/07/20/us/politics/climate-change-republicans-delay.html).

13 BMUV and Umweltbundesamt, *Umweltbewusstsein in Deutschland 2022. Ergebnisse einer repräsentativen Bevölkerungs-umfrage*, Berlin, 2023.

14 Silke Kersting and Dietmar Neuerer, 'Die Klimakrise könnte Deutschland 900 Milliarden Euro kosten', *Handelsblatt*, 07.03.2023 (https://www.handelsblatt.com/politik/deutschland /klimawandel-die-klimakrise-koennte-deutschland-900-milliar den-euro-kosten/29015520.html).

15 See also the meta-analysis by Lena Klaaßen and Bjarne Steffen, 'Meta-Analysis on Necessary Investment Shifts to Reach Net Zero Pathways in Europe', *Nature Climate Change* 13 (2023), pp. 58–66.

16 McKinsey Global Institute, 'The Net-Zero Transition: What It Would Cost, What It Could Bring' (https://www.mckinsey.com /capabilities/sustainability/our-insights/the-net-zero-transition -what-it-would-cost-what-it-could-bring). The figures given in the study have been criticized as greatly overstated: see Karl Burkart, 'No McKinsey, It Will Not Cost $9 Trillion per Year to Solve Climate Change', *Medium*, 01.02.2022 (https://medium .com/oneearth/no-mckinsey-it-will-not-cost-9-trillion-per-year -to-solve-climate-change-3d0e20af52a).

17 Klaaßen and Steffen, 'Meta-Analysis on Necessary Investment Shifts to Reach Net Zero Pathways in Europe'.

18 Daniel Römer and Johannes Salzgeber, *KfW-Energie-wendebarometer 2023. Energiewende im Spannungsfeld zwischen Handlungsbedarfen und finanziellen Möglichkeiten*, Frankfurt/M., 2023 (https://www.kfw.de/PDF/Download-Cen ter/Konzernthemen/Research/PDF-Dokumente-KfW-Energie wendebarometer/KfW-Energiewendebarometer-2023.pdf).

19 Dagmar Röhrlich, 'Warum der Umbau des Stromnetzes kompliziert ist', Deutschlandfunk, 07.09.2023 (https://www. deutschlandfunk.de/energiewende-umbau-der-stromnetze-100. html).

20 Klaus Stratmann, '"Mehr Tempo bei Investitionen" – Habeck geht auf die Stahlbranche zu', *Handelsblatt*, 04.02.2022 (https:// www.handelsblatt.com/politik/deutschland/klimaneutralitaet -mehr-tempo-bei-investitionen-habeck-geht-auf-die-stahl branche-zu/28039434.html).

21 To outline the scale of this conversion: it would take 3,600 modern wind turbines to produce the 130,000 tonnes of hydrogen required to replace the Thyssenkrupp blast furnaces currently in operation in Duisburg with hydrogen-powered direct reduction plants. The whole of North

Rhine-Westphalia does not have that many wind turbines: see Felicitas Boeselager, '50 Jahre "Schwarzer Riese": Die Transformation des Ruhrgebiets', Deutschlandfunk, 06.02.2023 (https://www.deutschlandfunk.de/50-jahre-hochofen-schwarzer-riese-die-transformation-des-ruhrgebiets-dlf-bc92c562-100.html).

22 Julian Olk, 'Habeck krempelt Subventionsregeln zur klimagerechten Transformation der Industrie um', *Handelsblatt*, 07.03.2022 (https://www.handelsblatt.com/politik/deutschland/foerderricht linie-habeck-krempelt-subventionsregeln-zur-klimagerechten-tr ansformation-der-industrie-um/29022234.html).

23 Ben Coates, 'Why Dutch Farmers Turned Their Flag Upside Down', *The New York Times*, 03.04.2023 (https://www.nytimes .com/2023/04/03/opinion/why-dutch-farmers-turned-their-flag -upside-down.html).

24 Daniel Kahneman and Amos Tversky, 'Prospect Theory: An Analysis of Decision under Risk', *Econometrica* 47:2 (1979), pp. 263–91.

25 A classic account is given in Anthony Downs, *An Economic Theory of Democracy*, New York, 1957.

26 Studies show, however, that willingness to support climate agreements depends on the specific design of the agreements: see Michael M. Bechtel and Kenneth F. Scheve, 'Mass Support for Global Climate Agreements Depends on Institutional Design', *Proceedings of the National Academy of Sciences* 110:34 (2013), pp. 13763–8.

27 There were many other catalysts for the movement, and in general it signalled opposition to redistribution from the bottom to the top.

28 Roland Czada, 'Energiewendepolitik. Aufgaben, Probleme und Konflikte', *GWP – Gesellschaft. Wirtschaft. Politik* 69:2 (2020), pp. 169–81.

29 BMUV and Umweltbundesamt, *Umweltbewusstsein in Deutschland 2022*.

30 Johannes Leithäuser, 'Die britische Regierung verwässert ihre Klimaziele', *Frankfurter Allgemeine Zeitung*, 20.09.2023

(https://www.faz.net/aktuell/politik/ausland/klimaschutz-rishi-sunak-verwaessert-grossbritanniens-klimaziele-19188088.html).

31 Paolo Agnolucci et al., 'Declining Coal Prices Reflect a Reshaping of Global Energy Trade', World Bank Blogs, 21.03.2023 (https://blogs.worldbank.org/en/opendata/declining-coal-prices-reflect-reshaping-global-energy-trade).

32 Julian Wettengel, '"Klimageld" to Return CO_2 Price Revenues to Citizens Not before 2025 – Econ Min Habeck', *Clean Energy Wire*, 24.01.2023 (https://www.cleanenergywire.org/news /klimageld-return-co2-price-revenues-citizens-not-2025-econ -min-habeck).

33 Michaël Aklin and Matto Mildenberger, 'Prisoners of the Wrong Dilemma: Why Distributive Conflict, Not Collective Action, Characterizes the Politics of Climate Change', *Global Environmental Politics* 20:4 (2020), pp. 4–27.

34 Roland Czada, 'Transformative Klimapolitik in der Zeitenwende. Konfliktlinien und Handlungsrestriktionen eines Jahrhundertprojektes', unpublished manuscript of a presentation for the Annual Colloquium of the Max Planck Institute for the Study of Societies on 3 and 4 November 2022 in Cologne.

35 Daniel Albalate et al., 'The Influence of Population Aging on Global Climate Policy', *Population and Environment* 45:3 (2023), pp. 12–34.

36 Andreas Reckwitz, *The End of Illusions: Politics, Economy, and Culture in Late Modernity*, Cambridge, 2021; Robert Ford and William Jennings, 'The Changing Cleavage Politics of Western Europe', *Annual Review of Political Science* 23 (2020), pp. 295–314.

37 However, it should be borne in mind that state support for companies can also be a form of 'social welfare'. This is particularly true if the support is not linked to clear conditions that result in a 'benefit' for the state. If this is not the case, the subsidies merely demonstrate the state's weak and subordinate position: Fabio Bulfone et al., 'No Strings Attached: Corporate Welfare,

State Intervention, and the Issue of Conditionality', *Competition & Change* 27:2 (2023), pp. 253–76.

38 See Lukas Haffert, *Die schwarze Null. Über die Schattenseiten ausgeglichener Haushalte*, Berlin, 2016.

39 An influential text in this area is Mariana Mazzucato, *The Value of Everything: Making and Taking in the Global Economy*, London, 2018. In Mazzucato's view, higher growth is linked to stronger state intervention in market processes.

40 See Philipp Lepenies, *Verbot und Verzicht. Politik aus dem Geiste des Unterlassens*, Berlin, 2022.

41 Mary Harrington, 'The Failure of Lockdown Localism', *UnHerd*, 10.05.2022 (https://unherd.com/2023/05/how-egg-poli tics-failed-britain/).

42 Claas Tatje, 'Verzicht macht die Welt nicht besser', *Zeit Online*, 19.09.2022 (https://www.zeit.de/2022/38/kreuzfahrten-tui-cruises-klimaschutz-interview).

43 Christopher Wright and Daniel Nyberg, *Climate Change, Capitalism, and Corporations: Processes of Creative Self-Destruction*, Cambridge, 2015.

44 See, for example: Fritz W. Scharpf, 'Notes Toward a Theory of Multilevel Governing in Europe', *Scandinavian Political Studies* 24 (2001), pp. 1–26.

45 Fritz W. Scharpf, 'Die Politikverflechtungsfalle: Europäische Integration und deutscher Föderalismus im Vergleich', *Politische Vierteljahresschrift* 26:4 (1985), pp. 323–56.

46 Till Ganswindt, 'Warum dauert es so lange, Windkraftanlagen zu bauen?', *MDR*, 14.11.2022 (https://www.mdr.de/nachrichten /deutschland/politik/windkraft-anlagen-planung-dauer-sachsen -100.html).

47 Czada, 'Energiewendepolitik'.

48 Another aspect of this is that climate activists are repeatedly attacked by drivers and passers-by. This is a further indicator of the high level of 'social stress' that climate change is now causing.

49 Dieter Rucht, *Die Letzte Generation. Beschreibung und Kritik*, Berlin, 2023.

50 Nils C. Kumkar, *Alternative Fakten. Zur Praxis der kommunikativen Erkenntnisverweigerung*, Berlin, 2022.

51 See also Juan Telleria and Jorge Garcia-Arias, 'The Fantasmatic Narrative of "Sustainable Development": A Political Analysis of the 2030 Global Development Agenda', *Environment and Planning C: Politics and Space* 40:1 (2022), pp. 241–59.

52 Forest Information System for Europe, '3 Billion Trees' (https://forest.eea.europa.eu/3-billion-trees/introduction).

53 Frank Adloff and Sighard Neckel, 'Futures of Sustainability as Modernization, Transformation, and Control: A Conceptual Framework', *Sustainability Science* 14 (2019), pp. 1015–25; Sighard Neckel, 'Der Streit um die Lebensführung. Nachhaltigkeit als sozialer Konflikt', *Mittelweg 36*:6 (2020), pp. 82–100, here p. 87. See also Joel Wainwright and Geoff Mann, *Climate Leviathan: A Political Theory of Our Planetary Future*, London and New York, 2018. The authors use the term 'Climate Mao' for an authoritarian climate regime of this kind.

54 Joel Millward-Hopkins, 'Why the Impacts of Climate Change May Make Us Less Likely to Reduce Emissions', *Global Sustainability* 5 (2022), e21 (https://doi.org/10.1017/sus.2022.20); Ross Mittiga, 'Political Legitimacy, Authoritarianism, and Climate Change', *American Political Science Review* 116:3 (2022), pp. 998–1011.

Chapter 5 Global prosperity

1 Jens Beckert and Wolfgang Vortkamp, 'Westlicher Universalismus?', *Neue Gesellschaft/Frankfurter Hefte* 43:5 (1996), pp. 410–15.

2 Walt Rostow, *The Stages of Economic Growth: A Non-Communist Manifesto*, Cambridge, 1960.

3 Per capita emissions in both countries are still far behind those of the United States, but these are the two most populous countries in the world. China's per capita emissions have now overtaken those of the European Union. This is due in part to the global division of labour. A large proportion of global industrial production takes place in China.

4 Harald Fuhr, 'The Rise of the Global South and the Rise in Carbon Emissions', *Third World Quarterly* 42:11 (2021), pp. 2724–46.

5 Klaus Hubacek et al., 'Global Carbon Inequality', *Energy, Ecology and Environment* 2:6 (2017), pp. 361–9.

6 World Resources Institute, 'Forest Pulse: The Latest on the World's Forests' (https://research.wri.org/gfr/latest-analysis-deforestation-trends).

7 Alex Cuadros, 'Has the Amazon Reached Its "Tipping Point"?', *The New York Times Magazine*, 04.01.2023 (https://www.nytimes.com/2023/01/04/magazine/amazon-tipping-point.html).

8 Ruth Maclean and Dionne Searcey, 'Congo to Auction Land to Oil Companies: "Our Priority Is Not to Save the Planet"', *The New York Times*, 24.07.2022 (https://www.nytimes.com/2022/07/24/world/africa/congo-oil-gas-auction.html).

9 Sonia Rolley, 'Congo Rejects US Request to Pull Oil Blocks from Auction', Reuters, 05.10.2022 (https://www.reuters.com/world/africa/congo-rejects-us-request-pull-oil-blocks-auction-2022-10-05/).

10 Maclean and Searcey, 'Congo to Auction Land to Oil Companies'.

11 David Bieber, 'Gasdeal mit Senegal: "Eine Partnerschaft auf Augenhöhe"', *WEB.DE*, 15.03.2023 (https://web.de/magazine/politik/gasdeal-senegal-partnerschaft-augenhoehe-37911330).

12 M. Graziano Ceddia, 'The Super-Rich and Cropland Expansion via Direct Investments in Agriculture', *Nature Sustainability* 3:4 (2020), pp. 312–18.

13 Corey Ross, *Ecology and Power in the Age of Empire: Europe and the Transformation of the Tropical World*, Oxford and New York, 2017, pp. 407f.

14 Jeffrey D. Sachs and Andrew M. Warner, *Natural Resource Abundance and Economic Growth*, NBER Working Paper 5398, National Bureau of Economic Research, Cambridge, MA, 1995.

15 Ross, *Ecology and Power in the Age of Empire*, pp. 407f.

16 Abdi Latif Dahir, 'An Oil Rush Threatens Natural Splendors across East Africa', *The New York Times*, 14.03.2023

(https://www.nytimes.com/2023/03/14/world/africa/oil-pipeline-uganda-tanzania.html).

17 Tim Schauenberg, 'Trotz Klimakrise "großer Moment" für Afrikas Gasindustrie', *Deutsche Welle*, 11.11.2022 (https://www.dw.com/de/gasf%C3%B6rderung-in-afrika-die-verlockung-des-schnellen-geldes/a-63711886); Jennifer Holleis and Martina Schwikowski, 'Erdgas für Europa: Afrika rückt nach', *Deutsche Welle*, 04.04.2022 (https://www.dw.com/de/erdgas-für-europa-afrika-rückt-nach/a-61006246). This argument is also used by oil companies to defend their high profits.

18 At the same time, falling prices for fossil fuels make them more economically attractive and thus increase demand for them (in the global South).

19 Hans-Werner Sinn, *The Green Paradox: A Supply-Side Approach to Global Warming*, Cambridge, MA, 2012.

20 Vivian Yee, 'Even as Egypt Hosts Climate Summit, Selling Fossil Fuels Is a Priority', *The New York Times*, 07.11.2022 (https://www.nytimes.com/2022/11/07/world/middleeast/egypt-climate-cop27-natural-gas.html).

21 The link between high world market prices for gas and the increase in CO_2 emissions can be applied more widely. The higher the gas price, the greater the incentive to rely more heavily on coal.

22 IEA, 'Total Primary Energy Consumption in Egypt from 2005 to 2021 (in quadrillion Btu)', Chart, *Statista*, 20.06.2023 (https://www.statista.com/statistics/994451/egypt-total-primary-energy-consumption/).

23 IEA, *The Future of Cooling: Opportunities for Energy-Efficient Air Conditioning*, Paris, 2018 (https://iea.blob.core.windows.net/assets/0bb45525-277f-4c9c-8d0c-9c0cb5e7d525/The_Future_of_Cooling.pdf); Christoph Hein, 'Der Klimaanlagen-Teufelskreis', *Frankfurter Allgemeine Zeitung*, 20.05.2023 (https://www.faz.net/aktuell/wirtschaft/klima-nachhaltigkeit/hitze-in-asien-der-klimaanlagen-teufelskreis-18905813.html).

24 Alfred Hackensberger, 'Afrikas grüner Wasserstoff', *Die Welt*, 27.04.2023, p. 6.

25 See also Diana Vela Almeida et al., 'The "Greening" of Empire: The European Green Deal as the *EU First* Agenda', *Political Geography* 105 (2023), 102925 (https://doi.org/10.1016/j.polgeo.2023.102925).

26 Galina Alova et al., 'A Machine-Learning Approach to Predicting Africa's Electricity Mix Based on Planned Power Plants and Their Chances of Success', *Nature Energy* 6:2 (2021), pp. 158–66.

27 Anna Osius, 'Wie Ägypten erneuerbare Energien ausbaut', Deutschlandfunk, 01.11.2022 (https://www.deutschlandfunk.de/erneuerbare-energien-aegypten-100.html).

28 Yee, 'Even as Egypt Hosts Climate Summit, Selling Fossil Fuels Is a Priority'.

29 Enerdata, 'Ägypten gibt die Entdeckung eines Gasfeldes mit geschätzten Reserven von 99 Mrd. m3 bekannt', 19.12.2022 (https://germany.enerdata.net/publikationen/energie-nachrichten/%C3%A4gypten-gasreserven-entdeckung.html).

30 IEA, 'World Energy Investment 2023: Overview and Key Findings' (https://www.iea.org/reports/world-energy-investment-2023/overview-and-key-findings).

31 IEA, *Financing Clean Energy Transitions in Emerging and Developing Economies*, Paris, 2021.

32 Catrin Einhorn and Manuela Andreoni, 'Ecuador Tried to Curb Drilling and Protect the Amazon. The Opposite Happened', *The New York Times*, 14.01.2023 (https://www.nytimes.com/2023/01/14/climate/ecuador-drilling-oil-amazon.html).

33 In a referendum in 2023, a majority of Ecuadorian voters voted in favour of ending production in one of the oil fields in Yasuní National Park within a year. The indigenous population has been fighting to stop production for over a decade. If this plan is actually implemented, Ecuador's oil production would be reduced by 12 per cent. Whether this will happen remains to be seen, not least because of pressure from the financial markets. See Dan Collyns, 'Ecuadorians Vote to Halt Oil Drilling in Biodiverse Amazonian National Park', *The Guardian*, 21.08.2023

(https://www.theguardian.com/world/2023/aug/21/ecuador-votes-to-halt-oil-drilling-in-amazonian-biodiversity-hotspot).

34 Susanne Götze, 'Klimafinanzierung in kleinen Schritten', *Der Spiegel*, 14.04.2023 (https://www.spiegel.de/wissenschaft/mensch/klimabericht-klimafinanzierung-in-kleinen-schritten-a-16c9 e482-ce91-4b42-a367-df6f35449328).

35 OECD, *Climate Finance Provided and Mobilised by Developed Countries in 2016–2020: Insights from Disaggregated Analysis*, Paris, 2022.

36 Fritz Schaap, 'Nigeria vor den Wahlen: Wie sich der afrikanische Gigant zum "Failed State" entwickelt', *Der Spiegel*, 29.01.2023 (https://www.spiegel.de/ausland/nigeria-wie-sich-der-afrikanische-gigant-zum-failed-state-entwickelt-a-84ab0314-3015-4f1b -9178-00525496c154).

37 Nicola D. Coniglio and Giovanni Pesce, 'Climate Variability and International Migration: An Empirical Analysis', *Environment and Development Economics* 20:4 (2015), pp. 434–68.

38 Jason Hickel, *Less Is More: How Degrowth Will Save the World*, London, 2020, pp. 116f.

39 Heiner von Lüpke et al., *Internationale Partnerschaften für eine gerechte Energiewende: Erkenntnisse aus der Zusammenarbeit mit Südafrika*, DIW Wochenbericht 90:5, Berlin, 2023.

40 European Commission, 'Joint Statement: South Africa Just Energy Transition Investment Plan', 07.11.2022 (https://ec.europa.eu/commission/presscorner/detail/en/statement_22_6664).

41 Somini Sengupta, 'How Africa Can Help the World', *The New York Times*, 16.06.2023 (https://www.nytimes.com/2023/06/16 /climate/africa-renewable-energy.html).

42 Anita Engels et al. (eds), *Hamburg Climate Futures Outlook 2023: The Plausibility of a 1.5°C Limit to Global Warming – Social Drivers and Physical Processes*, Hamburg, 2023, p. 121.

43 Daniela Gabor, 'The Wall Street Consensus', *Development and Change* 52:3 (2021), pp. 429–59.

44 Daniela Gabor and Ndongo Samba Sylla, 'Planting Budgetary Time Bombs in Africa: The Macron Doctrine En Marche',

Groupe d'Études Géopolitiques, 23.12.2020 (https://geopoli tique.eu/en/2020/12/23/planting-budgetary-time-bombs-in-africa-the-macron-doctrine-en-marche/).

45 FitchRatings, 'Fitch Downgrades Ecuador's Long-Term IDR to "CCC+"', 16.08.2023 (https://www.fitchratings.com/research /sovereigns/fitch-downgrades-ecuador-long-term-idr-to-ccc-16 -08-2023).

46 Llewellyn Leonard, 'Climate Change, Mining Development and Residential Water Security in the uMkhanyakude District Municipality, KwaZulu-Natal, South Africa: A Double Catastrophe for Local Communities', *Local Environment* 28:3 (2023), pp. 331–46.

47 Von Lüpke et al., *Internationale Partnerschaften für eine gerechte Energiewende*, p. 50.

Chapter 6   Consumption without limits

1 Uwe Jean Heuser and Marc Widmann, 'Die Gewalt in der Auseinandersetzung ist absolut unakzeptabel, [interview with RWE CEO Markus Krebber]', *Zeit Online*, 09.02.2023 (https:// www.zeit.de/2023/07/luetzerath-kohleausstieg-rwe-markus -krebber).

2 Jean-Marie Martin-Amouroux, 'World Energy Consumption 1800–2000: The Results', 14.03.2022 (https://www.encycloped ie-energie.org/en/world-energy-consumption-1800-2000-results/); Enerdata, 'World Energy & Climate Statistics – Yearbook 2022' (https://yearbook.enerdata.net/total-energy/world-con sumption-statistics.html).

3 On this calculation, see Eurostat, 'Energy Statistics – An Overview', May 2023 (https://ec.europa.eu/eurostat/statistics -explained/index.php?title=energy_statistics_-_an_overview& final_energy_consumption%e2%8c%aa) and OECD, 'Historical Population Sizes and Average Annual Growth Rates in Western Europe in Selected Years between 0 and 1998', *Statista*, 14.04.2022 (https://www.statista.com/statistics/1303831/western-europe -population-development-historical/).

4 Ralf Dahrendorf, *Inequality, Hope, and Progress*, Liverpool, 1976, p. 14.

5 In the pursuit of profit, the oil industry has even ensured that the oil consumption of American consumers is particularly high: Timothy Mitchell, 'Carbon Democracy', *Economy and Society* 38:3 (2009), pp. 399–432, here p. 409. On the global transformative power of the almost unlimited access to oil in the post-war period, see also Corey Ross, *Ecology and Power in the Age of Empire: Europe and the Transformation of the Tropical World*, Oxford, 2019.

6 CEIC, 'United States Private Consumption: % of GDP', 2023 (https://www.ceicdata.com/en/indicator/united-states/private -consumption--of-nominal-gdp).

7 Economic theory assumes that consumers' desire for more and more things is a natural propensity, meaning that wealth maximization is a fundamental psychological principle. However, this obscures the historically exceptional status of such behaviour and its embeddedness in the specific social structures of capitalist modernity.

8 E.P. Thompson, *The Making of the English Working Class*, Harmondsworth, 1968; Max Weber, *Economy and Society: An Outline of Interpretative Sociology*, ed. Guenther Roth and Claus Wittich, Berkeley, 1978.

9 Something similar can still be seen today in how cabdrivers organize their working hours. See Marcin Serafin, 'Cabdrivers and Their Fares: Temporal Structures of a Linking Ecology', *Sociological Theory* 37:2 (2019), pp. 117–41.

10 Colin Campbell, *The Romantic Ethic and the Spirit of Modern Consumerism*, Oxford, 1987, p. 18.

11 Early economic theory did not regard private consumption as an important factor at all; every supply finds its demand, according to the French economist Jean-Baptiste Say in the late eighteenth century. It was only in the 1930s, under the influence of the Great Depression, that economists began to focus their attention on the fragility of private demand. Informed by the experience

of the Great Depression, the British economist John Maynard Keynes showed that underutilization of production capacity and underemployment of workers can become entrenched in economic crises. In such situations, the state has to replace the missing demand through debt-financed spending programmes.

12 Walt Rostow, *The Stages of Economic Growth: A Non-Communist Manifesto*, Cambridge, 1960.

13 Philipp Lepenies, *Verbot und Verzicht. Politik aus dem Geiste des Unterlassens*, Berlin, 2022. Lepenies builds on the work of the economic historian Stefan Schwarzkopf, including: 'The Political Theology of Consumer Sovereignty: Towards an Ontology of Consumer Society', *Theory, Culture & Society* 28:3 (2011), pp. 106–29. See also Sophie Dubuisson-Quellier, 'How Does Affluent Consumption Come to Consumers? A Research Agenda for Exploring the Foundations and Lock-ins of Affluent Consumption', *Consumption and Society* 1:1 (2022), pp. 31–50.

14 Émile Durkheim (among others) argued that unlimited consumption does not lead to greater individual autonomy but to social pathologies because the regulative functions of morality are undermined. For more detail, see Pierre Charbonnier, *Affluence and Freedom: An Environmental History of Political Ideas*, trans. Andrew Brown, Cambridge and Medford, MA, 2021, pp. 109f.

15 Claas Tatje and Marc Widmann, 'Ich finde SUVs nicht massig, sondern schön', *Zeit Online*, 24.11.2022 (https://www.zeit.de/2022/48/markus-duesmann-audi-chef-suv-klimaschutz).

16 Samira El Ouassil, 'Die Argumentationstricks der Klimabremser', *Der Spiegel*, 27.04.2023 (https://www.spiegel.de/kultur/klima krise-rhetorisches-greenwashing-kolumne-a-dd625c2d-c8df-4a76-85ad-5af9b69214d8).

17 Sighard Neckel, 'Infrastruktursozialismus. Die Bedeutung der Fundamentalökonomie', in Neckel et al. (eds), *Kapitalismus und Nachhaltigkeit*, Frankfurt/M. and New York, 2022, pp. 161–76.

18 Ibid., p. 161.

19 See, for example, Pierre Bourdieu, *Distinction: A Social Critique of the Judgement of Taste*, trans. Richard Nice, London et al., 2010;

Don Slater, *Consumer Culture and Modernity*, Cambridge, 1997; Andreas Reckwitz, *The Society of Singularities*, trans. Valentine A. Pakis, Cambridge, 2020.

20 See Christoph Deutschmann, *Trügerische Verheißungen. Markterzählungen und ihre ungeplanten Folgen*, Wiesbaden, 2020, esp. Ch. 7.

21 Zenith, 'Advertising Spending Worldwide from 2000 to 2024 (in Million US Dollars)', *Statista*, 08.06.2022 (https://www.statista.com/statistics/1174981/advertising-expenditure-worldwide/).

22 Gregor Brunner, 'Unverhohlener Konsum ist nicht gefragt', *Frankfurter Allgemeine Zeitung*, 02.01.2023 (https://www.faz.net/aktuell/wirtschaft/unternehmen/was-die-werbebranche-in-der-krise-noch-tun-kann-18553574.html).

23 Tatje and Widmann, 'Ich finde SUVs nicht massig, sondern schön'.

24 Maximilian Pieper et al., 'Calculation of External Climate Costs for Food Highlights Inadequate Pricing of Animal Products', *Nature Communications* 11 (2020), 6117 (https://doi.org/10.1038/s41467-020-19474-6). The production of 1 kilogram of beef is associated with the emission of 13.6 kilograms of CO_2 equivalent, primarily through the methane gas emitted by the cattle: see Hannah Krolle, 'Der Klimasünder als wertvoller Werkstoff', *Handelsblatt*, 08.03.2023 (https://pyreg.com/wp-content/uploads/230309_Handelsblatt-print_Der-Klimasunder-CO2.pdf).

25 Klaus Stratmann and Martin Greive, 'Klimageld: Liberale fremdeln mit Vorstoß von Arbeitsminister Heil', *Handelsblatt*, 29.05.2022 (https://www.handelsblatt.com/politik/deutschland/ampelkoalition-klimageld-liberale-fremdeln-mit-vorstoss-von-arbeitsminister-heil/28381884.html).

26 The EU commission estimates that the law could lead to the avoidance of roughly 1.2 million tonnes of greenhouse gas emissions per year. This is about 0.03 per cent of total emissions in the EU: Hendrik Kafsack, 'EU einigt sich auf Recht auf Reparatur', *Frankfurter Allgemeine Zeitung*, 02.02.2024 (https://

www.faz.net/aktuell/wirtschaft/klima-nachhaltigkeit/eu-einigt-sich-auf-recht-auf-reparatur-19491212.html).

27 For more detail, see Jens Beckert, *Imagined Futures: Fictional Expectations and Capitalist Dynamics*, Cambridge, MA, 2016, Ch. 8; Campbell, *The Romantic Ethic and the Spirit of Modern Consumerism*.

28 Lieve Van Woensel and Sara Suna Lipp, 'What If Fashion Were Good for the Planet?', European Parliamentary Research Service, 2020 (https://www.europarl.europa.eu/RegData/etudes/ATAG/2020/656296/EPRS_ATA(2020)656296_EN.pdf).

29 Tatje and Widmann, 'Ich finde SUVs nicht massig, sondern schön'.

30 On this, see especially Lepenies, *Verbot und Verzicht*.

31 Ralf Fücks, 'Mit grünem Wachstum aus der Klimakrise!', *Wirtschaftswoche*, 13.01.2023 (https://www.wiwo.de/my/politik/deutschland/essay-mit-gruenem-wachstum-aus-der-klimakrise/28918038.html).

32 Our World in Data, 'Per Capita Consumption-Based CO_2 Emissions' (https://ourworldindata.org/grapher/consumption-co2-per-capita?tab=chart&country=USA~OWID_EU27~CHN~DEU~NGA~OWID_WRL). See also Lucas Chancel et al., *Climate Inequality Report 2023*, World Inequality Lab Study 2023/1 (https://wid.world/wp-content/uploads/2023/01/CBV2023-ClimateInequalityReport-3.pdf).

33 Laura Cozzi et al., 'The World's Top 1% of Emitters Produce over 1000 Times More CO_2 than the Bottom 1%' (https://www.iea.org/commentaries/the-world-s-top-1-of-emitters-produce-over-1000-times-more-co2-than-the-bottom-1).

34 Beatriz Barros and Richard Wilk, 'The Outsized Carbon Footprints of the Super-Rich', *Sustainability: Science, Practice and Policy* 17:1 (2021), pp. 316–22.

35 Joe Fassler, 'The Superyachts of Billionaires Are Starting to Look a Lot Like Theft', *The New York Times*, 10.04.2023 (https://www.nytimes.com/2023/04/10/opinion/superyachts-private-plane-climate-change.html); Grégory Salle, *Superyachten. Luxus und Stille im Kapitalozän*, Berlin, 2022.

36 This term was introduced by the American economist Thorstein
    Veblen over a hundred years ago: Thorstein Veblen, *The Theory
    of the Leisure Class*, Boston, 1973 [1899].
37 Chancel et al., *Climate Inequality Report 2023*.
38 See, for example, Thomas Piketty, *Capital in the Twenty-First
    Century*, trans. Arthur Goldhammer, Cambridge, MA, 2014.
39 Lucas Chancel, 'Global Carbon Inequality over 1990–2019',
    Nature Sustainability 5:11 (2022), pp. 931–8; Sighard Neckel,
    'Zerstörerischer Reichtum. Wie eine globale Verschmutzerelite
    das Klima ruiniert', *Blätter für deutsche und internationale
    Politik* 4 (2023), pp. 47–56, here p. 49.
40 Neckel, 'Zerstörerischer Reichtum', p. 56.
41 For example the head of TUI in an interview with *Die Zeit*,
    see Claas Tatje, 'Verzicht macht die Welt nicht besser', *Zeit
    Online*, 19.09.2022 (https://www.zeit.de/2022/38/kreuzfahrten
    -tui-cruises-klimaschutz-interview).
42 Die Bundesregierung, 'Nachhaltige Mobilität. Nicht weniger
    fortbewegen, sondern anders', 23.12.2022 (https://www.bundes
    regierung.de/breg-de/schwerpunkte/klimaschutz/nachhaltige
    -mobilitaet-2044132).
43 Rüdiger Kiani-Kress and Thomas Stölzel, 'Wolkenkuckucks
    flieger', *Wirtschaftswoche*, 22.05.2023 (https://www.wiwo.de/my
    /unternehmen/industrie/wasserstoffflugzeuge-wolkenkuckucks
    flieger/29156538.html).
44 Dipesh Chakrabarty, *The Climate of History in a Planetary Age*,
    Chicago and London, 2021, p. 12.
45 Increasing energy efficiency means that the same number of
    products are produced or supplied using less energy.
46 DIHK, 'Wohlstandsverluste durch das geplante Energie-
    effizienzgesetz?', *Das Wirtschaftsmagazin*, 25.04.2023 (https://
    tinyurl.com/4ee7as5e).
47 Carina Zell-Ziegler and Hannah Förster, *Mit Suffizienz mehr
    Klimaschutz modellieren. Relevanz von Suffizienz in der
    Modellierung, Übersicht über die aktuelle Modellierungspraxis
    und Ableitung methodischer Empfehlungen. Zwischenbericht*

zu AP 2.1 'Möglichkeiten der Instrumentierung von Energie-verbrauchsreduktion durch Verhaltensänderung', Texte 55, Berlin, 2018.

48 Nico Stehr et al. (eds.), *The Moralization of the Markets*, New Brunswick et al., 2006.

49 Anthony Leiserowitz et al., 'Sustainability Values, Attitudes, and Behaviors: A Review of Multinational and Global Trends', *Annual Review of Environment and Resources* 31:1 (2006), pp. 413–44.

50 Roger Cowe and Simon Williams, *Who Are the Ethical Consumers?*, Manchester, 2001.

51 The global clothing market is estimated at around 1.9 trillion US dollars, the market for ethical clothing at around 7 billion: Research and Markets, 'Ethical Fashion Global Market Opportunities and Strategies to 2032' (https://www.researchand markets.com/reports/5740762/ethical-fashion-global-market -opportunities#src-pos-2).

52 Jannis Engel and Nora Szech, 'A Little Good Is Good Enough: Ethical Consumption, Cheap Excuses, and Moral Self-Licensing', *PLoS ONE* 15:1 (2020), e0227036 (https://doi.org/10.1371/jour nal.pone.0227036).

53 Andreas Diekmann and Peter Preisendörfer, 'Green and Greenback: The Behavioral Effects of Environmental Attitudes in Low-Cost and High-Cost Situations', *Rationality and Society* 15:4 (2003), pp. 441–72.

54 Dingeman Wiertz and Nan Dirk de Graaf, 'The Climate Crisis: What Sociology Can Contribute', in Klarita Gërxhani et al. (eds), *Handbook of Sociological Science: Contributions to Rigorous Sociology*, Cheltenham, 2022, pp. 475–92.

55 Luise Land et al., '100 Prozent Meeresplastik, 59 Prozent Wahrheit', *Zeit Online*, 03.06.2022 (https://www.zeit.de/green /2022-06/got-bag-greenwashing-plastikmuell-meer-recycling -nachhaltigkeit).

56 'EU-Kommission plant Gesetz gegen Greenwashing', *Zeit Online*, 22.03.2023 (https://www.zeit.de/wirtschaft/2023-03/eu -werbung-greenwashing-mindeststandards-reparatur).

57 Astrid Geisler and Hannah Knuth, 'Das Label ist im Grunde tot', *Zeit Online*, 26.01.2023 (https://www.zeit.de/2023/05/klimaneut rale-produkte-rossmann-label-co2-zertifikate).

58 See Jürgen Schaefer and Malte Henk, 'Emissionshandel: Die Luftnummer', *Geo*, 16.12.2010 (https://www.geo.de/natur/oeko logie/4896-rtkl-klimawandel-emissionshandel-die-luftnummer); Hans-Josef Fell, 'Emissionshandel mit null Wirkung', *Geo*, 23.04.2022 (https://www.geo.de/natur/oekologie/4896-rtkl-klimawandel-emissionshandel-die-luftnummer).

59 Martin Cames et al., *How Additional Is the Clean Development Mechanism? Analysis of the Application of Current Tools and Proposed Alternatives*, Berlin, 2016. This is also confirmed by a more recent study: Thales A.P. West et al., 'Action Needed to Make Carbon Offsets from Forest Conservation Work for Climate Change Mitigation', *Science* 381:6660 (2023) (https://doi.org/10.1126/science.ade3535).

60 The largest of these companies, the Swiss company South Pole, was worth more than 1 billion euros at the beginning of 2023. It employs 1,500 people worldwide and has developed over seven hundred carbon offset projects. Research by the Dutch investigative platform *Follow the Money* revealed that the company had 'knowingly sold worthless CO_2 certificates' from a project in Zimbabwe: see Tin Fischer and Hannah Knuth, 'Taumelndes Einhorn', *Zeit Online*, 03.02.2023 (https://www.zeit.de/2023/06/south-pole-co2-zertifikate-kariba-projekt).

61 Sighard Neckel, 'Die Klimakrise und das Individuum: Über selbst induziertes Scheitern und die Aufgaben der Politik', *Soziopolis*, 17.06.2021, here p. 4 (https://www.ssoar.info/ssoar/handle/docu ment/80379).

62 Dubuisson-Quellier, 'How Does Affluent Consumption Come to Consumers?'. See also Nick Chater and George Loewenstein, 'The I-Frame and the S-Frame: How Focusing on Individual-Level Solutions Has Led Behavioral Public Policy Astray', *Behavioral and Brain Sciences* 46:e147, 05.09.2022 (doi:10.1017/S 0140525X22002023).

63 Sighard Neckel, 'Der Streit um die Lebensführung. Nachhaltigkeit als sozialer Konflikt', *Mittelweg 36*:6 (2020), pp. 82–100. On this type of protest behaviour, see also Carolin Amlinger and Oliver Nachtwey, *Offended Freedom: The Rise of Libertarian Authoritarianism*, Cambridge, 2024.

64 This is why it is anticipated that it will primarily be people on lower incomes who will continue to drive combustion engine cars. This is another argument in favour of targeted support for lower income groups in the transition to electro-mobility: see Anna Gauto, 'Das sind die neuen Strategien der Klimaschutzbremser', *Handelsblatt*, 04.04.2023 (https://www.handelsblatt.com/poli tik/deutschland/desinformation-das-sind-die-neuen-strategien -der-klimaschutzbremser/29074922.html).

Chapter 7   Green growth

1 See among others Jason Hickel, *Less Is More: How Degrowth Will Save the World*, London, 2020; Tim Jackson, *Prosperity without Growth: Foundations for the Economy of Tomorrow*, London and New York, 2017. On the circular economy, see Harry Lehmann et al. (eds), *Impossibilities of the Circular Economy: Separating Aspiration from Reality*, London, 2022.

2 Ulrike Herrmann, *Das Ende des Kapitalismus. Warum Wachstum und Klimaschutz nicht vereinbar sind – und wie wir in Zukunft leben werden*, Cologne, 2022.

3 UN Environment Programme, *Emissions Gap Report 2022: The Closing Window – Climate Crisis Calls for Rapid Transformation of Societies*, Nairobi, 2022 (https://www.unep.org/resources /emissions-gap-report-2022).

4 Hickel, *Less Is More*. See also Ch. 8, below.

5 Branko Milanovic, 'The Illusion of Degrowth in a Poor and Unequal World', blog post on *Degrowth*, 2017 (https://de growth.info/library/the-illusion-of-degrowth-in-a-poor-and- unequal-world).

6 Manfredo Tafuri, *Architecture and Utopia: Design and Capitalist Development*, Cambridge, MA, 1976.

7 See, for example, the work of Christoph Deutschmann: *Disembedded Markets. Economic Theology and Global Capitalism*, Abingdon, 2019; and 'The Capitalist Growth Imperative: Can It Be Overcome?', *Foro* 7:4 (July/August 2023) (https://www.revis taforo.com/2022/0704-01-EN). Tilo Wesche recently made an interesting proposal in relation to property rights: *Die Rechte der Natur. Vom nachhaltigen Eigentum*, Berlin, 2023.

8 Milanovic, 'The Illusion of Degrowth in a Poor and Unequal World'.

9 This can be seen, for example, in the production of solar panels, 95 per cent of which now takes place in China. The attempt to (re)build production capacities in Europe and the United States aims to free the Western world from strategic dependency. This is what the American Inflation Reduction Act and the European Green Deal are about.

10 Per Espen Stoknes and Johan Rockström, 'Redefining Green Growth within Planetary Boundaries', *Energy Research & Social Science* 44 (2018), pp. 41–9.

11 This assumption is highly controversial, however, as service activities often also have high energy consumption. Digitalization, for example, leads to a considerable increase in electricity consumption. In addition, the use of industrial goods such as steel, cement, and plastic, which are also required for tourism, financial services, and the organization of pop concerts, continues to increase globally.

12 Robert Boyer, 'Expectations, Narratives, and Socio-Economic Regimes', in Jens Beckert and Richard Bronk (eds), *Uncertain Futures: Imaginaries, Narratives, and Calculation in the Economy*, Oxford, 2018, pp. 39–61.

13 Ibid., p. 53

14 Michel Aglietta, *A Theory of Capitalist Regulation: The US Experience*, London, 2015.

15 Larry Fink, 'Larry Fink's 2022 Letter to CEOs: The Power of Capitalism', BlackRock, 2022 (https://www.blackrock.com/cor porate/investor-relations/larry-fink-ceo-letter).

16 Benjamin Braun, 'Asset Manager Capitalism as a Corporate Governance Regime', in Jacob S. Hacker et al. (eds), *The American Political Economy: Politics, Markets, and Power*, New York, 2021, pp. 270–94.

17 McKinsey Global Institute, 'The Net-Zero Transition: What It Would Cost, What It Could Bring' (https://www.mckinsey.com /capabilities/sustainability/our-insights/the-net-zero-transition -what-it-would-cost-what-it-could-bring).

18 IEA, *World Energy Outlook 2021*, Paris, 2021 (https://www.iea .org/reports/world-energy-outlook-2021).

19 See Neil Fligstein, *The Architecture of Markets: An Economic Sociology of Twenty-First-Century Capitalist Societies*, Princeton, 2001.

20 Daniela Gabor, 'The Wall Street Consensus', *Development and Change* 52:3 (2021), pp. 429–59.

21 William D. Nordhaus, *Managing the Global Commons: The Economics of Climate Change*, Cambridge, MA, 1994, and *The Spirit of Green: The Economics of Collisions and Contagions in a Crowded World*, Princeton, 2021. An excellent critical discussion of the marketing of ecological externalities can be found in Ève Chiapello and Anita Engels, 'The Fabrication of Environmental Intangibles as a Questionable Response to Environmental Problems', *Journal of Cultural Economy* 14:5 (2021), pp. 517–32.

22 CO_2 emissions permits are similar to direct taxation of greenhouse gas emissions in terms of their steering effects. Both utilize the price mechanism. Permits are less politically difficult because tax rates do not have to be constantly changed.

23 See, for example, Thomas Pellerin-Carlin et al., *No More Free Lunch: Ending Free Allowances in the EU ETS to the Benefit of Innovation*, Jacques Delors Institute, Policy Brief, 03.02.2022 (https://institutdelors.eu/en/publications/no-more-free-lunch -ending-free-allowances-in-the-eu-ets-to-the-benefit-of-innova tion).

24 The same applies to de-risking strategies in the financial sector, which withdraw financial capital from climate-damaging

production processes but leave it up to private investors alone to decide how climate neutrality is to be achieved.

25 Adrienne Buller, 'What's Really behind the Failure of Green Capitalism?', *The Guardian*, 26.07.2022 (https://www.theguard ian.com/commentisfree/2022/jul/26/failure-green-capitalism).

26 Jürgen Flauger and Kathrin Witsch, 'Milliardengeschäft Kohle: Warum RWE sogar an steigenden CO_2-Preisen verdient', *Handelsblatt*, 19.09.2021 (https://www.handelsblatt.com/tech nik/thespark/energiekonzern-milliardengeschaeft-kohle-warum -rwe-sogar-an-steigenden-co2-preisen-verdient/27617624 .html). RWE allegedly has so many permits that it sells some of them at a profit on the spot market. The financial markets even see the permits as a significant hidden reserve for the company.

27 Umweltbundesamt, 'Internationale Marktmechanismen im Klimaschutz', 22.06.2023 (https://www.umweltbundesamt.de/ daten/klima/internationale-marktmechanismen).

28 See Jürgen Schaefer and Malte Henk, 'Emissionshandel: Die Luftnummer', *Geo*, 16.12.2010 (https://www.geo.de/natur/oeko logie/4896-rtkl-klimawandel-emissionshandel-die-luftnummer).

29 Stefan Bach et al., *CO_2-Bepreisung im Wärme- und Verkehrssektor. Diskussion von Wirkungen und alternativen Entlastungsoptionen* (= Politikberatung kompakt 140, Deutsches Institut für Wirtschaftsforschung), Berlin, 2019.

30 Manuela Andreoni, 'A New Tax on Greenhouse Gases', *The New York Times*, 25.04.2023 (https://www.nytimes.com/2023/04/25 /climate/europe-greenhouse-gas-tax.html).

31 Stefan Bach et al., *Verkehrs- und Wärmewende: CO_2- Bepreisung stärken, Klimageld einführen, Anpassungskosten verringern* (= DIW Wochenbericht 23, Deutsches Institut für Wirtschaftsforschung), Berlin, 2023, pp. 274–80.

32 Sighard Neckel, 'Zerstörerischer Reichtum. Wie eine globale Verschmutzerelite das Klima ruiniert', *Blätter für deutsche und internationale Politik* 4 (2023), pp. 47–56, here p. 55.

33 Council of the EU, '"Fit for 55": Council Adopts Key Pieces of Legislation Delivering on 2030 Climate Targets', press release,

25.04.2023 (https://www.consilium.europa.eu/en/press/press-releases/2023/04/25/fit-for-55-council-adopts-key-pieces-of-legis lation-delivering-on-2030-climate-targets/).

34 It is easier for export-oriented growth regimes to introduce CO_2 taxes because the negative effects on consumption are less significant: see Jonas Nahm, 'Green Growth Models', in Lucio Baccaro et al. (eds), *Diminishing Returns: The New Politics of Growth and Stagnation*, Oxford, 2022, pp. 443–63. Furthermore, apart from dwindling coal production, the EU countries have no significant fossil fuel production of their own. Politically, therefore, less attention needs to be paid to this industry than in the United States, in fact quite the opposite: reducing oil and gas consumption reduces expenditure on imports, thus strengthening Europe's balance of payments and leading to reduced geopolitical dependency.

35 Energy Institute, 'Consumption of Coal in China from 1998 to 2023 (in Exajoules)', *Statista*, 26.06.2023 (https://www.statista .com/statistics/265491/chinese-coal-consumption-in-oil-equiva lent/).

36 Baysa Naran et al., *Global Landscape of Climate Finance: A Decade of Data: 2011–2020*, Climate Policy Initiative, 27.10.2022 (https://www.climatepolicyinitiative.org/publication/global-landscape-of-climate-finance-a-decade-of-data/).

37 Gabor, 'The Wall Street Consensus'.

38 Daniela Gabor and Benjamin Braun, 'Green Macrofinancial Regimes', unpublished MS, UWE Bristol and Max Planck Institute for the Study of Societies, 2023.

39 Lucas Chancel and Thomas Piketty, 'Decarbonization Requires Redistribution', in Greta Thunberg (ed.), *The Climate Book*, London, 2024, pp. 405–9, here p. 405.

40 Jonas Meckling and Nicholas Goedeking, 'Coalition Cascades: The Politics of Tipping Points in Clean Energy Transitions', *Policy Studies Journal* 51:4 (2023), pp. 715–39; Nicolas Schmid et al., 'Explaining Advocacy Coalition Change with Policy Feedback', *Policy Studies Journal* 48:4 (2020), pp. 1109–34.

41 Anthony Shorrocks et al., *Global Wealth Report 2023: Leading Perspectives to Navigate the Future*, UBS, 2023 (https:// www.ubs.com/global/en/family-office-uhnw/reports/global-wealth-report-2023.html).

42 Saijel Kishan, 'There's $35 Trillion Invested in Sustainability, but $25 Trillion of That Isn't Doing Much', *Bloomberg*, 18.08.2021 (https://www.bloomberg.com/news/articles/2021-08-18/-35-trillion-in-sustainability-funds-does-it-do-any-good).

43 Magdalena Senn et al., *Die Grenzen von Sustainable Finance. Wie das Finanzsystem zu einem stärkeren Hebel für eine nachhaltige Wirtschaft werden kann*, Berlin, 2022, p. 15.

44 On the power wielded by index providers, see also Johannes Petry et al., 'Steering Capital: The Growing Private Authority of Index Providers in the Age of Passive Asset Management', *Review of International Political Economy* 28:1 (2021), pp. 152–76.

45 See especially Adrienne Buller, *The Value of a Whale: On the Illusions of Green Capitalism*, Manchester, 2022, Ch. 4. However, the European Securities and Markets Authority (ESMA) now appears to be taking greenwashing in the financial industry more seriously and is tightening the standards that apply to European ESG labels. Since 2021, the EU has had a binding regulation (SFDR) on what may be advertised as a sustainable investment. This defines standards for the use of certain labels and obliges fund companies to disclose their sustainability criteria. Previously, the standards were so lax that more than half of all fund products could be classified as sustainable. Following the revision, this is likely to change. A study by ESMA of three thousand funds currently classified as sustainable in the EU came to the conclusion that, with the new criteria, less than 1 per cent of these funds will still be allowed to use the sustainability label: Julien Mazzacurati et al., *TRV Risk Analysis. EU Ecolabel: Calibrating Green Criteria for Retail Fund*, Paris, 2022.

46 Senn et al., *Die Grenzen von Sustainable Finance*, pp. 11f.

47 Buller, *The Value of a Whale*; Jan Fichtner et al., 'Mind the ESG Capital Allocation Gap: The Role of Index Providers, Standard-

Setting, and "Green" Indices for the Creation of Sustainability Impact', *Regulation & Governance* 18:2 (2024), pp. 479–98.

48 Tomaso Ferrando et al., 'Indebting the Green Transition: Critical Notes on Green Bonds in the South', *EADI Blog*, 31.03.2022 (https://www.developmentresearch.eu/?p=1167).

49 Larry Fink, 'Larry Fink's 2018 Letter to CEOs: A Sense of Purpose', BlackRock, 2018 (https://www.blackrock.com/corpo rate/investor-relations/2018-larry-fink-ceo-letter).

50 Ibid.

51 Joseph Baines and Sandy Brian Hager, 'From Passive Owners to Planet Savers? Asset Managers, Carbon Majors and the Limits of Sustainable Finance', *Competition & Change* 27:3–4 (2022), pp. 449–71. See also Benjamin Braun, 'Exit, Control, and Politics: Structural Power and Corporate Governance under Asset Manager Capitalism', *Politics & Society* 50:4 (2022), pp. 630–54.

52 David Gelles, 'How Environmentally Conscious Investing Became a Target of Conservatives', *The New York Times*, 28.02.2023 (https://www.nytimes.com/2023/02/28/climate/esg-climate-backlash.html).

53 Matthew Goldstein and Maureen Farrell, 'BlackRock's Pitch for Socially Conscious Investing Antagonizes All Sides', *The New York Times*, 23.12.2022 (https://www.nytimes.com/2022/12/23 /business/blackrock-esg-investing.html).

54 However, this amounts to only around 15 per cent of primary energy consumption. Even in Germany, which prides itself on its transition to renewable energy, about 80 per cent of energy came from fossil fuels in 2022: see Umweltbundesamt, 'Primärenergieverbrauch', 22.03.2023 (https://www.umweltbun desamt.de/daten/energie/primaerenergieverbrauch#definition -und-einflussfaktoren).

55 IWR, 'Trendwende: In Deutschland sind 2022 knapp 10.000 MW neue Wind- und Solarleistung in Betrieb gegangen', 13.01.2023 (https://www.iwr.de/news/trendwende-in-deutschland-sind-2022-knapp-10-000-mw-neue-wind-und-solarleistung-in-betrieb

-gegangen-news38202); Bundesnetzagentur, 'Bundesnetzagentur veröffentlicht Daten zum Strommarkt 2023', 06.01.2024 (https://www.bundesnetzagentur.de/SharedDocs/Pressemitteilungen/DE/2024/20240103_SMARD.html#:~:text=Insgesamt%20lag%20in%202023%20die,(100%2C6%20TWh%20)).

56 This figure does not yet include the dismantling of 350 old turbines, which, however, had a significantly lower output than new wind turbines: see Bundesnetzagentur, 'Bundesnetzagentur veröffentlicht Daten zum Strommarkt 2023'.

57 See Bundesverband WindEnergie, 'Deutschland in Zahlen' (https://tinyurl.com/5n738yza).

58 Agora Energiewende, 'Klimaneutrales Stromsystem 2035. Wie der deutsche Stromsektor bis zum Jahr 2035 klimaneutral werden kann', 23.06.2022 (https://www.agora-energiewende.de/publikationen/klimaneutrales-stromsystem-2035).

59 McKinsey & Company, 'Global Energy Perspective 2021' (https://www.mckinsey.com/~/media/mckinsey/industries/oil%20and%20gas/our%20insights/global%20energy%20perspective%202020 21/global-energy-perspective-2021-final.pdf).

60 IEA, *World Energy Outlook 2022*, Paris, 2022 (https://www.iea.org/reports/world-energy-outlook-2022/key-findings).

61 IRENA, *World Energy Transitions Outlook 2023: 1.5 °C Pathway*, Vol. 1, Abu Dhabi, 2023.

62 Catiana Krapp and Kathrin Witsch, 'Das sind die Strategien der Energiekonzerne', *Handelsblatt*, 18.01.2023 (https://www.handelsblatt.com/unternehmen/energie/bp-equinor-vattenfall-das-sind-die-strategien-der-energiekonzerne-/28923918.html).

63 Klaus Stratmann and Kathrin Witsch, 'Stromlücke droht: Warum die Ziele aus dem Koalitionsvertrag kaum zu meistern sind', *Handelsblatt*, 06.12.2021 (https://www.handelsblatt.com/politik/deutschland/energie-stromluecke-droht-warum-die-ziele-aus-dem-koalitionsvertrag-kaum-zu-meistern-sind/278616 76.html).

64 Stoknes and Rockström, 'Redefining Green Growth within Planetary Boundaries'; Timothée Parrique et al., *Decoupling*

Debunked: Evidence and Arguments against Green Growth as a Sole Strategy for Sustainability, Brussels, 2019.

65 Martin Müller, 'Kein Zurück zur Natur', *Frankfurter Allgemeine Zeitung*, 07.02.2023 (https://www.faz.net/aktuell/karriere-hoch schule/kritik-der-klimarettung-kein-zurueck-zur-natur-186419 35.html).

66 Joeri Rogelj et al., 'Mitigation Pathways Compatible with 1.5°C in the Context of Sustainable Development', in Valérie Masson-Delmotte et al. (eds), *Global Warming of 1.5°C. An IPCC Special Report on the Impacts of Global Warming of 1.5°C above Pre-Industrial Levels and Related Global Greenhouse Gas Emission Pathways, in the Context of Strengthening the Global Response to the Threat of Climate Change, Sustainable Development, and Efforts to Eradicate Poverty*, Cambridge and New York, 2018, pp. 93–174.

67 Oliver Gedeni et al., *The State of Carbon Dioxide Removal*, Oxford, 2023.

68 Rogelj et al., 'Mitigation Pathways Compatible with 1.5°C in the Context of Sustainable Development'.

69 Marcus Theurer, 'Die CO_2-Speicherung ist einer der größten Hebel', *Frankfurter Allgemeine Zeitung*, 22.12.2022 (https://www.faz.net/aktuell/wirtschaft/die-co2-speicherung-ist-einer-der-groessten-hebel-18539046.html).

70 IEA, *World Energy Outlook 2022*, pp. 172–3.

71 Gedeni et al., *The State of Carbon Dioxide Removal*.

72 The discussion around eFuels is very similar. The hope pinned on such fuels reduces the pressure to switch to electric cars and can therefore be seen as a delaying tactic.

73 Brad Plumer, 'In a US First, a Commercial Plant Starts Pulling Carbon from the Air', *The New York Times*, 09.11.2023 (https://www.nytimes.com/2023/11/09/climate/direct-air-capture-carbon.html).

74 Thomas Stölzel, 'Kohlendioxidfänger: Große Erwartungen, bescheidene Bilanz', *Wirtschaftswoche*, 28.08.2023 (https://www.wiwo.de/my/technologie/umwelt/direct-air-capture-kohlendi

oxidfaenger-grosse-erwartungen-bescheidene-bilanz/29350542
.html).
75 Susanne Götze et al., 'Der Bunkerplan', *Der Spiegel*, 11.05.2023
    (https://www.spiegel.de/wissenschaft/mensch/der-bunkerplan
    -a-2c1925c4-8b2f-422f-a837-7fae20c1ce3a).
76 IEA, *Direct Air Capture: A Key Technology for Net Zero*, Paris,
    2022 (https://iea.blob.core.windows.net/assets/78633715-15c0
    -44e1-81df-41123c556d57/DirectAirCapture_Akeytechnology
    fornetzero.pdf); Habib Azarabadi et al., 'Shifting the Direct Air
    Capture Paradigm', BCG, 05.06.2023 (https://www.bcg.com/pub
    lications/2023/solving-direct-air-carbon-capture-challenge).
77 Thomas Stölzel and Martin Seiwert, 'Die fatale Verehrung des
    E-Autos', *Wirtschaftswoche*, 08.02.2023 (https://www.wiwo.
    de/my/technologie/mobilitaet/e-fuels-die-fatale-verehrung-
    des-e-autos/28785172.html).
78 Klaus Stratmann and Kathrin Witsch, 'Die Speicherung von CO_2
    boomt – aber Deutschland zögert', *Handelsblatt*, 09.02.2023
    (https://www.handelsblatt.com/unternehmen/energie/ccs-die-
    speicherung-von-co2-boomt-aber-deutschland-zoegert/289674
    78.html).
79 Arjun Appadurai and Neta Alexander, *Failure*, Cambridge, 2020,
    p. 125.

Chapter 8 Planetary boundaries

1 Johan Rockström et al., 'Planetary Boundaries: Exploring the Safe
   Operating Space for Humanity', *Ecology and Society* 14:2 (2009),
   32 (https://ecologyandsociety.org/vol14/iss2/art32/).
2 Andrew Simms, *Ecological Debt: The Health of the Planet and the
   Wealth of Nations*, London et al., 2005.
3 United Nations, 'Ensure Sustainable Consumption and
   Production Patterns' (https://unstats.un.org/sdgs/report/2019
   /goal-12/).
4 Monika Dittrich et al., *Green Economies around the World?
   Implications of Resource Use for Development and the
   Environment*, Vienna, 2012.

5 Sven Beckert and Ulbe Bosma, 'Ever More Land and Labour', *aeon*, 06.10.2022 (https://aeon.co/essays/the-capitalist-transfor mations-of-the-countryside).

6 Walter Rüegg, 'Die toxische Seite der Solarpanels', *Neue Zürcher Zeitung*, 31.01.2023 (https://www.nzz.ch/meinung/solarstrom -er-ist-dreckiger-als-viele-denken-ld.1723091).

7 Dorian Schiffer, 'Lithiumabbau: Unabsehbare Schäden für die Umwelt', *Der Standard*, 13.07.2022 (https://www.derstandard .de/consent/tcf/story/2000137382763/lithiumabbau-unabseh bare-schaeden-fuer-die-umwelt); Amit Katwala, 'The Spiralling Environmental Cost of Our Lithium Battery Addiction', *Wired*, 05.08.2018 (https://www.wired.co.uk/article/lithium-batteries -environment-impact).

8 Sebastián Carrasco and Aldo Madariaga, 'The Resource Curse Returns?', *NACLA Report on the Americas* 54:4 (2022), pp. 445–52; Sebastián Carrasco et al., 'The Temporalities of Natural Resources Extraction: Imagined Futures and the Spatialization of the Lithium Industry in Chile', *The Extractive Industries and Society* 15 (2023), 101310 (https://www.sciencedirect.com/ science/article/abs/pii/S2214790X23001004).

9 Marcus Theurer, 'Der Wechsel zum Elektroauto kommt schneller als erwartet', *Frankfurter Allgemeine Zeitung*, 06.04.2023 (https:// www.faz.net/aktuell/wirtschaft/auto-verkehr/mercedes-chef-e-auto-wechsel-kommt-schneller-als-erwartet-18803833.html).

10 See also Diana Vela Almeida et al., 'The "Greening" of Empire: The European Green Deal as the *EU First A*genda', *Political Geography* 105 (2023), 102925 (https://doi.org/10.1016/j.polgeo .2023.102925); Maristella Svampa, *Neo-Extractivism in Latin America: Socio-Environmental Conflicts, the Territorial Turn, and New Political Narratives*, Cambridge, 2019.

11 Claus Hecking et al., 'So soll die Nordsee zum größten Kraftwerk der Welt werden', *Der Spiegel*, 25.07.2023 (https://www.spiegel .de/wirtschaft/windraeder-so-soll-die-nordsee-zum-groessten-kraftwerk-der-welt-werden-a-58991c91-642d-46fc-8e86-3f7f8ea6ea9f).

12 Carrasco and Madariaga, 'The Resource Curse Returns?'.
13 Claus Hecking, 'Norwegen will nicht Europas Batterie sein', *Der Spiegel*, 30.04.2023 (https://www.spiegel.de/wirtschaft/energiest reit-in-norwegen-wir-wollen-nicht-die-batterie-europas-sein-a -4afcf7e0-8bfa-4617-a542-c3e4565881a1).
14 IEA, *The Role of Critical Minerals in Clean Energy Transitions. World Energy Outlook Special Report*, Paris, 2022 (https://iea .blob.core.windows.net/assets/ffd2a83b-8c30-4e9d-980a-52b6 d9a86fdc/TheRoleofCriticalMineralsinCleanEnergyTransitions .pdf).
15 Jason Hickel, *Less Is More: How Degrowth Will Save the World*, London, 2020, p. 159.
16 Agora Verkehrswende, 'Zusammensetzung der Treibhausgas-Emissionen in der Herstellung von Batterien für Elektroautos nach Bestandteilen/Fertigungsschritten (in kg CO_2-Äquivalenten pro kWh der Batterie; Stand: 2019)', *Statista*, 01.05.2019 (https:// de.statista.com/statistik/daten/studie/1074324/umfrage/zusam mensetzung-der-co2-emissionen-bei-der-herstellung-von-e-autobatterien/).
17 Martin Wietschel, *Ein Update zur Klimabilanz von Elektrofahrzeugen*, Working Paper Sustainability and Innovation No. S 01/2020, Fraunhofer-Institut für System- und Innova-tionsforschung ISI, Karlsruhe, 2020 (https://www.isi.fraun hofer.de/content/dam/isi/dokumente/sustainability-innovation/ 2020/WP-01-2020_Ein%20Update%20zur%20Klimabilanz% 20von%20Elektrofahrzeugen.pdf). See also Elena Shao, 'Just How Good for the Planet Is That Big Electric Pickup Truck?', *The New York Times*, 18.02.2023 (https://www.nytimes.com/interac tive/2023/02/17/climate/electric-vehicle-emissions-truck-suv .html).
18 Elsa Semmling et al., *Rebound-Effekte. Wie können sie effektiv begrenzt werden?*, Umweltbundesamt, Dessau-Roßlau, 2016 (https://www.umweltbundesamt.de/sites/default/files/med ien/376/publikationen/rebound-effekte_wie_koennen_sie_effek tiv_begrenzt_werden_handbuch.pdf).

19 Hickel, *Less Is More*, pp. 154f.
20 Aaron Kolleck, 'Does Car-Sharing Reduce Car Ownership? Empirical Evidence from Germany', *Sustainability* 13:13 (2021), 7384 (https://doi.org/10.3390/su13137384). In addition, these schemes are most profitable where there is already a very good transport service, that is, in densely populated urban centres. The schemes do not contribute to solving the 'last mile' problem, which is the reason why many people use private cars.
21 Tim Niendorf, 'Das E-Scooter-Versprechen ist gescheitert', *Frankfurter Allgemeine Zeitung*, 15.04.2023 (https://www.faz.net/aktuell/politik/inland/e-scooter-warum-staedte-neue-regeln-fuer-die-flitzer-brauchen-18821738.html).
22 Ruben Rehage, 'Bitte anschnallen!', *Zeit Online*, 03.03.2024 (https://www.zeit.de/2024/10/klimaneutrale-flugzeuge-luftfahrt-umweltschutz).

Chapter 9 What next?

1 Martin Müller, 'Kein Zurück zur Natur', *Frankfurter Allgemeine Zeitung*, 07.02.2023 (https://www.faz.net/aktuell/karriere-hochschule/kritik-der-klimarettung-kein-zurueck-zur-natur-18641935.html).
2 Jason Hickel, *Less Is More: How Degrowth Will Save the World*, London, 2020.
3 Nancy Fraser, *Cannibal Capitalism: How Our System Is Devouring Democracy, Care, and the Planet – and What We Can Do about It*, London and New York, 2022, p. 85.
4 Especially as it would not be enough to change the prevailing relationship between humans and nature, but would also require a restructuring of property rights, among other things. See Christoph Deutschmann, 'The Capitalist Growth Imperative: Can It Be Overcome?', *Foro* 7:4 (July/August 2023) (https://www.revistaforo.com/2023/0704-01-EN).
5 Wolfgang Streeck, *How Will Capitalism End? Essays on a Failing System*, London, 2016.

6 Reiner Grundmann, 'Climate Change as Wicked Social Problem', *Nature Geoscience* 9 (2016), pp. 562–3. See also above, Ch. 1.

7 Of course, the opposite is also possible. For example, a collapse of multilateralism, economic crises, social destabilization owing to the accelerating effects of the climate crisis, and the absence of implementable technological solutions could all reduce the chances of establishing effective climate protection policy in the future. See also Anita Engels and Jochem Marotzke, 'Klimaentwicklung und Klimaprognosen', *Politikum* 6:2 (2020), pp. 4–13.

8 Timothy M. Lenton et al., 'Quantifying the Human Cost of Global Warming', *Nature Sustainability* 6 (2023), pp. 1237–47.

9 Rebecca Elliott, *Underwater: Loss, Flood Insurance, and the Moral Economy of Climate Change in the United States*, New York, 2021; Andreas Reckwitz, 'Auf dem Weg zu einer Soziologie des Verlusts', *Soziopolis*, 06.05.2021 (https://www.soziopolis.de /auf-dem-weg-zu-einer-soziologie-des-verlusts.html).

10 Eric Klinenberg et al., 'Sociology and the Climate Crisis', *Annual Review of Sociology* 46:1 (2020), pp. 649–69.

11 Mike Davis, 'Who Will Build the Ark?', *New Left Review* 61 (2010), pp. 29–46, here p. 36.

12 See above, Ch. 3.

13 On the role of barriers to political strategies, see also the review article by Jonas Meckling and Valerie J. Karplus, 'Political Strategies for Climate and Environmental Solutions', *Nature Sustainability* 6:7 (2023), pp. 742–51.

14 The discussions around the creation of subjective, enforceable rights for the natural world represent an important legal development. In a similar way to companies, nature could be given the 'legal fiction' of a legal personality within the legal system. The natural environment could thus be given stronger legal representation, although its interests would of course have to be defined and articulated by humans. This is nothing unusual in the legal system, where the interests of other 'legally mute' entities – such

as the unborn, children, people with mental disabilities, or those who are comatose – are represented by third parties. However, the question arises as to who should actually define and represent the rights of nature and how the conflicting 'interests' of different living entities should be assessed. Some attempts have been made to define and establish rights for nature, particularly in the global South, usually with the intention of protecting indigenous population groups: see Frank Adloff and Tanja Busse, *Welche Rechte braucht die Natur? Wege aus dem Artensterben*, Frankfurt/M., 2021.

15 See also Michael M. Bechtel and Massimo Mannino, 'Ready When the Big One Comes? Natural Disasters and Mass Support for Preparedness Investment', *Political Behavior* 45 (2023), pp. 1045–70.

16 Michael M. Bechtel et al., 'Improving Public Support for Climate Action through Multilateralism', *Nature Communications* 13 (2022), 6441 (https://doi.org/10.1038/s41467-022-33830-8).

17 Sighard Neckel, 'Der Streit um die Lebensführung. Nachhaltigkeit als sozialer Konflikt', *Mittelweg* 36:6 (2020), pp. 82–100, here p. 95.

18 Nikhar Gaikwad et al., 'Creating Climate Coalitions: Mass Preferences for Compensating Vulnerability in the World's Two Largest Democracies', *American Political Science Review* 116:4 (2022), pp. 1165–83.

19 Joel Millward-Hopkins, 'Why the Impacts of Climate Change May Make Us Less Likely to Reduce Emissions', *Global Sustainability* 5 (2022), e21 (https://doi.org/10.1017/sus.2022.20).

20 See also Sachverständigenrat für Umweltfragen, *Politik in der Pflicht: Umweltfreundliches Verhalten erleichtern*, Berlin, 2023.

21 Alice Garvey et al., 'A "Spatially Just" Transition? A Critical Review of Regional Equity in Decarbonisation Pathways', *Energy Research & Social Science* 88 (2002), 102630 (https://doi.org/10.1016/j.erss.2022.102630).

22 See Davis, 'Who Will Build the Ark?'; Wolfgang Streeck, 'Vorwort zur deutschen Ausgabe', in Foundational Economy

Collective (eds), *Die Ökonomie des Alltagslebens. Für eine neue Infrastrukturpolitik*, Berlin, 2019, pp. 7–30.

23 Mancur Olson, *The Logic of Collective Action: Public Goods and the Theory of Groups*, Cambridge, MA, 1965; Garrett Hardin, 'The Tragedy of the Commons', *Science* 162:3859 (1968), pp. 1243–48.

24 The economist Albert O. Hirschman has convincingly pointed out in a number of texts how important projections of a desired future society are as a source of motivation for altruistic or self-sacrificing behaviour in the present. This is an important idea, familiar also from theology, which helps explain why people can motivate themselves to act even when they are aware of the uncertainty of success or when free-riding is the more obvious option: see, for example, Albert O. Hirschman, *Shifting Involvements: Private Interest and Public Action*, Princeton, 1982.

25 Anne M. van Valkengoed and Linda Steg, 'Meta-Analyses of Factors Motivating Climate Change Adaptation Behaviour', *Nature Climate Change* 9:2 (2019), pp. 158–63.

26 See Jürgen Habermas, *The Theory of Communicative Action*, Vol. 2, trans. Thomas McCarthy, Boston, 1987. The research undertaken by political scientist Elinor Ostrom shows how communities can successfully maintain collective goods over long periods of time: see Elinor Ostrom, 'Handeln statt Warten: Ein mehrstufiger Ansatz zur Bewältigung des Klimaproblems', *Leviathan* 39 (2011), pp. 267–78; and *Governing the Commons: The Evolution of Institutions for Collective Action*, Cambridge, 1990.

27 See Wolfgang Streeck, *Zwischen Globalismus und Demokratie. Politische Ökonomie im ausgehenden Neoliberalismus*, Berlin, 2021, p. 480. Also, more widely, Amitai Etzioni, *The Active Society: A Theory of Societal and Political Processes*, London, 1968.

28 Sighard Neckel, 'Infrastruktursozialismus. Die Bedeutung der Fundamentalökonomie', in Neckel et al. (eds), *Kapitalismus und Nachhaltigkeit*, Frankfurt/M. and New York, 2022, pp. 161–76, here p. 170.

29 Émile Durkheim, *Suicide: A Study in Sociology*, trans. John A. Spaulding and George Simpson, London 2002 [1897].

30 Frank Adloff and Sighard Neckel, 'Futures of Sustainability as Modernization, Transformation, and Control: A Conceptual Framework', *Sustainability Science* 14 (2019), pp. 1015–25.

31 Erik Olin Wright, *Envisioning Real Utopias*, London, 2010; Anita Engels et al., *Erlaubt, machbar, utopisch? Aus dem Forschungstagebuch eines Projekts zur klimafreundlichen Stadt*, Munich, 2023.

32 Sighard Neckel, 'Die Klimakrise und das Individuum. Über selbstinduziertes Scheitern und die Aufgaben der Politik', *Soziopolis*, 17.06.2021 (https://www.soziopolis.de/die-klima krise-und-das-individuum.html); Anita Engels, 'Über die not-wendige Verknüpfung von Institutionen- und Individualethik. Warum Lebensführung und Institutionen nicht gegeneinander ausgespielt werden sollten', *Zeitschrift für Wirtschafts- und Unternehmensethik* 22:2 (2021), pp. 196–200.

33 Sara M. Constantino and Elke U. Weber, 'Decision-Making under the Deep Uncertainty of Climate Change: The Psychological and Political Agency of Narratives', *Current Opinion in Psychology* 42 (2021), pp. 151–9.

34 Ashlee Cunsolo, 'Climate Change as the Work of Mourning', in Ashlee Cunsolo and Karen Landman (eds), *Mourning Nature: Hope at the Heart of Ecological Loss and Grief*, Montreal and Kingston, 2017. More generally on the role of emotions in the climate crisis, see Sighard Neckel and Martina Hasenfratz, 'Climate Emotions and Emotional Climates: The Emotional Map of Ecological Crises and the Blind Spots on Our Sociological Landscapes', *Social Science Information* 60:2 (2021), pp. 253–71.